The Hadrami Diaspora

The Hadrami Diaspora

Community-Building on the Indian Ocean Rim

Leif Manger

berghahn
NEW YORK · OXFORD
www.berghahnbooks.com

First published in 2010 by

Berghahn Books

www.berghahnbooks.com

©2010, 2014 Leif Manger
First paperback edition published in 2014

Library of Congress Cataloging-in-Publication Data

Manger, Leif O.
    The Hadrami diaspora : community-building on the Indian Ocean rim / Leif
Manger.
        p. cm.
    Includes bibliographical references and index.
    ISBN 978-1-84545-742-6 (hardback) – ISBN 978-1-84545-978-9 (institutional
ebook) – ISBN 978-1-78238-397-0 (paperback) – ISBN 978-1-78238-398-7 (retail
ebook)
    1. Hadrami (Arab tribe)—Migrations. 2. Hadrami (Arab tribe)—Ethnic identity.
3. Hadrami (Arab tribe)—Indian Ocean Region—Social conditions. 4. Hadramawt
(Yemen : Province)—Emigration and immigration. 5. Indian Ocean Region—
Emigration and immigration. I. Title.
    DS219.H34M36 2010
    305.892'75335—dc22

                                                                        2010013188

British Library Cataloguing in Publication Data

A catalogue record for this book is available from the British Library

Printed on acid-free paper

ISBN: 978-1-78238-397-0 paperback
ISBN: 978-1-78238-398-7 retail ebook

For al-Qaddal, a friend

❋ Contents

❈ Preface

This book is a very different book from the one I set out to write. When I started traveling to Yemen in the early 1990s, I went with the intention of doing a conventional ethnography of the Hadramaut people living in South Yemen. Hadramaut is a name used for a region that includes *wadi* Hadramaut. The narrow valley is home to famous towns like Shibam, Seyun, and Tarim, and its inhabitants have historically depended on flood-irrigated agriculture. There is a plateau, *al Jol,* running north and south of the valley where pastoralists live, and a coastal strip where people engage in agriculture and fishing. There are also some important towns, like the historical center of Shihir, and the present capital, Mukalla.

My focus was on developmental issues, including the changing interaction between production systems of agriculture, pastoralism, and fishing. I was interested in land tenure, particularly the changes brought about by the shift from Communist rule in the earlier People's Republic of Yemen, to the union between the People,s Democratic Republic of Yemen (PDRY) and North Yemen in May 1990. State and collective farms dating from the socialist era were no longer viable units; the new state promoted private land ownership. Land that had been seized under Communism was returned to the old landowning groups. This fact was interesting to me as it showed how a highly stratified society had evolved within different social and political contexts.

I wanted to look at the structures of development administration in the unified Yemen, to see to what extent the unification of two state structures had affected policy-making and administrative efficiency in the productive sectors. These were my initial aims. My first rounds of fieldwork were indeed directed at such issues, and some writing was completed (Manger n.d.). But as I started my work in Hadramaut, I was also drawn towards the very long history of Hadrami migration. This history included movement throughout the Indian Ocean, the Gulf and in Yemen itself. Migration is a basic element in the Hadrami way of life. The continuation of those patterns, and particularly the revitalization of some ancient links after Yemeni unification, fascinated me. Because of this, my focus shifted, and I started to follow up on some of these diasporic links. This interest exposed me to the literature and ways of thinking that I had not focused on before. Debates on diaspora and diasporic identities became central to my research. I began to interrogate literature on globalization and approach questions of how to conceptualize larger systems. It was also necessary to look at various problems related to the relationships between anthropology and history.

Finally, the shift in focus also involved a new approach to fieldwork. I had to engage in what Marcus has termed "multi-sited fieldwork," (1999) rather than staying in Hadramaut for a longer period as originally planned. The present book is thus the end result of a rather long anthropological journey, filled with interesting moments of discovery but also a feeling of anxiety as I struggled with my inclination to deal with the "totality" of Hadarami migration history: My anthropological instincts told me to settle for a discussion of things less speculative, more focused on stories in which we can see real people.

Several contexts for this work should be mentioned. In the mid 1980s, Gunnar Håland began talking about Hadramaut and migration history throughout the Indian Ocean. At that time he had done some work in the region (Håland 1985, 1986) and wanted to link up with like-minded people. For that purpose, Abdalla Bujra was brought to Bergen as a visiting researcher, dividing his time between the Center for Development Studies at the University of Bergen and, later, at the Chr. Michelsens Institute. Bujra had written the first monograph on Hadramaut (Bujra 1971), and had published on other aspects of South Arabian society (1970) and the Hadrami migration (1967). In Bergen, Bujra produced a framework for a study on the Hadrami migration (1987). People began to take an interest in this type of studies.

At the same time, people were busy with other things. We drifted in different directions, myself being involved in a research project in Eastern Sudan (Manger et al. 1996). But the interest did not go away. In the early 1990s, after the unification of North and South Yemen in May 1990, I was able to make several journeys to Yemen and Hadramaut. My previous research in Sudan's Red Sea Hills also brought me into contact with Hadramis living in eastern Sudan. In 1996 I applied for funds from the Norwegian Research Council in order to establish a small network of scholars interested in studies on Hadramaut and the Hadrami migration. The network was called "The Indian Ocean Program — Hadrami Diaspora: Migration of People, Commodities and Ideas." With this, the research became more focused. The network revitalized an interest that had been dormant since the 1980s. I was able to link up with colleagues in Bergen, as well as an increasing number of international scholars who were involved in relevant studies.

The interest in Yemen increased a great deal after unification, and studies on the Indian Ocean region also developed rapidly during the 1990s. This was a consequence, in part, of the fall of the Berlin Wall and the subsequent opening up of possibilities previously closed. The Indian Ocean Program ended with a conference at the end of 2000, but new programs were coming up. One program directed by historians in Bergen ("Trade, Migration and Cultural Change in the Indian Ocean") shared the focus on the Indian Ocean. In anthropology, two programs were developing related lines of thinking, one on Southeast Asia ("Migrants and Entrepreneurs in Insular Southeast Asia: Negotiating Globalization and Marginalization") and one on the Pacific region ("Islands Connected: Making Pacific Worlds"). These programs had their own agendas, of course, but we shared interests in the study of large systems, in globalization, in historical connections and in grounding the study of such large scale processes in ethnographic realities.

All through this period I have benefited from the collaboration with and help from a great many people. From the early days, Gunnar Håland and Abdalla Bujra provided inspiration. In Yemen, Abdel Rahman Bamatraf was helpful, introducing me to his family in Mukalla, where his brother Ali helped me, and also to his colleagues at the faculty of Agriculture at the University of Sana'a and the Agricultural Research and Extension Services (AREA). In Sana'a, I am also grateful for assistance from the Yemen Center for Studies and Research, the American Institute for Yemeni Studies and the French Institute for Yemeni Studies. In Hadramaut, I benefited from the generosity of Saleh Basura, president of Aden University, and Mohamed Felhoum, dean of the Faculty of Education, in Mukalla. Several individuals at the Faculty of Education helped and provided friendly company.

But my time in Mukalla and Aden would not have been as pleasurable without the company of the late Muhamed Saeed al-Qaddal. He was a friend and colleague from the University of Khartoum, and he was the son of the man who built modern educational institutions in Hadramaut. Muhamed Saeed married into a Hadrami family in the Sudan, and when I met him he was Professor at the University of Aden, teaching both in Mukalla and in Aden. Muhamed Saeed acted as colleague, advisor, and mentor, and as a door-opener. But most of all he was a friend with whom I shared a great deal of time. He returned to Khartoum after his stay in Aden but remained an important contact point for my engagement with the Hadramis until his untimely death early in 2008.

In Wadi Hadramaut, I benefited from contacts in the Museum in the Seyun Palace, the local branch of AREA, the Wadi Hadramaut Agricultural Development Project, and the local office of the Ministry of Agriculture. Salam Hotel was my base in Seyun and the staff there was friendly and helpful. From there I was able to travel around Wadi Hadramaut and visit people. Special thanks go to "Al-Khail" Bajaber, in Andel, who in his capacity as overseer of the distribution of irrigation water in the village taught me a lot about the local irrigation system. Participants in the Indian Ocean program have all

helped me a great deal. Thomas Pritzkat and Sylvaine Camelin, Mikhail Rodionov, Ulrike Freitag, Mustafa Aideros, Abdel Aziz Lodhi, Anders Bjørkelo,
Christian Meyer, Richard Pierce, Anwar Osman, and Anne Bang have all
played their part.

Special thanks are due to N. Sudhakar Rao, Abdul Taha, and Hothur Ma-
hammad for assistance in carrying out a survey on the Hadrami communities
in Hyderabad, and to Samia al Hadi al Naqar, and Getachew Kassa for help-
ing me carry out surveys on the Hadrami communities in Sudan and Ethiopia.
Samson Abebe was also of great help in Ethiopia. All three introduced me
to Hadramis in the different areas, as did Syed Farid Alatas in Singapore and
elsewhere in Southeast Asia. In all the places I have traveled, I owe thanks to
many individuals, particularly to those connected to the various associations
in areas where I did surveys.

After fieldwork comes writing. My writing-up was greatly facilitated by
a sabbatical stay at Northwestern University in Evanston, Illinois. During
the fall term of 1999 and spring term of 2000, I was provided with excellent
working conditions, first at the Program of African Studies (PAS), then at
the Department of Anthropology. Throughout this period, I received support
from Northwestern University Library and particularly the Africana Library.
Many individuals should be mentioned but I limit myself to the department
leaders at that time: Jane Guyer and Akbar Virmani at PAS, Tim Earle in
Anthropology, and Mette Shayne in the Library. I thank all institutions for
providing me with a space to work, for allowing me to present material in
their seminars, and for receiving me in such a friendly way.

I have to mention Caroline Bledsoe and William Murphy especially, for
providing professional as well as social company. This was important both for
me and my son, Åsmund, who stayed with me during my year at Evanston,
enrolled as a student at Evanston Township High School (ETHS), and for my
daughter Ane and my wife Karin who came on shorter visits. Mohamed Mahmoud at Tufts University in Boston also helped, by inviting me to speak in his
Religious Studies Department seminar and for putting up Ane, Åsmund, and
myself while we "did the East Coast." The same goes for John Magistro, who
provided hospitality and introduced me to his colleagues at the Atmospheric
Research Center in Boulder, Colorado. We had a wonderful year in Chicago
and in the United States, and I acknowledge my debt to you all.

Some people have read and commented on earlier versions of various
chapters. I thank Gil Stein at Northwestern, Ulrike Freitag in Free University, Berlin, and Randi Håland, Richard Pierce, Christian Meyer, Anwar Osman, Bruce Kapferer, and Frode Storås in Bergen for sharing their throughts
with me. Also, Wendy James has provided valuable insights. Towards the
end, as this manuscript took shape, Betty O'Reilly was helpful in shaping
up my "Norwenglish." Finally, Carol Berger did a tremendous job in further

improving matters of style and readability, and Erlend Eidsvik helped with the map.

The homefront is important, as always. My wife Karin, daughter Ane, and son Åsmund have once again suffered from my absences. I am happy they could all enjoy at least periods of my stay in Evanston, but it seems my debt to my family can only be acknowledged, never repaid.

Bergen, June 2009
LM

Hadrami routes in the Indian Ocean. Map produced with the assistance of Erlend Eidsvik.

❋ Introducing the Issues

A Hadrami migration history

This book aims to contribute to an understanding of the fascinating migration history of the Hadramis of South Yemen and the resulting emergence of Hadrami diasporic communities throughout the Indian Ocean region. Migration from Hadramaut was always a result of many different factors. It was initiated by drought and tribal wars at home in Hadramaut, but was also the result of people pursuing trading opportunities in the Indian Ocean region. Some Hadramis traveled as Islamic missionaries. The migration has brought the Hadramis to South East Asia, parts of India, the Comoro Islands in the Indian Ocean, the Swahili and Somali coasts, as well as African countries bordering the Red Sea. In the process, the migrants have had to deal with very different local conditions, characterized by different ecologies, economies, political systems, and sociocultural and civilizational frameworks.

A Hadrami diaspora has emerged, with various links between these communities and their homeland. Political and economic links played important roles in the homeland, as did the religious links based on the Shafie school of Islam and sufi-inspired practices. Since the most common migrant in the early centuries of migration was a man who was both a trader and a religious missionary, most often from the Sada group, we may call the evolving diaspora both a "trade diaspora" and a "religious diaspora." We shall also see that poor Hadramis, from non-Sada groups, also traveled, encouraged by the various labor needs within the global economy of the nineteenth century. These groups also became part of the Hadrami diaspora, and from the nineteenth century on we may also talk about a Hadrami "labor diaspora" (see, for example, R. Cohen 1997).

But rather than get lost in typologies and processes of classification, we should take a closer look at the underlying diasporic processes. What we see then is a diaspora which takes on various shapes and forms. The Hadramis, in their various diaspora communities, do not constitute any pre-given community, society, or group. The Hadrami diaspora has no center except for a point of origin and is characterized by being highly adaptive. At certain times, movements appear as organized in ways that we may term diasporic; in other periods this is not necessarily the case. This view is in contrast to the alternative understanding of the Hadrami diaspora as an ever present, special type of society, with predefined cultural characteristics that originate in the homeland. There is thus a need to focus more explicitly on the complexity of the diaspora concept by paying more attention to the intersectionality of many processes. In this sense, diaspora space is a contested space, and the collective "we" must be problematized. This means that we need to look at institutions, discourses, and practices rather than assume ahistorical constructs. Rather than assume fixity, we need analyses of historical dynamics and a narrative that can show historical process. In short, historical agency must be problematized.

Hadramis in an Indian Ocean world: Establishing diasporic communities

My historical analysis clearly shows that the Hadrami migration must be understood in relation to elements we now think of as typical of "globalisation"; i.e., that the migration was part of larger waves of population movement across the ocean generated by global economic and political forces. We first meet the Hadramis towards the end of the eighteenth and the beginning of the nineteenth century, at a time in which the European presence in the Indian Ocean region is changing from one based on commercial interests alone to the imperialistic ambition that led to the occupation of ever extending territories. Various centers were being subjected to Western rule and exploitation, with the mechanisms being trade as before, but also plantation agriculture, mining, cash cropping, and intensified forms of slavery. Leading groups of Hadramis maintained various forms of links to power holders and elite groups, and were indeed, in many places, part of such ruling elites. But new groups of Hadramis also traveled in these periods, ending up as part of impoverished groups that were exploited in colonial economies.

The diaspora thus has a clear internal power dimension. Because of this, class differences within the diaspora must be accounted for. In the Hadrami case, an economic and political elite lived as diasporic cosmopolitans, experiencing the reality of the diaspora as a site of novel possibilities, and saw their history as a participation in a glorified process. Another segment of the same group, however, was at the bottom of the ladder of stratification, experiencing life in the diaspora as defined by discrimination and exclusion, either ignoring the glorified history of the elite or actively resisting it.

To capture some of the variation in this migration history and its adaptive consequences, I present in Part One some specific cases of Hadrami diasporic communities. In Singapore (chapter one), Hadramis arrived not long after Raffles had taken control of this strategic place in 1819, and became part of the enormous commercial development that characterized the development of that global city. They became part of the regional imperial competition between England and Holland, and several families had considerable economic success.

In Hyderabad (chapter two), the Hadramis became famous in the nineteenth century for the role they played as soldiers in the army of the Nizam, thus playing a role in a period of Indian history in which the imperial control of the Mughal Empire was weakened, and regional power centers such as Hyderabad developed into political units in their own right. In Sudan (chapter three) and Ethiopia (chapter four), we see small-scale traders engaged in local petty trade and participating in regional trade networks that linked agropastoral communities throughout the Horn of Africa. The Hadramis remained small players in this trade, but their trading careers were built within contexts defined by the dynamics of Egyptian geopolitical interests in the region and the actions of the various European colonial powers, as well as the Omani Sultanate in Zanzibar.

During the period of colonialism, the adaptational processes of the Hadramis can clearly be understood as a conventional diasporic adaptation, but with different effects. The most successful traders in Singapore (and in other Southeast Asian areas of Indonesia and Malaysia) and the most successful soldiers in Hyderabad came to play significant roles in their home countries, economically as well as politically. Of particular importance is their role in the political consolidation of Hadramaut during the nineteenth and early twentieth centuries through the emergence of two dominant Sultanates, Qaiti on the coast, with Mukalla as its capital, and Kathiri, in the wadi Hadramaut, with Seyun as its capital. Both were established as a consequence of Hyderabadi-based soldier families' involvement with tribal groups at home.

Established in the second half of the nineteenth century, the two Sultanates competed for external support, particularly from the British and the Ottomans. Various political settlements prepared the ground for both sultanates to become part of the British Empire as protectorates in the 1930s, later to be part of the colony of Aden. During this period, the area remained traditional, with adaptations based on irrigated agriculture and animal husbandry, but we see a clear involvement of leading diasporic families in economic development and in education. But the effects of the diaspora were not only seen on this elite level of an economic bourgeoisie. Among the majority of people, remittances from the diaspora played a significant role in their struggle for survival at home (Arai 2004; Freitag 2001, 2003; Lekon 1997).

Due to the increase in numbers of Hadramis who traveled in the nineteenth and early twentieth centuries, the demography of Hadrami communities changed in many places and brought reconfigurations within the Hadrami diaspora. Some of the migrants married local women and disappeared into local communities, no longer acknowledging their Hadrami identity. But the majority maintained links to other Hadramis and were thus part of the diaspora in a more direct way. Often they were linked to the successful Hadramis, the big traders and influential religious leaders, by living in their rest houses, visiting the mosques, and participating in the various religious ceremonies surrounding the sheikh, particularly pilgrimages to tombs. All these processes helped both to diversify the Hadrami diaspora and to create linkages among Hadrami diasporic populations that were organized around groups of leaders and followers.

The groups were organized on the basis of home area in Hadramaut, which produced systematic variation in the migration patterns. People from Wadi Hadramaut itself tended to go to southeastern Asia, whereas people from the coast went to India and to East Africa. People from Wadi Daw'an traveled to the areas around the Red Sea. But whatever the geographical variation, such organizational structures helped new Hadramis find their place in a community, helped them find work, and directed them in their choices of spouses and the upbringing of their children, thus giving coherence to the community.

Hadramis within nation states

This pattern changes when we move to the period of national independence. National independence in Singapore, India, and Sudan, as well as modern developments in Ethiopia, did not totally cut off the links between Hadramis in the diaspora and the homeland but it certainly changed the rules of the game. Stricter rules of movement between nation states played a role, as did stricter rules about national identities and various national policies for dealing with "non-national" populations. The developments in Hadramaut also played a significant role. The Qaity and the Kathiri sultanates had both become part of the new, independent state of South Yemen, a state that was dominated by the socialist and communist forces that had spearheaded the struggle against the British colonialist. The regimes of the new People's Democratic Republic of Yemen (PDRY) did not stop the diasporic links, but certainly affected the movement of both people and capital.

Together, such changes produced a situation in which the active diasporic relations faded out and were replaced with adaptations that were more national in character, making the Hadramis appear as part of the various nation states in which they lived. In Singapore, independence in the 1960s signaled the start of a phenomenal economic development that also changed the fortunes of the Hadramis, particularly vis-à-vis the Chinese. In Hyderabad, Indian independence in 1947 signaled the end of the independent Hyderabad state, and its inclusion into India turned the tables for the Hadramis in dramatic ways, from being allies of a ruling dynasty to becoming citizens in a Hindu-dominated state.

In Sudan, this tension was not so strong because the Hadramis in eastern Sudan were among fellow Arabs and Muslims, and Sudanese independence in 1956 did not make any dramatic change in the position of the Hadramis in that country. Ethiopia was never a colony, but the national developments of the country placed the Hadramis in a problematic position. In the early years of the Eritrean struggle for independence, they were accused of being on the side of the "Arab forces"; during the Ogaden crisis, they were accused of being "Somalis"; and during the socialist reign of Ethiopia, they were accused of being "capitalists."

Oil, God and diaspora

We see yet another significant change in the dynamics within parts of the Hadrami diaspora in the latter part of the twentieth century. Again, we need to relate our discussion to broader, global processes. The Hadramis have always been key actors within the Muslim diaspora, and members of the Sada groups are indeed among the important forces of Islamization in areas around the Indian Ocean. But the Muslim diaspora we see emerge in the latter decades of the twentieth century is a diaspora with new dynamics. Osama Bin Laden has become the most famous symbol of this diaspora, and since he stayed in the Sudan during the 1990s, Bin Laden became a part of the story both as a member of the traditional Hadrami diaspora, and also as a prominent individual signifying the new diasporic realities of the contemporary world. But my aim is not to contribute to the mythmaking around Osama Bin Laden. Rather, I use his case as a starting point for a historical exploration of the changes in the dynamics of the Hadrami diasporic that characterize the second half of the twentieth century.

These developments are related, among other things, to the development of the oil economies in Saudi Arabia and in the wider Gulf. These developments made it easy for Hadramis living at home in Yemen to seek labor in these areas, rather than move across the Indian Ocean. The Bin Laden family, as well as many other Hadrami families, exploited these opportunities. Some succeeded and others failed, but whatever happened, it was clear that Saudi Arabia and other Gulf countries had taken over as a major migration center. The Gulf provided new opportunities for the diasporic Hadramis living in various nation states. This was true both for big traders whose riches grew, and for others who were struggling with poverty and marginality. The result was that many Hadramis met in these areas, without ever visiting their homeland. But Yemen remained of importance, although now in a more indirect way. Although never having visited their homeland, the migrants certainly tried to appear as Hadramis and as Arabs and Muslims, in order to facilitate their adaptation into the booming labor markets.

But the most important effect of this new pattern of migration for the Hadramis was that some of them became part of the upsurge of religiously inspired resistance against the Western world. My aim is not to explain all the details of this complex modern history, but rather to place the Hadramis within them. As it turns out, Osama Bin Laden is not the first Hadrami to participate in Muslim responses to Western imperialism and empire-building in the Indian Ocean (Ho 2004). Hadramis, in earlier periods, had engaged in acts of resistance against the dynamics of a spreading global capitalism. Certainly, contemporary developments are unique in many ways (see, for example, Devji 2005), but for all the cases it is necessary to combine an understanding of the various ways people are formed by Islam as a religion and way of life with an understanding of the ways in which religion gives direction to people's understanding of their marginal position within global political and economic forces. Being part of a global Muslim community is thus more important than loyalty to a government or nation state. A Muslim system based on Islamic religious universalism could be established in opposition to normative claims of the superiority of Western modernity.

Forming a diasporic consciousness

The point about historical agency relates particularly to the normative dimensions of diaspora and the ways through which historical processes provide material for different *interpretations* among people and, therefore, leads to discussions of change. It is not enough to discuss the social form of diasporas; one must also look at the formation of *diasporic consciousness*. Thus, we may ask whether diaspora is an objective or subjective phenomena. Movement between homeland and diaspora spaces, whether physical and real or cognitive and imagined, is exercised through a myriad of networks, including kinship, trade, and religious networks and is affected by technologies of travel and communication. The diasporic reality may also be established through literature, or be displayed in museums. Or it may only be available in associations in which diasporic links are celebrated.

My aim here is to approach the issue not by making diaspora consciousness a special type of consciousness, but to discuss it in the context of broader processes through which consciousness and meaning is established. Some narrate the present as a configuration of the past; others argue that the flux in the present is novel and that what went on in the past cannot be taken for granted. It is not possible to predict how such debates will surface, nor what the specific topics will be, but they do relate to the existence of different modes of historicity. This question of historicity demands a better understanding of a group's self-definition. We need to be concerned with people's own narratives, through which we can see the group memory evolve, and at the same time see how such claims to historical truths are debated.

The Hadrami diasporic history shows many interesting examples. Going back to the general period of colonialism, we see that this period shows ideological developments, from the "civilizing projects" of the colonialists and imperialists, to various reactions among the colonized, such as the Muslim "awakening" in the nineteenth century, expressed in neo-sufism and in discourses of social reform. In some migrant circles, the social reality experienced was transformed into religious teachings with great social and political implications.

Among the Hadramis, such "reformers" often came from the groups of well-established migrants who had the means to engage in education, travel, and networking. The Sada represented this type of group. Through education in the Hijaz, and links to Islamic centers such as Istanbul and Cairo, combined with their economic successes in the diaspora, the rhetoric of the Sada combined a continuation of their dominant position in relation to the poor with a sense of responsibility towards improving the lives of those who were less successful. The elite groups, as community leaders, could then make demands to the power holders, whether they were colonial authorities or the various sultans in the areas in which they lived.

At other times, we see that internal differences among the Hadramis, among the religious elites and common people, among the Sada and the non-Sada, were problematized, and the assumed sense of unity collapsed. Instead of appearing to be community leaders, the Sada were attacked for being part of the colonial elites, economic exploiters and, in religious terms, Sufis who venerated their ancestors more than God. Such debates thus brought the history of new groups into perspective, showing that the Hadrami diaspora had other sides to it than the hegemonic discourses had revealed, and that this silenced history also depicts a diasporic reality.

Such an actualization of history in different historical periods is given direction by the various spheres of experience people have, which help create horizons of expectations. Such horizons may be local and particularistic in their orientation, or generalizing, linking local events to broader historical contexts. But the process of creating self-awareness is dynamic and takes place within specific contexts. This requires a broad exploration, not only of ideas, but also of the historical context within which such ideas are produced, reproduced, and changed.

In pursuing analyses along these lines, I have tried to understand how the transfer of collective memories relates to various methods of transmission, ranging from genealogical structures, commemorative rituals in specific places at certain times, oral storytelling and the spread of literacy, the availability of printed books, and the emergence of cassettes, television, and the Internet. The construction of memories is affected by the various types of technologies that may be involved in the narration. The various "revolutions" of the nineteenth century, both in transportation and in general telecommunications, and also in the development of a printing press that allowed for the spreading of books and newspapers, all affected what types of stories people heard, and what "truths" local people came to believe in.

In our contemporary world, the use of cyberspace and the establishment of Internet sites that bring people of different political orientations and goals together play a similar function. But it is important to note that in both the nineteenth and twentieth centuries, the ensuing debates show disagreement and contestation as often as they show agreement and shared points of view. Narratives may thus produce different understandings of the diasporic realities. While a diasporic history may be important to some, it may be ignored and forgotten by others.

What comes out of this type of argument is not a call for a noncommittal "multiple voices" type of approach but rather a call for systematic models of diversity and inequality. Such models assume that everything is culturally construed and that people realize cultural meanings through their practice of social relationships. Diaspora, then, is a particular way of seeing and interpreting the world and is part of how people structure and make sense of the particular reality in which they live. Such meanings and schemes of classification are always evaluative. Our task is to see how such systems of meaning are constructed and how people understand and act upon them. The discussion in Part Two pursues such analyses.

Is there a Hadrami ethnic identity in the diaspora?

An important issue in any discussion of the Hadrami diaspora is the maintenance of various types of collective Hadrami identities during the long diaspora history. The following questions must be asked: Is there a shared identity? What are the mechanisms that maintain such identity processes in various diasporic contexts? A discussion of these questions is the focus of Part Two. Chapter five focuses on the various ways the Hadramis have maintained an *ethnic identity*. One possibility is to accept that the reproduction of a Hadrami identity is related to primordial cultural elements that the diasporic Hadramis brought from their homeland.

Classical anthropological kinship theories have of course told us that identities are often situated within systems of descent and configurations of ancestors. My analysis in chapter five indeed shows that the cultural elements that define the Hadramis as an ethnic group in the various diasporic communities to a certain extent depends on "primordial" characteristics, like kinship and marriage, and other aspects of Hadrami "culture." The marriage practices followed by the Hadramis, through which one tends to marry within one's own stratificational group (*kafa'a*), is an important factor in maintaining identity both at home and in the diaspora. But we need historical contexts as well. What we see in the chapter is how important the emergence of *nation states* has been for the creation and maintenance of the various types of Hadrami identities that can be observed today. This is a general fact applying to many other groups as well and has to do with the general organization of the multi-ethnic communities within nation states.

In the colonial world, race and ethnicity were used to classify people and to place them in a colonial order. This order was increasingly characterized by capitalist relationships, wage work, and commercialization. Opposition against this order led to anti-colonial resistance, and eventually to the emergence of new nation states. The new nations had a different take on the issue of identities: New leaders aimed at establishing purely *national* identities. Nation-state projects such as the building of national bureaucracies, national military, and police forces, establishing an educational system, and the emergence of the mass media all aimed to create a new world in which old tribal, sectarian, religious, and ethnic identities could be replaced.

The Hadrami cases show that this was also a defining moment in Singapore, India, Sudan, Ethiopia, and Somalia. The challenge has been to balance several types of group identities—as Hadramis, Arabs, Yemenis, and Muslims—in a context in which the pressure has been towards assimilation into national cultural identities defined through bureaucratic categorization. Thus we see that the reproduction of a Hadrami ethnic identity within the various nation states is tied to the existence of specific Hadrami organizations in the diaspora. These organizations work to maintain the use of the Arabic language and to provide Islamic education, but also help to ensure the continued existence of Hadrami folklore such as songs, dances, food, and clothing. Such organizations are not primordial at all, but arise as a consequence of new ways of organizing community interests in the nationalistic period. The way diaspora is expressed in different historical periods is thus related to changes in norms, practices, and institutions, as well as in normative processes of interpretations of these changes, creating forms of community and belonging in the process.

The Hadrami adaptation also shows very clear gender dimensions. The cosmopolitan life of Hadrami migrants is a man's world. Women are based locally and play a crucial role in the construction of local identities of new generations of Hadramis. These observations make necessary a distinction between the identity *category* of Hadrami and the *cultural content* of the same identity. Calling oneself Hadrami may be a general feature of some people in all diasporic communities, but what that identity implies locally may differ. This is partly as a consequence of the interaction of Hadramis with members of different cultural and civilizational groups, but also as a consequence of the relationships to those arenas in which Hadraminess is being played out. As the problems facing Hadramis vary in the different places, we also see that their concerns are not identical and that solutions to such concerns have repercussions for the maintenance of identity.

Another feature of the Hadrami identity arising from the long history of migration, and the intermarriage between Hadramis and individuals from the different regions in which they live, is the emergence of a mixed identity, *muwallad*. In chapter five I discuss this type of creolized identity among the Hadramis and show that it is a type of identity that changes meaning over time, from an unproblematic identity to a stigmatized identity that reflects varying notions and discourses of the "purity" and "impurity" of identities.

Chapter five argues first that Hadrami identities should not be reified but seen as the outcome of people's engagement with their own complex realities; second, that cultures are characterized by variation, which means that individual persons within a group do not share culture but in fact may have widely differing life experiences; third, that while people may not share culture, this does not keep them from organizing themselves into groups in which they may appear unified around one collective identity; and finally, that the nation state is enormously important as a distributor of national resources and to the ways in which groups and individuals operate to get access to what they want from the state.

Diasporic consciousness and social stratification: Negotiating the homeland

Whereas my focus in chapter five was on the outer boundaries of Hadrami society, the focus in chapter six is on various internal boundaries within Hadrami society itself. My aim in this chapter is to show that basic properties of Hadrami culture, such as the system of social stratification, have emerged through historical processes, and that their content and form are under debate. I argue that this requires a model of diversity in which the criteria for social differentiation (class, ethnicity, caste, race, power, honor, knowledge, kinship, gender, and age) must be broken down into more basic processes.

For each general form of social differentiation, there will be different play-ers, different arenas and different games. And in each form, various types of "values" will be negotiated in certain ways. Such "value games" are embedded in historical processes shaped by conscious actors pursuing basic concerns in their lives. I try to show the usefulness of this way of thinking through a discussion of the central role the Sada group occupies in Hadrami history. Al-though the awareness of group distinctions among the Hadramis has changed through the generations, one divisive line seems to be maintained among the Hadramis themselves, that between the Sada and the non-Sada. But let us start with the system of stratification itself.

The major groups are the Sada (Seiyd), people who claim descent from Prophet Mohammed and who have historically been at the top of the reli-gious and social hierarchy; the Mashaikh (Sheikh) who also have consider-able status but cannot show links of descent to the Prophet, rather being local lineages who through historical processes have acquired status in the region; the Qabail (Qabila), who are tribal groups; and the Da'fa (Da'if), among whom are traders and various market laborers. Then there are the Akhdam (Khaddam), or servants, who are involved in various occupations in this lo-cal system. Although this general system has been taken to be uniform, for instance as described in various colonial reports, such uniformities should be treated with caution and not form the basis for easy generalizations. Clearly, there are factors that work towards the maintenance of the system—for in-stance the so-called *kafa'a* marriage (i.e., the rule that there should be no marriage outside the group, and particularly that girls cannot be married to lower status men). But there is no total agreement on this. Rather, we see arguments about ranking in general and about where individual persons and families belong in particular.

My point is that a system of stratification such as that of the Hadrami must not be taken as a timeless, norm-driven equilibrium, but must be theorized within broader historical contexts of economics and politics. Concentrating on the way the difference between the Sada and the non-Sada groups evolved in the twentieth century, I show particularly how the Tariqa al-Alewiyya, a Sufi-oriented brotherhood, profoundly affected the way the Sada could de-velop their adaptive strategies in the Indian Ocean. I argue that the spread and importance of the Tariqa al-Alewiyya must be combined with the Sada's involvement in and success in trade. Such developments have helped the Sada maintain their identity as well as maintaining their position on top of the Hadrami stratification system.

But my discussion also shows that there is no automatic consensus among the Hadramis about what position the Sada should have in Hadrami soci-ety. I provide some examples of how that position has been debated among the Hadramis. New dynamics in the diaspora, as well as in the homeland, lead to new understandings and new evaluations about how the world is to be understood and to what extent various Hadramis accept a conventional view of "being Hadrami." Through such discussions we can illustrate how the acceptance of certain positions, for instance on Sada social and religious supremacy, depends on the acceptance of specific versions of Hadrami history, placing certain groups as religious experts, in command of religious knowledge, and others as receivers of that knowledge. But we can also show how this can be contested by members of other groups who perceive their position in Hadrami history in a different way.

Whereas the Tariqa al Alewiyya reproduces groupness by organizing around religious networks, and special constraints on marriage help maintain that groupness, others are less focused on history and genealogy, and reproduce their identities more through existing, contemporary relationships based on occupational relationships, on commercial success and on their immediate families. Rather than focusing on long lines of descent, people in this second category focus on a genealogy going back only three generations. In this case, the reproduction of identity is not a reflection of engagement with the history of the group but rather a product of specific contexts, some of which encourage links to the homeland while others do not.

The issue of Sada dominance cannot be reduced to one of religious organizations and theology. Dynamics in the religious field must be linked to social and economic factors among the Hadramis themselves, such as the wider stratification system, the political system, position in the market, and so on. Hence, I conclude by arguing that history is not only the acting out of certain basic cultural schemas; people are also influenced by politics and power when positioning themselves in these schemas. My point is that the maintenance of Hadraminess is not so much dependent on agreement about cultural schemas—it depends more on people's willingness to engage in the discourses relating to the understanding of being Hadrami. Such a reflexive engagement also brings awareness of one's own identity.

Muslim universalism against Western globalization

One basic and defining property of the Hadrami diaspora is the fact that they are Muslims. The Hadramis have thus participated in an Indian Ocean world that is part of a wider *dar al-islam*, a dynamic world in which the Hadramis were active players as missionaries, traders, sailors, or whatever other occupations they represented. They have been part of an imperial history of political expansion, of waves of political rise and decline, but also processes of intellectual development and tides of reformism and accommodation, processes that may not reflect the sequences of political and economic developments. The history of Islamic civilization thus fits into broader schemes of the rise and fall of civilizations. It should be understood in the context of civilizations and social forms that preceded it, and those that have followed it, as well as in the context of the ones with which it has coexisted.

Also, here there is a need to develop a historical understanding of the Indian Ocean in a long durée and to make Islam one part of that larger system. In the final chapter, chapter seven, I focus more on the global processes with which the Hadramis have been involved. In the centuries before the European colonial powers became dominant, the Muslim Arabs, among them the Hadramis, were themselves part of what Ellen Meiksins Woods calls an "Empire of Commerce" (2003). Islam was a basic organizational vehicle of an empire which competed with Venice and Florence, and was later superseded by other Muslim forces, including the Mughals and the Ottomans, and, finally, by the new imperial European powers. It is these latter developments that are my concern here, particularly during the time of the colonial British Empire, based on the control of territory, and the time of the American Empire, without colonial territories but with a dominance revolving around trade and commercial hegemony and expressed in cultures of mass consumption.

The historical periods we are dealing with also represent processes of globalization, represented by technological developments, political reconfigurations, and cultural adaptations or upheavals. By focusing on such processes related to the spread of global capitalism, chapter seven shows clearly that there are global world system processes at play. It also argues that the Hadramis and other Muslims are not passive recipients of the effects of such processes. My aim in the chapter is to carry out what Raymond Williams called "epochal analysis," in which "a cultural process is seen as a a cultural system, with determinate, dominant features, such as feudal culture or bourgeoisie culture" (Williams 1977: 121; see also Hall 1991). Williams emphasizes "countercurrents," represented by alternative cultural formations coexisting with the hegemonic one (Ortner 2005), and it is also one of my aims to discuss such countercurrents.

On the general level, my starting point is to build on an earlier argument (Manger ed. 1999) in which I stated that it is possible to look at Islam as a "world system" on its own. Not Wallerstein's capitalist system that led to *homo oeconomicus* (Wallerstein 1974), but to a system of ideas and informal networks of scholars and saints, organized around the messages of the Quran, building a righteous social order; in short, a system of *symbolic interaction* (Eaton 1990, Voll 1994). It is within such a "universalizing global culture" that Muslims around the world can experience themselves as members of the *umma*.

This experience has been affected by a host of developments, political conquests as well as defeats, trade routes that provided contacts across culture areas, the confinement of Muslims within nation states, Muslims in control of that state, being discriminated against by the state or victims of outright persecution, and Muslim reaction to Western and Eastern domination, secularism and consumerism, but also Muslim dependence on Western labor markets, modes of information, and travel. These are all factors that Hadramis, alongside other Muslim groups, have had to deal with. What is needed then, I argue, is to allow specific histories of these processes to come more clearly to the surface. Muslim lives need to be portrayed against that history not only as lives shaped by integrated localities organized according to Islamic principles alone, but also as lives lived in arenas in which complex historical processes have taken place and indeed do take place.

What we see from this history is a dynamism that counteracts notions of Muslims captured in a static, Islamic tradition. We see how processes of cumulative societal transformations in the Indian Ocean have not led to greater homogeneity but rather to a continuous diversification into different social and cultural worlds and imaginaries. This variation is captured by John Voll (1994), who identified four different types of Muslim reaction to the Western encroachments: a *pragmatic, adaptionist style* through which Muslims were able to exploit the new opportunities and settle in strange territories; a *conservative style*, in which they were trying to preserve earlier gains; a *fundamentalist style*, in which Muslims looked to the Quran for guidance and emerged as political activists upsetting social stability; and a *personal acceptance of the religion*, focused on local holy men, on the Mahdi or the Shi'a Imam as political representatives. All these types of reactions can also be found among the Hadramis.

My more specific interest is therefore both the evolving systems of dominance and Muslim reactions to them, particularly as they also represent Hadrami involvement. We all know the latest form of reaction represented by Osama Bin Laden. Bin Laden's rhetoric is based on the Islamic *jihad*, in promotion of a war against the infidels, with clear references to a Muslim historical tradition, but also applied to the contemporary world with the aim of exploiting the globalizing effects of the media. But Bin Laden stands in a line of earlier Hadrami rebels. Leading Hadramis were involved in particular acts of resistance against the Portuguese in Malabar in the 1570s (Ho 2004), and against the British in the same area in the 1840s and 1920s (Dale 1980, 1997). They were also active against the Dutch in Acheh towards the end of the eighteenth century (Reid 1967). Towards the end of the twentieth and into the twenty-first century, there is Bin Laden himself.

But these reactions, or cases of resistance, are not about being Hadrami. The issue here is not ethnic but one of religion. The issue is about being Muslim in a context defined by the encroachment of the Western world, and Western ways of life, into the various peripheries in which Muslims live.

Although Westerners have operated in the area since the sixteenth century, it was not until the eighteenth century that the effects of Western colonialism and imperialism were really felt, leading to basic changes in the region. In these periods the commentaries, whether by Hadramis or other Muslim intellectuals, are comments on the emergence of a Western "modernity" and continued Western influences through the current phase of "globalization."

We hear non-Western narratives about "the West," narratives that oppose Western notions such as liberal secularism. Such voices have become dominant in the global discourse on Islam following the events of September 11, 2001, but the chapter also shows other Muslim voices, voices that argue for an Islamic liberalism, for a Muslim modernity in peaceful interaction with the West. While Muslim commentaries on these historical factors vary internally among Muslims, at the same time they also represent a distinct Muslim type of commentary that draws on basic principles from within the Muslim tradition.

PART ONE

Diasporic Communities Within Empires and Nation States

CHAPTER ONE

❋ Singapore
Making Muslim Space in a Global City

First visit to S'pore

Concierge Recommends

Welcome to Singapore ... the Garden City. For the first time visitors, the multi-cultural society of this Lion City will fascinate you with their warm hospitality and ensure your pleasant stay throughout. And for those who have been here before, the rapid infrastructure development will make you feel as if you have missed out on many things and places in our previous visits. There's certainly more for you to see and experience during your stay here. Let Concierge Ali offer you some tips on how to best make your stay an enjoyable and memorable one.

I found this ad in the tourist magazine *This Week in Singapore* (7–13 November 1998). Frankly, I did not notice Ali at first. My attention was on the place where he worked. Ali was chief concierge at The Elizabeth Hotel. I had discovered, on my Scandinavian Airline flight SK 973 from Copenhagen, via Bangkok to Singapore, that this hotel was mentioned as one of two "SAS business hotels" in Singapore. My immediate reaction was that this might be a place to check on Norwegians in Singapore. Not a very anthropological reaction I admit, but I was soon brought back to anthropologyland. A picture following the ad revealed that Ali was Ali Alsagoff, and although the spelling of the name was unconventional, the picture revealed that Ali indeed could be of Arab descent, and even more, if he was an Arab he might be of the famous al-Saqqaf family from Hadramaut. So I ended up in the lobby bar of The Elizabeth, asking for Ali Alsagoff.

Certainly, he was a Hadrami. His father was a Sagoff, his mother an Alatas, both from Johore in Malaysia. They had settled in Singapore and Ali had gone to Singaporean schools, but a brother was still in Johore. We made jokes about what old Hadramis would think of us if they saw us in the bar of The Elizabeth Hotel, discussing the old world of Hadrami traders and Islamic missionaries who had come to Singapore from the early and mid nineteenth century. Ali definitely saw the irony and wondered, laughingly, that perhaps he should have been sent to a religious school and had a period back in Hadramaut in order to get into a career other than being a chef concierge.

"But it could have been worse," he laughed. "Have you met Moe?"

No, I had not met Moe, and who is Moe, anyway?

"Moe Alkaff," he said. "The DJ. He runs Moezik Enterprise down at Tembeling Road. Why don't you see him?"

The Ba'alewi Mosque

Before I had time to find Moe Alkaff, I met Hassan al-Attas, the imam of the Ba'alewi mosque on Lewis Street. On my first Friday in the meeting room in the mosque I met Hadramis from Singapore, Johore in Malaysisa, and Jakarta, Indonesia. Of the Hadramis from Singapore, one was working in a Center for Conversion, another for Malaysia Airlines. The latter was there with his younger brother who was on his way to Jeddah, to do the *umrah*. A third told me about himself and his brother in Kuala Lumpur and their trip back to Hadramaut to participate in the *ziyara Nebbi Hud*. I also met some Sudanese who were working with the Saudi Embassy and some Pakistanis, one of whom was a director for Shell. There was also a Muslim scholar from Egypt, a former student of Al Azhar, who had had a long stay in Banjarmasin, Kalimantan. A Malay Member of Parliament from the residential area of the mosque was there, as was the Malaysian High Commissioner to Singapore.

I have to admit that to me this was certainly a group of people who seemed to represent the traditional Hadrami cosmopolitanism that I knew from Hadramaut itself, at least when compared to the more "Westernized" appearance of Ali Alsogoff. I had been directed to Imam Hassan by Dr. Syed Farid Alatas, an associate professor in the Sociology Department of the National University of Singapore (NUS). Farid was born in Holland, during the time his father studied there. The father, Syed Hussein Alatas, was a leading academic who worked for many years as a professor and head of the Department of Malay Studies at the National University of Singapore. He also wrote a much-cited work on Southeast Asian modernization, and also a critical assessment of Raffle's contribution to the history of the region.

An established scholar in his own right, Dr. Syed Farid Alatas followed his father to the Sociology Department at NUS, and his father moved to Kuala Lumpur. In KL, his uncle, Professor Syed Muhammad al-Naquib al-Attas, is also an established scholar and the founder-director of the Institute of Islamic Thought and Civilization (ISTAC) at the International Islamic University of Malaysia who writes contributions relating to what is now called "the Islamization of knowledge." All three are close relatives of Imam Hassan and have ancestors from Hureidha in Hadramaut. The name of the mosque itself, Ba'alewi, comes from the Ba'alewi mosque in Hureidha.

The family also has close links to Bogor, Indonesia, an important religious center. The al-Attas family that I encountered in Singapore thus represents a history of religious and academic learning that I was better prepared for than my encounter with Concierge Ali. Of course, we have not forgotten that Ali's mother was an al-Attas from Johore, indicating more complexity to the family history. The reader familiar with Hadramaut has of course also discovered the connection to Abdalla Bujra's seminal monograph on the al-Attas in Hureidha in Wadi Amd, in Hadramaut. Things were certainly falling into place. And there was more to come.

The Arab Association

During a visit to the Arab Association, Al-Wehdah, I was received by the secretary, Abdel Kader Alhadad. He took me around the premises of Al-Wehdah, showing me its kindergarten, classrooms and also a general meeting point. Al-Wehdah tries to extend education in Arabic to children of Arabic descent, and also to be a general meeting place for Arabs in Singapore. Abdel Kader is a pilot for Singapore Airlines and is married to a Javanese woman. He has one brother in Java and another in Malaysia. His family comes from outside Tarim in Hadramaut and his relatives have reestablished the educational institution in the home town known as "*ribat* Tarim." They are heavily into education, and his cousin, Tahir Mohammad Eisa Alhaddad (whom I also met), runs several schools in Singapore and rents space in Al-Wehda for his educational enterprises. The association also handles all the *waqf* property that was still owned by Hadramis in Singapore.

The association works with the Singaporean Muslim *waqf* committee, in part because of the difficulty of locating people who had rights in such *waqf* property. Besides, a lot of the property had been confiscated over the years by the authorities. Al-Wehdah also issues scholarships for young boys to go to Hadramaut to attend the *ribats* there. The cost is $2,500 (U.S.) for a year, full board. There are also people who arrange trips to *ziara* Nebbi Hud. In the year of my visit, the group numbered about twenty people; a similar number went in a group from KL.

While at the Arab Association, I also met Ali al-Lajam. His family comes from Shibam. In the 1950s and 1960s, Ali attended schools in Ghail Bawasir, Mukalla and Aden. He left Yemen just before the Communist takeover in 1967. Now he works in the Saudi Embassy, where he is a colleague of the Sudanese I had met earlier in the Ba'alewi mosque, and does work as a volunteer for Al-Wehdah.

Some days later I attended a big celebration in the Arab Association. Apart from the Arab community living in Singapore, Saudi dignitaries were present, including senior executives from Saudia Airlines and Egypt Air. Both companies gave away flight tickets from Singapore to Jeddah and Cairo. The Qadi of Singapore, bin Sumeit, was also among the dignitaries. After dinner there was traditional Hadrami dancing accompanied by a band brought in from Jakarta, the female singer being a Bawasir while the lead male singer a Saqqaf.

The Honorary Consul for Yemen

After my stay in Singapore, I was scheduled to go to Hadramaut and so I needed a visa to enter Yemen. To inquire about ways to obtain this while staying in Southeast Asia, I went to the offices of the Honorary Consul for Yemen, Helmi bin Talib. The problem of the visa turned out to be easy to solve. It could be obtained from the Yemeni Embassy in Kuala Lumpur, Malaysia, and as I was going there shortly, that problem was solved. More interesting, however, was our conversation about the Hadramis in Southeast Asia. I had already met the Consul's brother in Sana'a and talked about the family history of settlement in Southeast Asia and in Cairo, so this information was not entirely new to me. But the consul also talked about the wish of older people to maintain their Hadrami Arab identity, and also how younger people tended to assimilate into the global culture of Singapore. The issue of identity had apparently become a major subject of discussion in the Arab community in Singapore in the early 1990s, following a TV program in which the Arabs had been referred to as "Malays of Arab descent."

My first visit to Arab Street

From the Consul, I went to Arab Street, where I knew I would find a Hadrami shop owned by Abdalla al Juneid. Abdalla, the father, was not there, but I met the son, Muhamed, who is now running the shop. They do batik, a classic item of Hadrami trade in Southeast Asia, but business was poor and they had stopped importing the white cloth used to create the batik. Now they imported the cloth ready-made from Hong Kong and Indonesia and applied the patterns themselves. While I was in the shop, some Kuwaitis came in to buy perfume and *bokhor* for marriage. Almost every day, Muhamed told me, the shop gets telephone calls from the Middle East, asking about their products.

The Al-Juneids are also involved in the administration of *waqfs* in Singapore. Al-Juneid and others act as agents collecting rent from houses in Chinatown and Little India. They pay property tax and send money to Hadramaut. The father, Abdullah, is president of the Arab Association and actively maintains links to Yemen and Hadramaut. Two of his sons had been back to

Hadramaut, but they told me jokingly that they could not stay too long because it was "too boring."

But differences between living in Singapore and in Hadramaut aside, there was no doubt that the family took pride in both their history in the city and their links to their homeland. One token of this pride was a book that I was given, *The Spice of Life That is Aljuneid*. This book from 1996 is a political propaganda book for politicians and Members of Parliament representing the political constituency in Singapore called al-Juneid. As the name indicates, this area takes its name from the family of al-Juneid, and the first page of the book is dedicated to the history of this family in Singapore, the text being set over a photo of the first family home in the city. The last page carries a photo of "A Branch of the al-Juneid Family Tree" with members of the family presently living there. Apart from being political PR for politicians, then, the book serves as a proud reminder of the importance of the al-Juneid family in the history of Singapore.

The early Hadramis

From this quick overview of field notes written during my first visit to Singapore, we see a fascinating group of individuals. Some represent traditional Hadrami adaptations while others represent adaptations not known to the Hadramis a generation ago. All have adapted to contemporary Singaporean realities and as such are representatives of a Hadrami diaspora community living in what is now a "global city." I shall have more to say about such adaptations, but first we have to return to the history of the Hadramis in Singapore. Let us start by looking at the book I picked up on Arab Street and present the Preface in full:

> Aljuneid Road and Aljuneid Constituency were named in honour of the Arab family which were pioneers of Singapore.
>
> Record has it that Syed Sharif Omar Aljuneid, a young prince and descendant of Prophet Mohammad, uprooted his family in Palembang and moved to Temasek (Singapore) in 1819 when he heard that a Englishman intended to develop the island into a centre of free trade.
>
> Mr. Syed Omar was welcomed by Thomas Stamford Raffles because the Arab had established himself as a businessman as well as an important leader of the Arab community in the East.
>
> Soon after arriving in Singapore, Mr. Syed Omar built a house near the present day junction of High Street and North Bridge road. He imported spices from Indonesia and exported them to the Middle East and London, and imported cotton from England under his own brand name, then sent them to Indonesia for batik printing. Mr. Syed Omar had an acute sense for business and his wealth grew.

Just as his business flourished, the charitable side of Mr. Syed Omar also became known and much appreciated. Among his gifts to the people were the land and the Masjid Kampong Melaka in Chinatown, the land for the St. Andrews Cathedral, and the land for Dr. Tan Tock Seng paupers' hospital. Mr Syed Omar also donated land in Victoria Street for a Muslim cemetary and built another mosque in Bencoolen Street.

After Mr. Syed Omar's death, Mr. Syed Abdullah, one of his sons, and Mr. Syed Ali, a cousin, carried on the family's work of accumulating and sharing wealth.

One of Mr. Syed Ali's earliest contributions was the building of four community wells at his own expense. He also donated land for the Bukit Wakaff Cemetary at Grange Road, and a large piece of land in Victoria Street and Arab Street for the Tan Tock Seng Hospital, which was later resited to Moulmein Road. Mr. Syed Ali's brother, Mr. Syed Alwi Ali Aljuneid, was also a philantropist. He is best known for filling in a swamp purchased by his father Mr. Ali Mohammed Aljuneid—land that would become Weld Road and Jalan Besar. Three bridges in the area were also built at his expense.

In 1855, Mr. Syed Abdullah Omar, rebuilt the masjid Kampong Melaka, and named the road next to it after his father—Omar road.

The family home was eventually sold and the Aljuneids moved to a new house in Belestier Road, owned by Mr. Syed Omar's other son, Mr. Syed Abu Bakar Omar Aljuneid. Mr. Sayed Abu Bakar is one of the founders of the Singapore International Chambers of Commerce and the only non-European member of the Board of Governors of the Singapore Harbour Board, now known as Port of Singapore Authoriy, in its pioneering years. Mr. Syed Abu Bakar later passed on the house to his daughter, Sharifah Alawiyyah Abu Bakar Aljuneid. Madam Sharifah is the wife of Mr. Syed Abdul Rahman Juneid Aljuneid. Mr. Syed Abdul Rahman is the Founder of the Aljuneid Islamic School in Victoria Street.

In this house, Mr. Abdullah Haroon Aljuneid, President of the Arab Assiociation of Singapore, and his three brothers were born. Mr. Abdullah provided this picture of his old family home in Balestier Road. Mr. Abdullah is a fifth generation Aljuneid in Singapore, directly from the lineage of Mr. Syed Sharif Omar Aljuneid. The house has since been sold. Recently, Mr. Abdullah moved out of his Lorong J Telok Kurau residence of 30 years. The land will be redeveloped.

Currently, there are some 300 Aljuneids living in Singapore. True to tradition, the Aljuneids continue to prosper in Singapore and the region. Like their forefathers, they have carried on the practice of giving to society what they have gained from it.

Hadrami pioneers—"the big four"

Let me first correct the impression given by the Aljuneid book that Syed Omer was the first Aljuneid to arrive in Singapore. In fact, his uncle, Syed Mohamed bin Harun Aljuneid, had started a business in 1819, the same year that Syed Omar bin Ali Aljuneid arrived in the city. Both had come from Palembang on Sumatra. Omer was known as the *"Pengeran Sherif,"* meaning he was looked upon as a prince by the Malays and was a man of considerable fame in the Malay world (Pearson 1955). Sir Thomas Stamford Raffles, is said to have welcomed his arrival as he knew that Omar would be followed by many Arabs. Raffles wrote to William Farquhar: "The Pengeran Sherif Omar who recently arrived on a mission from Palembang to Borneo, being desirous of remaining under our protection … I have to request you will allot him a proper residence and a suitable support while he remains under your authority" (Pearson ibid.: 92).

Later, in a glowing note of introduction, Raffles wrote: "I particularly recommend to your attention Pengeran Sherif Omar … as a man in whose character and abilities every confidence may be placed" (Pearson ibid.: 92–93). With Raffles's help, Mohamed and Omar found land on which to build a house and compound. With them begins the history of the Hadramis in Singapore, a history that Ulrike Freitag (2001) has outlined in some detail. Mohamed died in 1824, and Syed Omer took over the business until Mohamed's son was old enough to take over. Omer visited Hadramaut from 1834 to 1838, and he sent his sons there to study. He also brought a nephew from Hadramaut to marry one of his daughters. Syed Omer also intervened in politics at home by supporting the renewal of the Kathiri state. His trade seems to have been in cloth, and he may have been the person who introduced muslin for men's clothing in Hadramaut (Freitag ibid.). Omer died in 1852.

Both these pioneer men, Mohamed and Omer, were buried in Syed Omar's Cemetery. And family members continued the involvement in business. One of Omer's sons, Abu Bakr (1845–1891) was cofounder of the Singapore Port Company. The family was also involved in so-called "tax farming," and in 1872 an association of businessmen led by al-Juneid bought the right to tax local farmers in the Tebrau Valley in the Sultanate of Johore. They were the only non-Chinese doing this, and after receiving the tax rights, the association subcontracted the work to a Chinese businessman (Clarence-Smith 1997: 302).

The Aljuneids were followed by others. In 1824, Abd el Rahman al-Saqqaf and his son Ahmed came from Hijaz. They had been involved in the spice trade in Malacca. In 1848 they established the Alsagoff and Company to conduct trade between the islands, including the Javanese town of Gresik. Ahmad married the daughter of the wealthy Bugis Sultana Hadjee Fatima and was thereby able to link his own shipping ventures with the considerable fleet of his mother-in-law (a wealthy merchant of Malaccan origin, who was also the Sultana of Gowa in the Celebes).

After her death, he built a mosque in her name on Beach Road. Using their ties to Hijaz, they became active in business connected to pilgrim traffic to Mecca. The family moved between Seyun, Mecca, Jedda, and Singapore. Mohammad al-Saqqaf, the only son of Ahmed, owned the first steamship registered in Singapore. He expanded the family business by adding plantations of rubber, sago, coconuts, coffee, cocoa, and pineapples on Kukub Island (where he issued his own currency). He founded the Straits Cycle and Motor Company and the Express Saw Mill Company, in addition to running pilgrim traffic.

The traffic in people travelling to Mecca on the *haj* was important. According to William Roff (1964), by the mid nineteenth century, some 2,000 Indonesian pilgrims traveled annually to Mecca; by the end of the century, the numbers were more than 7,000. Most of them traveled via Singapore, partly to avoid Dutch discriminatory measures at home, and also to earn the necessary money. Many stayed for years before they had acquired sufficient funds, and the term *haji Singapura* is still, according to Roff, understood in Indonesia as referring to those migrants who never made it to Mecca. This business was generally in the hands of the Hadramis.

Pilgrim *shaykhs* registered possible *hajjis* independently or on behalf of Meccan *shaykhs*. The same agents were also involved in organizing the Malays, Baweanese, and Javanese into bonded labor, clearing land for settlement in Johore, a practice which continued until the 1920s (Li 1989). Al-Saqqaf was also involved in this, extending loans to poor Javanese and employing cheap labor at his plantation (the Constantinople Estate) on Kukub Island (Mandal 1997: 190).

Mohammad b. Ahmad al-Saqqaf may have also served as Ottoman Consul in Singapore in the 1880s. According to Freitag (2001b), however, the issue remains unclear. It was certainly a time when the British were keenly watching contact between the Arabs and the Ottomans for fear of a pan-Islamic and Ottoman involvement in anti-Dutch rebellions in Sumatra. Maybe also because of his links with the Ottomans, Mohammed was accused of using his trade in pilgrim traffic to put people in debt and then hiring them out as coolie labor. This information came from the British Consul in Jidda, and led to investigations in Singapore, but the case was later dismissed.

With business interests in Jiddah, close relations with the Sharif of Mecca, the Maharajah of Johore and Indonesian rulers, Mohamed was certain to arouse British suspicion. When rumors had it that he had been appointed Ottoman Consul, the British looked into the matter. In Istanbul, however, it was claimed that the consul was "a certain Djuneid" (Abdalla b. Umar al-Junayd, and after his death his brother Junayd [1842–1891] [Freitag ibid.]). Whoever might have been Ottoman Consul, the position was of limited significance as the British rulers refused to acknowledge such positions. But it is certain that in 1883 Mohamad was a member of the Municipal Board of Commissioners. It is also true that the family wielded a great deal of influence.

His son Ahmad, nephew Omer, and the nephew's son, Ibrahim, were all appointed at different times as justices of the peace. Omer b. Mohammad al-Saqqaf was, until his death in 1927, the head of "the merchant prince family" of the Arabs and entertained guests at the Alkaff Mansion on Mount Washington (Jumabhoy 1981). Omer's son Ibrahim was born in Mecca and did not arrive in Singapore until the late 1920s, later taking over the family business. While in Mecca, Ibrahim was a member of its Legislative Assembly there, first under King Hussayn (the former Sharif Hussayn) and, in 1926, under King Abd al-Aziz b. Saud. He was a founding member of the Islamic World League and served as the Iraqi and Saudi Honorary Consul-General for Singapore and the Federation of Malaya.

Ibrahim b. Omer al-Saqqaf also contributed to the al-Nahda school in Seyyun in 1919, a breeding ground for young reformers in Hadramaut. This shows that the famous "Alewi-Irshadi conflict" was not as potent in Singapore as in Indonesia. This conflict originated in different views on education among the Hadramis in Indonesia, and it created a split between the Alewi "traditionalists" and the Irshadi "reformers." The conflict had repercussions throughout the Southeast Asian diaspora communities, as well as in the homeland, Hadramaut. But it seems that the Hadramis in Singapore were not as positioned in this conflict as were the Indonesian communities. And Ibrahim b. Omer al-Saqqaf's position may illustrate this. For instance, in seeking to find a compromise in the conflict he also negotiated with Ahmad Surketti, the leader of the Irshadiyyin.

Another influential person to come from the Alsagoff family was Syed Abdul Rahman Bin Taha Alsagoff (1880–1955), or Engku Aman. His maternal great-grandmother was Hajjah Fatima, and Mohamad b. Ahmad was his uncle. Engku Aman was one of the first two trustees of the (Sayed Mohamad bin Ahmed) "SMA Alsagoff Trust Fund." Syed Abdul Rahman oversaw the building of the Alsagoff Arab School in 1912 and was its supervisor for 43 years, from 1912 to 1955. It is the oldest girls' school in Singapore, and was the island's first Muslim school. In the 1920s he presided over the reconstruction of the Hajjah Fatima Mosque in Java Road, Kampong Glam, which is now a national monument. In 1911, 1912, and 1943, he was president and secretary of the Muslim Trust Fund Association, founded in 1904 to serve the spiritual and material welfare needs of Singaporean Muslims. Today the association is responsible for the running of Muslim orphanages, the mosque, and the Alsagoff Arab School (*Sunday Straits Times*, 4 September 1994).

The first al-Kaf, Sheikh bin Abdel Rahman Alkaff, came to Singapore in 1852. He had first traveled from Hadramaut to India, together with his brother Mohamed. They dealt in spices from the Far East to India, trading with the East Indian Company. From India, Sheikh traveled to Surabaya, Java, and from there to Singapore. He was doing all kinds of business, including scrap iron and clothing. Eventually he entered the property market, a move that was very successful (Alkaff 1982).

Shaikh Alkaff built the Arcade Building around 1888, as well as the Hotel de l'Europe, in the same class as the famous Raffles Hotel, which was also at one time owned by the Saggaf family. Owning a hotel in Singapore involved a balancing act for the Alkaffs, and they were criticized for serving alcohol in their hotel. They also owned the Alkaff Mansion on Mount Washington (Turnbull 1977: 98–99ff). The Alkaffs also tried to involve themselves in the textile industry, but World War II interfered with their plans. They also organized themselves into clubs, including the Persekutuan Islam Singapora, or Muslim Association of Singapore, which was founded in 1900. Following the death of his brother Mohammed, Shaikh named his second brother in Hadramaut, Abdalla, as his new partner.

The bin Talibs came in the early part of the last century. They are Qabilis, not Sayyids like Aljuneid, Sogoff, and Alkaff. The family is of Kathiri descent from al-Hawta in Wadi Hadramaut. The first person to go to Southeast Asia was Mohamad, who came to Surabaya on Java. His son, Salim, was involved in trade with the Dayak in Kalimantan, and also with Vietnam. He moved to Singapore around 1902 and later, during World War I, traded in rubber, benefiting from world shortages and subsequent high prices. He invested his profits in real estate, buying property that was undervalued because of the war. Salim was also involved in shipping.

While becoming a successful businessman, he did not, however, display the usual Sada pattern of creating charities and acting as a philanthropist. Instead, he sent money back to his family in Hadramaut. They were *qabilis* and were often involved in tribal feuds. Salim married one wife in Hadramaut and three wives in Southeast Asia; in all, he had seventeen children. He was concerned that the life abroad was corrupting him and he was active in maintaining links to the homeland. Towards the end of his life he arranged for his family to return to Hadramaut. The story has it that they got as far as Aden, but that Salim died there in 1937, and the family rushed back to Singapore.

A Hadrami success story

Although trade remained important to the Hadramis, it was as houseowners, property, and estate owners that the most successful Hadramis made their mark in Singapore around the turn of the twentieth century. In 1885, 25 percent of Hadrami investments in real estate in the region were in Singapore; 18.8 percent were in Surabaya in Java; and 15.6 percent were in Batavia. By 1931 the few Arabs, only some 0.34 percent of the total population, were the biggest real estate owners in the city. Before 1920 some 80 percent of Arabs in

Singapore lived on revenue from house rents; by the early 1960s, the portion was still some 30 percent to 40 percent (Clarence-Smith 1997).

Hadramis in Indonesia and India also invested in Singapore. Because they needed local representatives, the job of handling agent was much sought after. We have mentioned the company S.O. Alsagoff, Landowners, Merchants and Commission Agents, which handled the Kathiri Sultan's properties and family trust in Singapore. Alkaff and Co. dealt with Indonesian Arabs, people from Aden and some from Hadramaut (Freitag 2001b). The management of what remains of this considerable property is still important.

The Hadrami fortunes built in Singapore were the basis of the formation of a number of trust funds or *awqaf* (sing. *waqf*) among the leading Hadrami families. Such trusts were important in keeping parts of the family wealth together. At the same time, the trusts became important instruments in Hadrami activities both in Singapore and in Hadramaut. Let us first introduce the *waqf* as an institution.

In Shari'a law only a third of a person's fortune is allowed to be passed on through a will. The rest should be divided according to Shari'a law. Hence, the family trust became a traditional mechanism among Muslims for keeping capital together. All Islamic schools of law allow Muslims to endow part of their property as *waqf*, either during the person's lifetime or as a testament. The donor (*waqif*) must have full right over the property and property that is endowed must be of tangible and permanent nature and yield revenue. This includes rural and urban real estate, but also movables like animals, books, and furniture.

The endowed object is endowed for perpetuity, meaning that it is withdrawn from circulation. It cannot be given away as gift, inherited, sold, or mortgaged. And it should be *fi sabil Allah*, for the sake of God: The revenues must revert to a charitable purpose, such as to a mosque, a hospital, or for the relief of the poor. If revenues go directly to charity it is called *waqf khayri* (charitable). The revenue may also go to relatives, and other private people. After these named people are dead, however, the revenues revert to charitable purposes. This is called *waqf dhurri*, or *waqf ahli* (family). Such a waqf is administered by a *mutawalli*.

Mohamed al-Saqqaqf started a *waqf* called the Sayyid Muhammad bin Ahmad (SMA) Wakaff Fund. Such trusts became a common way for Hadramis to invest capital and also to keep the capital from being split by inheritance The SMA Wakaff Fund yielded approximately 120,000 Singaporean dollars annually in 1983, which was to be divided into three divisions which added up to 100 shares. The shares were designated for the following purposes: for the upkeep of the Hadjee Fatimah Mosque; for the weekly distribution, on Fridays, of food for the poor; for the maintenance of poor relatives in Singapore; for the maintenance of poor relatives outside Singapore and Hadramaut; for the poor in Seyun; for the poor in Hadramaut outside Seyun; for the support of "poor students for the Mohammedan Priesthood" in Seyun; for the poor in Mecca and Medina; and for the upkeep of the Alsagoff Arab School in Singapore.

In addition, there were shares for the reading of the Koran in Mohamed al-Saqqaf's name in Singapore, Mecca, and Seyun; for providing food for the poor in Ramadan; for the burial of Muslim strangers in Singapore; the return of Muslim strangers to their homes; the renting of houses in Mecca for the poor; the support of pilgrims; the illumination of the *Rubat Sadayat Medina;* and, finally, "three such shares to be applied in making once a year the sacrifice for my soul" (quoted in Freitag ibid.).

The riches made by the al-Kaf family were also administered in a *waqf kheyri*. This is the probable source of the capital the family invested in its homeland of Hadramaut. This involvement, begun in the 1880s, had made them the favorites of the British by the 1930s. The family spent large amounts of money in Hadramaut in the 1930s, building the al-Kaf Road and supporting schools. They also worked for the Hadrami peace from 1936 to 1937 (for which Abu Bakr b. Shaykh was knighted) and threw their support behind the military force of the sultanate.

But the al-Kaffs were not alone in maintaining links to the homeland. The golden period for the Hadramis, during the 1920s and 1930s, was also the period of frequent visits between the diaspora and Hadramaut. There were new sailing routes and generally improved modes of transport. The early Saudi-based Hadrami traders had to travel via the western Indian cities of Bombay and also Ceylon. The development of steamships in the early part of the twentieth century made it possible to travel directly from Aden to Singapore.

The Hadramis were also active in publishing and were instrumental in making Singapore a center for the production of religious literature. Students from all over the archipelago who wanted to further their Islamic studies went either to Mecca or to the Straits Settlement, where they met and "sat at the feet of itinerant scholars from the Hadramaut, and from Patani, Acheh, Palembang, and Java—most of whom had themselves studied in Mecca" (Roff 1964). The city was at the center of a communication network which brought "orthodox" Muslim ideas and thought from the Hejaz into Southeast Asia. The carriers of such ideas were part of an urban-based, mercantile society, insistent upon fundamental Islamic values, untainted by the "impurities" of the local syncretism or the eclecticism of indigenous religious life. This "fundamentalist" trend was greatly helped by the printing presses that sprang up in Singapore.

The spread of literacy was also important, particularly in Malay, but also in Arabic. Although limited to a rather narrow elite of Arabs, Malay, and *Jawi Pernakan* (locally born Muslims, offspring of South Indian Muslim and Malay unions) (Roff 1964: 83), these developments facilitated the spread of Arabic literature throughout the region, particularly writings that originated in Egypt. Jutta E. Bluhm (1983) discusses the impact in Singapore of the Cairo-based *Al-Manar* during its period of publication from 1898 to 1936. Articles from the journal, edited by Muhamed Abduh and Rashid Rida in Cairo, were reprinted in *Al Imam*, published in Singapore from 1906 to 1908, and in *Al Munir*, published in Padang. A number of articles written by Southeast Asian Muslims also appeared in *Al-Manar*.

A third major field of investment for the Hadramis was education. Funding for schools was taken from the capital of *awqafs*, and helped maintain and expand the Hadrami interest in education that had begun centuries before back in their homeland. The Tariqa al-Alewia had taught literacy to the tribes in Hadramaut, and had written texts for use by teachers. These texts were used by educators in the Hadrami diaspora. One example of such a text is *a-Risalat al-jami'a fi bayan usul al din-wa 'l fiqh wa'l tasawuf li-madaris Zinjibar*, by Ahmad Zayn al-Hibshi (1658–1733). The book has a Malay translation, and was also translated into Swahili by Bin Sumeit in Zanzibar (Bang 2003).

The book presents the duties (*fard*) incumbent upon Muslims. The five pillars constitute the core, of course, but the book also discusses what differentiates the Muslim from the non-believer. What food to eat and not to eat is important in this respect, as is the avoidance of "sins of the tongue, eyes, ears and heart" (Bang). Sins of the flesh (*farj*) are also mentioned, completing a list that shows that the Hadrami educational manuals could indeed be used to teach new generations in the diaspora about their place in the world.

Religious activities remained central to the Hadramis. They operated as religious leaders, as Imams in mosques and as *qadis*. We have already introduced the Ba'Alewi Mosque in Lewis Street. The mosque itself, its founder and his family history can tell us a lot about this part of Hadrami involvement in Singapore, and also how religious affairs were conducted in the region as well as back in Hadramaut (see Abaza 1997).

The Lewis Street property where the mosque was built was purchased by Shaikh Abu Bakar bin Mohamad Hassan Ashiblie in 1947. He and Syed Mohammad bin Salim bin Ahmed bin Hassan al-Attas acted as trustees. Al-Shiblie retired from the trust in 1957 and Syed Ali Bin Salim bin Ahmad bin Hassan al-Attas was appointed in his place. The mosque was built in 1952 and run by Syed Mohamed bin Salim al-Attas. As we know, the al-Attas family originates from Hureidha in Hadramaut, the place of Bujra's feldwork. Van der Meulen and von Wissman noted the following on their visit to Hureidha and S. Hasan al-Attas in 1931: "A brother of Hassan and 'Aluwi come to greet us. This brother has had a Dutch education, 'Aluwi an Egyptian, and Hassan an Indian education. The uncle was an officer in the Hadrami regiment of the Nizam of Hyderabad" (Van der Meulen and Von Wissman 1932: 90).

Syed Mohamed bin Salem was born in Hureidha in 1906, and named after Ali bin Mohamed al-Habshi (d. 1915). At the age of ten he went to Tarim to study with Shaikh Mohamed bin 'Awad Ba-Fadl, and remained there for seven years. At twenty-seven he went to Hyderabad as an *alim* and *da'i* (preacher). In 1935, after three years in India, Mohamed went to Penang, where he lived for four years. From Penang he went to Bogor, Indonesia, staying for seven years. There he took the *ijazah* (license to teach) from Abdullah bin Muhsin al-Attas (grandfather of the sociologist Syed Hassan Alatas we mentioned earlier). Mohamad came to Singapore during the Japanese occupation and was the first imam of the Mosque Hajji Yussof. In 1952, he built the Ba'Alewi Mosque from donations and started to teach there. He returned to Hadramaut in the 1960s, visiting relatives, repairing his grandfather's house and renovating the mosque of his grandfather, Muhsin bin Hasan al-Attas. He died in 1976.

Standing in this line of tradition, the ongoing work of Imam Hassan with the Malay community today resembles that of a social worker. He attends weddings and funerals, counsels Malays (particularly women), organizes seminars, and receives people traveling through Singapore.

Hassan was born in Singapore but has traveled to the Middle East, in particular to Saudi Arabia. He did his elementary studies in Singapore and went to Hadramaut for a year when he was eighteen, receiving his *ijazah* from the *monseb* of Einat, Ahmed bin Shaikh Abu Bakr and Shaikh Fadil bin Mohamed Awad Ba Fadl. Returning to Singapore, he followed his father around the region and eventually took his place in the mosque. In Mecca, he was taught by Abdel Qadir al-Saqqaf and Hassan bin Abdullah al-Shateri. In Singapore, he studies with Omer al-Khatib, Shaikh Bin Abdullah Alhabshi and Yusuf Zawawi, the latter also being his father-in-law. Yusuf Zawawi's family originated from Pontianak, but he was raised in Egypt and studied at Al Azhar. While following the Maliki law school, he also worked as a Shafi'e mufti in Terengganu, Malaysia. He issued liberal *fatwas*, for instance in defense of women working as flight attendants.

Every year there is a *hawl*, a commemoration of the death of Imam Hassan's father, on the last Thursday of the month of *Rabi' al Thani*. His funeral had been attended by large crowds, such was his influence in the community. In the 1980s people came from Saudi Arabia also to attend. Hassan had links to and worked with Ali al-Atas in Johor, the head of the Malay Chamber of Commerce there, the All Malaya Muslim Organization (PERKIM) and the president of the Rabitah al-Arabiyyah in Johor Bahru. The two brought in the *hawlia* of Ali's grandfather Ali bin-Mohamed bin-Hasan bin-Ahmed al-Attas and combined it with that of Imam Hassan's father.

People come from Pahang, Terengganu, Melaka, Penang, Perlis, and Negeri Sembilan. During the *hawlia, majlis* are performed by visiting *ulema* (from

Johor, Sarawak, Brunei, Sudan, and Egypt), during which they give speeches testifying to the internationalization of Muslim relationships. Imam from Bosnia, Sudan, and Moscow all bring news about Muslims living in their home regions. The *hawl* is also a time when food is distributed to the poor.

The *ratib* on Thursdays is a specific event that brings Muslims together. It is like the *dhikr* of the sufis. The *ratib al-Attas* was written by Omer Abdul-Raman. His teacher again was Hussein bin Abu Bakr bin Salem from Einat. The *ratib* is available in Malay and Tamil and is widely read in Singapore, Indonesia, Malaysia, Saudi Arabia, Hadramaut, parts of Africa, and England. Hassan's father helped to spread its use. It is chanted on Saturdays and Sundays in Majid Sultan and Masjid Mujahidin in Singapore. It is also read in India, Cambodia, and Burma by members of the Tariqa al-Attasia. Hassan's great-grandfather (on his mother's side) spread the *tariqa* in Rangoon.

Great-grandfather Ahmad b. Hasan b. 'Abd Allah al-Attas (1841/2–1915) was born in Hureidha. He became blind at an early age but received a religious education in Hadramaut. He was in Mecca in the 1850s, meeting with Ahmad Zani Dahlaan and Fadl b. 'Alawi b. Sahl, whom we heard about among the Mappilas in Southwest India. In the 1860s he became *mansab* of the al-Attas in Hureidha, mediating between tribes and the Quayity state. He also traveled to spread knowledge to rural people (*da'wa*), and was known as a sufi, maintaining links with al Dahlaan.

Ahmad also worked towards institutionalizing Islamic knowledge, traveling to Egypt in the 1890s, associating with al-Azhar shaykhs and learning about the reforms going on there. He wrote about his *rihlas* to Egypt from 1890 to 1891, to Mecca in 1907, and one trip to Wadi Do'an. He also wrote about sufism and the 'Alawi *silsila*. But he was more than a religious scholar; he was also a political activist. As such, he continued the quest of the eighteenth-century revitalization of Abd Allah al-Haddad. The activism may be seen as a move from "doctrine to practice," and an attempt to bring religious knowledge to indigenous people in their vernacular language (Bang 2000).

As we see, education was part of the drive of the Ba Alewi towards the "inner mission." Back in Hadramut, the aim was to educate the nomads, so that they in turn could educate their children. In Southeast Asia, education was part of the general process of modernization. In addition to regular Muslim teaching, schools focused on general social aims. Hadrami teachers appear to have been as much activists—social and political reformers —as regular teachers. This produced the much-debated Alewi-Irshadi, in which people with a new understanding of the world challenged the role of the Sayyids as traditional religious and social leaders in the Hadrami community.

But modern education also produced a new type of dilemma that was central both to the maintenance of Hadrami identity and to the continuation of Hadrami business enterprises. Should children get their education at home in Hadramaut, or should they go to Muslim schools in Singapore, such as the al-Saqqaf and al-Juned Schools? Or should private teachers be brought in? Should they be exposed to a more Western education, for instance through the Raffles institution? At base was a choice about Hadrami identity, about how to balance the need to equip children to make a living in an increasingly globalized city like Singapore, and at the same time prepare them for running family enterprises in the expected way.

The emergence of such dilemmas foreshadows a new era for the Hadramis, and indicates the new realities that have affected people living in the contemporary Hadrami diaspora in Singapore. It is now time to focus on these changes, and to turn to the modern history of Singapore.

Becoming Malay—social and economic changes

Of course, the four pioneer families were not the only Hadramis in Singapore. And not all Hadrami stories are success stories. A member of a Sada family not mentioned yet, Sayyid Muhsin b. Salih al-Jufri, was in Singapore in the 1840s and is an example of the not-so-successful Hadramis. He had started his career as a *nakhoda*, or captain. He opened a shop in Arab Street and invested in shipping between Saigon and Suez. Unable to compete with the faster steamships after the opening of the Suez canal, his business was ruined and he died a poor man in 1894 (Clarence-Smith 1997). Rajabali Jumabhoy (1981) talks a little bit about other families, apart from "the early four." The descendants of such families are there, he says, engage d in different careers, "one in Parliament, one a doctor."

Also, the Almenoar family is mentioned, particularly the son, Tan Sri Esa Almenoar. The magazine *Al-Mahjar* (1998, vol. 3, issue 2, p. 6) published a list that shows how complex the Hadrami migration to Singapore must have been. The title is "One Hundred Twenty Arab Family Clans in Singapore," and it is a long and impressive list indeed. But in terms of numbers it is unclear how many Hadrami Arabs are currently living in Singapore. We do, however, know something about their numbers from the earliest times of settlement: 15 in 1824 (from a total population of 10,683), 115 in 1860 (81,734), 465 in 1871 (97,111), 919 in 1901 (226,842), 1,282 in 1921 (418,358), 2,591 in 1947 (938,144) and 3,471 in 1957 (1,445,929), 2,491 in 1980 (2,413,945) and 5,923 in 1990 (number of Arabs from Freitag 2001; other from Pan 1998: 200).

The population of Hadramis grew slowly and they remained but a tiny part of the total Singaporean population. In this context their successes have been remarkable. But the small Hadrami community in Singapore was vulnerable. During the golden decades of Hadrami fortune building, young men came to

Singapore after having been educated in Hadramaut or Mecca. They came looking for similar riches to those of their grandfathers. If newly arrived people did not have relatives, there were hostels run by the already established Hadramis.

Given the direct sealine between Aden and Singapore, this city became an point from which people could travel on to other destinations in Southeast Asia. Some stayed and married local Hadrami women. Some had even been encouraged by local Hadramis to come precisely for that purpose. Such strategies brought a certain amount of stability to the community, but it could not solve the basic problem of Hadramis everywhere—how to find socially acceptable spouses for their daughters so that their children again would have the "right" identity and social status. The problem was different with boys. They could marry anyone, and their children would still be part of the father's group. The problem also relates to how best to maintain a Hadrami identity. Again, solutions were gendered.

Some families sent their members "home" for education. But in reality this was mostly true for the sons only. Mothers and daughters mostly "refused" (Freitag 2001). With the central position of women in the raising of new generations and thus the transfer of social and cultural values, what happened to Hadrami women was important. If local spouses were available from other Hadrami families in Singapore, it was good. The influx of men migrating from Hadramaut itself also helped. But the flow of such men was affected by immigration policies. The Alien Ordinance of 1936 spelled the beginning of immigration control in Singapore by regulating that no ship could carry more than twenty-five Arabs. The effects were soon to be seen.

Before 1931, 25 percent of Arabs had been born in Hadramaut, whereas in 1947 this portion had sunk to 9 percent (Harn n.d.: 8). Later, the Immigration Law of 1953 made it difficult to bring women from outside Singapore at all. But whatever the availability, families sought to provide their members with "proper" marriage partners. The definition of what is proper, however, began to change. A survey of the al-Saqaff's family shows that out of seventy marriages, thirteen were between direct cousins, thirty-seven were interclan (with other al-Saqqafs), seven were with Arabs outside the clan, and thirteen were with non-Arab Muslims (Lim Lu Sia 1986/87). The family of Abdullah Haroon Aljuneid, for example, maintained the Hadrami custom. In a photo of the family reprinted in the book from the Aljuneid constituency mentioned above, the in-laws of the Aljuneids are two, Alsagoff and Alaidross.

But it is also certain that many families did not follow this pattern. Many Hadrami men married local Malay women and over time became Malay. And even if they recognized themselves as Hadramis or as Arabs, they tended to register as Malays as such identities opened for advantages in a Singapore that was soon to change from colony to nation state. The problem was not only about marriages between individuals but also what role that the Hadramis were to play within the wider Muslim community in Singapore.

The Hadramis may have been community leaders, but the vast majority of the Muslims were Malay. From the time of Singapore's establishment, Malays had been underrepresented among the most successful groups. If the successes of the Chinese, Indians, and Arabs grew out of their ethnically organized communities, which allowed for joint action and protection, Malay kampongs were different. They consisted of individual Malays who were not related, and who were not necessarily working for other Malays. This made the Malays in Singapore different from the other groups in that city, as well as from the kampongs of mainland Malaysia.

They were organized into ethnic residential enclaves, but did not operate economically or combine resources as did other groups, particularly the Chinese. But in the twentieth century the Malay were beginning to make their presence felt in Singapore. One avenue was education, and with it, development of Malay nationalism (Roff 1994). Leadership of the Arabs and the Jawi-Peranakans was challenged by a new generation of Malays who had been educated in England and returned home with Western ideas. Mohamed Euonos bin Abdullah, Dr. Abdul Samad (the first Malay doctor) and Tengku Kadir all objected to the Muslim Association of Singapore (Persekutuan Islam Singapora) as a rich man's club and founded a rival Muslim Institute to care for the needs of ordinary Malays (Turnbull 1977: 144). In 1926 the Singapore Malay Union (Kesatuan Melayu Singapora) was founded, excluding both Arabs and Indian Muslims.

This was only the beginning. Over the following decades there was an important shift in the collective Hadrami identity, from being an Arab group to a Malay-Muslim one. I have mentioned that intermarriage with other groups started to increase. Also, Hadrami family names may have been dropped, making the identification with the homeland more difficult. And the visits to the homeland were made increasingly difficult, both by the British colonialists and the new Communist rulers, after South Yemeni independence in 1967. In the celebrated field of education, Hadramis continued their earlier promotion of schools, but now within the new context of Malayization. A member of the Sagoff family, for instance, started a Malay-Muslim scholarship fund to encourage Malay youth to pursue secondary and higher education. No wonder, then, that old man Jumabhoy complains that it is no longer possible to know who people are in Singapore. Everyone dresses and behaves in similar ways.

Economically, Arab influence also changed. Whereas investments in profitable sectors of the economy made by the wealthy Arabs were helped by the rise in land prices in the interwar years, World War II signaled major changes in British policies in Singapore. In 1947, rent controls were introduced on pre-war buildings, striking a blow to the revenues of Hadrami trusts. For a time, families shifted their investments to Aden during the boom there in the 1950s. But their relationships with the homeland were also changing. Both Aden and Hadramaut were pretty much closed after 1967, when the British left Aden.

In Singapore, increased national sovereignty also brought new developments that profoundly affected the Hadramis, both in terms of the management of their properties and the management of their identity. Centralized urban planning policies saw the seizure of Hadrami properties. In 1962, the Perseverance Estate of the al-Saqqaf was acquired by the government for urban renewal under the Land Acquisition Act. As Hadrami properties were scattered small holdings, it was difficult to develop them into modern buildings. Faced with falling revenues from their properties, Hadramis developed trade links with Saudi Arabia and Africa. Some also sold their land. A tighter government control of *awqaf* affairs since 1968 led to fewer *awqafs* being endowed. This part of the story belongs to the period of Singaporean independence.

Modern Singapore 'governmentality'

Since independence in 1965, but particularly since the 1970s, Singapore has pursued an aggressive policy of economic growth. This growth has been primarily based on export manufacturing and trade. With Singapore's phenomenal economic success, there has been an impressive rise in living standards. Throughout this entire period, Singapore has been controlled by the People's Action Party (PAP). Its policies of transforming Singapore into a global city of regional importance in Southeast Asia has profoundly affected its inhabitants.

This transformation has been engineered by PAP and the Chinese majority. During the 1980s, opposition parties were allowed to play a certain role in politics, but the government's "developmental paternalism" continues to be the main force in Singaporean politics. What we are discussing then is the development of forms of Singaporean "governmentality" (Foucault 1991). Our interest, however, is in the effects of these policies on the Muslims of Singapore, the group in which we find both the majority of Muslim Malays and Arabs.

Over the past thirty years, the Singaporean Malay-Muslim community has been transformed from a traditional, rural and suburban community into an urbanized, industrialized component of Singapore. Monthly household income rose by roughly twenty times between 1970 and 1990. There was also a dramatic shift in housing patterns. In the early 1960s, the Housing and Developing Board (HDB) started to provide improved housing. A policy of ethnic integration was followed, which actively sought to spread the population into new residential areas, with no group dominating but with everyone living in close proximity to the majority Chinese. Residents' committees (RCs) and community centers (CCs) were established to work for the production of the new Singaporean citizen.

Economically, the strategy has been promoted through the Central Provident Fund (CPF), a savings scheme in which a portion of an employee's monthly wage is saved together with a matching sum from the employer and then deposited into an account to provide capital for the buying of an HDB-managed home. The effects of this policy on the Malays is clear. In 1970, 7.3 percent of Malays were living in HDB flats, and by 1990 the percentage had increased to 97.2 percent.

Muslim organizations have participated in the interplay of various social, educational, political, and economic policies in Singapore, but such organizations are now administered within the bureaucratic context of a secular state. Islamic religious affairs are governed by the Administration of Muslim Law Act (AMLA) of 1966, under which the Majlis Ugama Islam Singapora–Islamic Religious Council of Singapore (MUIS) was created in 1968. Its origins, however, go back to the Muslim and Hindu Endowments Board of 1906, which was set up to administer religious endowments (Cheman 1991). Together with the Sharia Court and the Registry of Muslim Marriages, MUIS is the regulatory center of Muslim community life in Singapore. All are administratively under the Ministry of Community Development, and they report to the minister in charge of Muslim affairs.

From its inception, MUIS was given the task of collecting *zakat* and distributing such *zakat* to the needy. Secondly, it is supposed to administer the *awqaf* (Muslim trusts). There is also a fatwa committee under the leadership of the mufti, Bin Sumeit. From 1975, MUIS has also gradually taken over the responsibility of organizing the *haj*. Since 1991, they have issued licenses for travel agencies to handle such travels. Further management of this process was made necessary after 1995 when the Saudi government instituted a quota of 3,000 pilgrims from Singapore to be allowed into Mecca.

MUIS also oversees Islamic schools (*madrasas*). In 1975, a mosque-building fund was established to build mosques in new housing estates. Each housing estate should also have a *dakwah* committee for organizing religious classes and events within the Muslim calendar. Muslim life is thus now part of a state-run administrative system. They also keep in touch with Muslims in the region through their attendance at gatherings of the Meeting of Ministers of Religious Affairs of Brueni Darussalam, Indonesia, Malayasia, and Singapore (MABIMS). Fasting times have been standardized so that celebrations take place on the same day. MUIS is also member of Rabitah Al-Alami Al-Islami, a Saudi-based forum. Hadramis are part of the leading committees of MUIS.

In addition to the *mufti*, Bin Sumeit, several Aljuneids and Saggafs are members of committees.

The field of education has also been transformed, with government-run secular schools that provide English-language instruction dominating. Some attention is, however, given to Muslim education. In the 1980s it was made known that Malay children were not performing as well as Chinese and Indian children, and that this was a policy concern for the Singaporean leadership. This led to the founding of Council for the Education of Muslim Children (MENDAKI) in 1981. The Singapore Malay Youth Organization (Taman Bacaan) and the Prophet Mohammad's Birthday Scholarship Fund (LBKM) also focus on education. Adult education is the concern of the Association of Muslim Professionals (AMP), including a skills-upgrading program for Malay-Muslim workers. There are also organizations such as Muhammadiyah, the Muslim Converts' Association of Singapore (MCAS) and the Islamic Theological Association of Singapore (Pertapis) that focus on religious education and Arabic-language courses. Social issues like drug abuse and family breakdown that leads to divorce are also addressed by groups like Taman Bacaan's Drug Rehabilitation Halfway House.

There are also organizations for non-Malay Muslims (making up 14.5 percent of all Muslims in Singapore). These include the Kadayanallur Muslim League, Singapore Bawean Association, South Indian Jami'athul Ulama, Tamil Muslim Jama'at, Malabar Muslim Jumaath, Singapore Arab Association, and Muslim Converts Association. A more broad-based voluntary organization, Jamiyah (Muslim Missionary Society), draws members from all of the above. National statistical surveys show that Muslim community organizations and social networks appear to be strengthening the role of religion in the lives of Singaporean Muslims. In the 1990 census, 84.3 percent reported that they carried out religious practices at home. The number of children attending religious educational facilities is also increasing. Two public holidays, Hari Raya Puasa (*Id al-Fitri*), which marks the end of the fasting month, Ramadan; and Hari Raya Haji (*Id al-Adha*), which observes the completion of the *haj* ritual, are both celebrated (Siddique 1995).

Another development that has had a profound effect on Muslims in Singapore is electronic communication. Since the 1990s, "computer literacy" has been promoted as part of the new "information highway" in Singapore. This strategy has as its expressed aim that every home, office, school, and factory will link up to a computer and make Singapore the "intelligent island."

The Economic Development Board (EDB) has created a zone for Direct Foreign Investment (DFI), in which transnational companies can invest. In these investment zones, Singapore is developing what others have invented, optimizing its regional position at a crossroads of sea and air routes. Such regional cooperation is important for Singapore. Within ASEAN they are part of the "growth triangle" consisting of Singapore, Malaysia's Johor, and the Indonesian Riau Islands. Within the triangle, Singapore acts as industrial and technological leader, while Johor provides land and semiskilled labor, and Riau has land and low-cost labor (Mittelman 1994: 436).

Asian values

What is emerging is a Singaporean version of Asian values, of a culture of Asian difference and superiority in a new, globalized world. But the choices themselves are not new. Ever since independence, the Chinese-dominated leadership has faced the choice of looking back, towards a colonial past, or forwards, where the emerging power of a communist China lurks. The leaders have made their choices. They definitely are looking forward, but with an extreme commitment to economic achievement, and a national identity grounded in rational and pragmatic values. In the words of a government minister, "Knowing where you are going is more important than knowing where you are coming from."

Singaporeans should let pragmatic solutions be directed by the world market, a policy that succeeded into the 1970s. Even Raffles has been reinvented to represent Singaporean identity. He is no longer portrayed as a colonialist but as an enemy of slavery and monopoly trade, a champion of the free market and civil society in the context of ethnic heterogeneity. In short, Raffles is now seen as a leading pragmatist, with exemplary self-discipline and a will to submit to duty—all central Singaporean virtues (Holden 1999).

But in Singapore different ethnic groups are part of the reality. Unification has been achieved through the HDB policy discussed above, in which ethnic groups (CMIO) were mixed. But differences remain. The revitalization of Confucianism with the "Speak Mandarin Campaign" in the late 1970s attempted to promote Singapore nationalism but it also created some tension. Similarly, a Malay emphasis on a Muslim *umma* is also potentially decisive. In schools, the use of the English language is supposed to unite the students, but every student must also have a second language that is supposed to be his or her "mother tongue," also promoting memories of a past that is not necessarily Singaporean.

To become "the intelligent island," Singapore must rely on its educated and affluent middle class. To create this class, the government has begun to loosen its political grip, to allow space for the development of this new Singaporean globalized citizen (Birch 1999). But with it comes civil society debates that are difficult to monitor and control. There are questions as to why parts of the Chinese population feel they have been left behind, why the share of wealth among Indians is declining, and why the Malay population still finds it hard to enter into Chinese-dominated businesses, the upper echelons of the civil service, and the military (Mittelmann ibid.).

In the middle of all this, a new Singaporean authenticity is being constructed. Singaporeans are addressed as individuals, as citizens and as a nation. Mainly through the media, but also in museums, galleries, and libraries, and via monuments and statues, institutional history and collective memory, they are being mobilized to create a new unity. The public discourse of everyday Singaporean life, however, with its power positioning and unequal relationships, holds the potential for future conflict between its many different peoples.

CHAPTER TWO

Hyderabad

From Winners to Losers

A small, yellow book

During one of my visits to Hyderabad, my friend and colleague Dr. Sudhakar Rao brought me a book he had picked up in a local bookshop. The title was *Hyderabad of "The Seven Loaves,"* which didn't tell me very much. The subtitle said a bit more and was potentially of importance to my work: *A Historical Account of the Asaf Jahi Dynasty, with an Autobiographical Sketch of the Author, Covering the Events of Hyderabad's Merger with the Indian Union* (el Edross 1994). But the most important thing was the fact that the author was Major-General Syed Ahmed el Edross, a man of Hadrami descent who had been a soldier in the nizam's army and ended up as its commander-in-chief. He held the position in 1948, at the time when Hyderabad was taken over by the newly established Indian nation state.

A Hadrami in such a prominent position was of course of great interest to me, and also to Sudhakar, who had worked with me collecting material on the Hadramis in Hyderabad. The book opens with a "dedication" from Sultan Ghalib Al-Qu'aity, the last sultan of the Al-Qu'aity sultanate in Hadramaut. It reads: "As the sponsor of the publication of this book, I dedicate it to the 'Loaves,' the unknown soldier and the civilian, and secondly, to the emigrés from Hadramaut through the ages, in recognition of their aptitude and enterprise." At this point I began to appreciate Sudhakar's excitement over the book, and I realized, as he had, that the book could provide new information and take us further in our understanding of the history of the Hadramis in Hyderabad.

Hadrami soldier and commander-in-chief

Syed Ahmed el Edross was a member of the Aydarus family (as it is written in Hadramaut), a family that has played a central role in Arab migration to

India, as religious teachers and businessmen, and as soldiers in Hyderabad. Syed Ahmed's grandfather, Ahmed bin Ali, arrived in Calicut with his son (Syed Ahmed's father), Mahdar, and later traveled on to Hyderabad, where Ahmad became a religious advisor. Major-General's Syed Ahmed's mother came from Zubair in the Persian Gulf and belonged to a family of Persian officers who had been deported by the British to Bangalore and who later joined the nizam's army in Hyderabad.

Syed Ahmed el Edross was born in 1889 and raised by his maternal grandfather. He attended St. George's Grammar School in Hyderabad, a school attended mostly by European children, and joined the army after his father died in 1913. In Hyderabad, the obvious career path for Hadramis was the nizam's army. Several Hadrami soldiers played important roles in the development of Hadramaut. Both the Quaiyti and the Kathiri sultanates were founded and led by men who had made their fortunes in Hyderabad. Syed Ahmed began his military career as a member of the "Arab Battalion."

In 1916 he was transferred to the imperial Service Lancers and in 1917 to the First Hyderabad Lancers, then stationed in Palestine. After serving in British Palestine, he returned to Hyderabad and continued his peacetime regimental duties. Included in these were the recruitment of soldiers to the Hyderabad army; and he was involved in bringing in more Hadramis as soldiers, as well as Pathans from the Northwest Frontier, Meos from Alwar, and Moplahs from the Malabar coast.

In addition to his active recruitment of Hadrami soldiers, Syed Ahmed traveled to Aden in 1942 to request that a military mission from Hyderabad come to Hadramaut to train soldiers (Ibid.: 82). In 1945 he returned to Aden to deal with a dispute between British and Hyderabadi officers there; he was also involved in the British handling of the famine in Hadramaut and a rebellion in Al-Ghurfa, a small town in Wadi Hadramaut.

The autobiography of Major-General Syed Ahmed el Edross thus takes us in different directions in our discussion of the Hadramis in Hyderabad. The story of Syed Ahmed, as a soldier building a military career, is typical of many other Hadrami individuals who arrived during the nineteenth and twentieth centuries, but few can match his level of success. As commander-in-chief of the Haydrabad Army, he played a major role in negotiations with the British over the position of smaller Indian states like Hyderabad in a future Indian Federation. The negotiations, however, led nowhere, India became independent, and eventually the Indian states either joined the newly established Pakistan, or were included in the newly independent Indian nation state. Hyderabad opted for independence, but was forcefully annexed to the Indian union during the so-called Police Action in 1948. And so ended the history of an independent Hyderabadi state, the reign of Mir Osman Ali Khan, the seventh nizam, and Hadrami fortunes as soldiers in Hyderabad.

For those Hadramis who remained in Hyderabad, their futures were gravely affected. They experienced decades of marginalization, as the majority Hindu population of Andhra Pradesh took over political and economic power. From the 1970s, however, the situation for Hadramis improved, as labor migration to the Arabian Gulf and Saudi Arabia improved their economic prospects. With the opening up of new financial opportunities came a revitalized interest in the history of Hadramis in Hyderabad, and stronger assertions of a Hadrami identity. Major-General Syed Ahmed el Edross did not live to see this. He passed away in the early 1960s, in Bangalore, but the book about his life takes us directly into this wider history of the Hadramis in Hyderabad. Let us start by looking backwards.

In the service of the nizam of Hyderabad

The history of Hadrami soldiers in Hyderabad relates closely to the so-called Asaf Jah dynasty in Hyderabad. The dynasty was founded in 1724 at a time when the Mughal emperors in Delhi were fighting for power after the death of the great Aurangzeb in 1707, losing control over the situation in southern India in the process. Mir Kamruddin had been a central player in the Mughal system and, as he saw the chaotic situation arising after the death of Aurangzeb, he decided to establish himself as a ruler in Hyderabad. He became the first Nizam ul-Mulk Asaf Jah, thus starting a line of nizams that only ended with the seventh one, Mir Osman Ali Khan, in 1948.

Returning to El Edross's book for a moment, the "seven loaves" of the title actually refers to this line of seven nizams. More specifically, it relates to a legend about the first nizam, who is said to have received a gift of seven loaves from an Islamic holy man, with a prophesy that the seven loaves represented the number of successors that the holy man would see after Mir Kamruddin. Over the centuries, the different nizams related to the Mughals, to other, smaller Indian political units, to the British colonizers as well and, eventually, the political elites of the emerging Indian nation state. The downfall of the regime during the reign of the seventh nizam can be seen as the fulfilment of the prophesy of the seven loaves. Whatever the case, throughout the history of Hyderabad, the military played a central role, and it is in this context that we see the early arrival of Hadramis in Hyderabad.

The first record of "Arab" soldiers in Hyderabad is around 1797, when a contingent of guards escorted the nizam's *diwan* (minister), Arastu Jah, on a journey from Poona to Hyderabad. Information pointing directly to a Hadrami among the Arab soldiers emerges from the Anglo-Maratha war in 1817. Among the soldiers who moved to Hyderabad at this time was Umar ibn Awad Al-Quaiti, the father of the man who later was to become founder of the Quaity sultanate in Hyderabad. When the British crushed the Maratha chiefs opposing them, Arab soldiers in the army were given a choice of return-ing to Arabia or staying on in India. Omar Khalidi (1997: 4–5) quotes con-temporary sources as saying that when the terms of surrender were granted to the Arabs in the battle of Nagpur (1817), *wilayati* (Hadramawt-born) Arabs were deported to Arabia while *muwallads* (Arabs of mixed origin) became a problem for the British government.

The nizam of Hyderabad, as a fellow Muslim, offered *aman* (refuge) to the *muwallads*. The nizam's motive may have been a desire to better balance vari-ous groups in his army against each other. The army included a number of Sikhs and local Hindus and Marathas. By including Muslim soldiers, includ-ing Arab soldiers, the two groups would be less powerful, the Arab soldiers being seen as having a greater loyalty to the Muslim nizam. More Hadramis came to Hyderabad in 1857, when the nizam absorbed the army of the Raja of Wanaparthy into his own army. The new unit was known as His Highness the Nizam's Field Force, later the famous Second Lancers; it was not disbanded until almost a century later, in 1950.

Arab and Hadrami soldiers acquired important positions with both Muslim and Hindu rulers and were paid better than any other soldier in eighteenth- and nineteenth-century India. The importance of the Arabs is reflected in this quote from Khalidi: "By 1854, every man of any substance or influence in the Nizam's Dominion retained armed Arab guards either for personal safety, collection of rents and debts, or for the security of treasuries" (O. Khalidi 1997: 6). Positions as soldiers also became a base for Hadrami participation in the *jagirdari* system, which provided senior soldiers with land as well as local populations of farmers as labor.

The term *jagir* (of Persian origin) literally means "a person who holds or occupies a place" and was a system the Mughals had used. According to the usage of the term in the nizam's government, it was an assignment of land or a territory to a state servant, including the right to collect revenue accruing from it for his own use, and to govern the people living on the land. Some-times the holder of such a right was required to render public service, such as collecting levies and maintaining a certain number of troops.

The grant was generally for the lifetime of the holder, and the land would revert to the state upon the person's death. It was left to the nizam's discre-tion whether to grant, amend or cancel the nature of the tenure. Prominent soldiers acted as landlords, exploited the labor of local farmers and ruled over the farmers' lives. This made them key figures in maintaining the economic, social, and political structure of the state.

Many Arabs held such *jaghirs*, and these *jamadars* kept Arab soldiers or ir-regular troops with them. The most successful of them became very rich and influential. After acquiring wealth, some Arab *jamadars* started up businesses and lent money, using their soldiers to collect debts. In this regard, Leonard notes:

> To collect the revenue, and then prevent the government from reclaiming the land assignments, the bankers employed military men, predominantly Arab and Pathan mercenaries, who acted as their agents. These military men acted as personal bodyguards for bankers too; almost all men of any standing in the city employed Arab troops to protect their interest. (Leonard 1981: 184)

It seems certain, therefore, that prominent Hadrami families, such as Al Quaiti, Al Awlaqi and Al Kathiri, financed their involvement in Hadrami politics with their Hyderabad affairs, thus providing a direct link between the history of Hyderabad and the eventual emergence of the two dominant sultanates in Hadramaut, the Quaity and the Kathiri (see Khalidi 1995; Hartwig 2000; Freitag 2003). Umar bin Awadh Al Quaiti is a case in point. I've already mentioned that he joined the nizam's army after the Anglo-Maratha war in 1817. In Hyderabad, he joined the army of the nizam as *jamadar* of a unit consisting of one hundred Arab soldiers. He was given the titles of Janbaz Jang and Shamshir al-Dawlah and a grant of *jagir* that provided an annual income of 100,000 rupees to cover the contingent's expenses. His annual personal revenue (*jagir zat*) from the land was Rs. 23,293.

Being a special grant, on the death of Umar bin Awadh Al Quaiti in 1865, the land grant was allowed to be transferred to two of his sons, Sultan Nawaz Jang and Baraq Jang. The former became the first Quaiti Sultan of Shihr and Mukalla in Hadramawt.

Other Hadrami also found wealth and influence in Hyderabad. Abdullah Ali Al Awlaqi joined the nizam forces around 1830. He held the titles of Sayf-ud-Dawlah and Mukaddam Jung and was *jamadar* of 1,500 Arab soldiers. With the income from the *jagirs* granted to him he bought fertile land in Hadramawt and built a castle, Hisn al-Sudaa. Muhsin Al Kathiri also came from Hadramawt around 1830 and quickly rose to the rank of *jamadar*. His land provided him with an annual income of Rs. 6,000, which allowed him to take part in politics in his homeland.

The Arab *jamadars* enjoyed great hospitality at the homes of their employers. The nobles patronized them because of their qualities as fighters, and even referred to themselves as "prisoners of Arabs." The British Resident Temple inferred from an interview with Minister Salar Jang (in power from 1853 until his death in 1883) that the nobility greatly depended on the Arab troops. He writes: "From his account it was clear that the Nizam, the Minister, and even the Treasury, were in the hands of the Arabs; and the Salar Jang admitted that they were afraid of the Arabs, mainly because their houses, their persons, and almost their lives, were at their mercy" (Temple 1887: 132).

The end of an era

A military career is thus a central story of the Hadramis in Hyderabad, and Major-General Syed Ahmed el Edross serves as an important example. While enjoying great success, he was also to witness the collapse of the system upon which his success had depended. A number of decisive events stand out: first, the final years of the nizam's regime, with violence and militancy on both the Muslim and Hindu sides, eventually leading to the Police Action in 1948, in which Major-General El Edross played a central role; second, the establishment of Andhra Pradesh as a new state in 1957, which changed the borders of the old Hyderabad state, which in turn lost areas to Maharashtra and Karnatak and gained the coastal areas to the east, thus acquiring both Andhra and Telengana; and third, Telegu becoming the language of the state.

Politically, the all-Indian development away from the dominance of the Indian National Congress, seeking some sort of secular Indian state, towards more Hindu and Muslim sectarianism, or communalism, led to an increasing number of communal riots. The period saw members of some elites, those close to the nizam and his regime, emigrate. Let us briefly discuss some of these events.

Although officially a Muslim state, the majority of the population of Hyderabad state were Hindu. The Hindu-Muslim issue had been a constant theme for a long time, but it came out more dramatically during the years leading up to Indian independence. For the Hindus, both the nizam and the British were seen as foreign rulers. Because of this, Hindus actively participated in and supported India's freedom struggle. Mahatma Gandhi's entry into this struggle in 1919 injected new hopes for independence. His visit to Hyderabad in March 1934 helped boost the optimism. New organizations also played a role. The State Congress for Independence was founded in 1938 not only for political reasons, but also as a religious reaction to intensified attempts by Muslims to Islamize Hyderabad state during the rule of the last nizam, Osman Ali Khan.

The Congress movement was largely Hindu, both in membership and ideology, and was strongly supported by the fundamentalist Arya Samaj. Muslims, meanwhile, launched the *tablig* missionary and revival movements to convert Hindus to Islam (Metcalf 1999). A Muslim communal organization called Majlis-Ittihad-ul-Muslimin had been founded in 1927 and received support and encouragement from the government to protect the interests of Muslims and the nizam. The leader of the Muslim League, Mohammed Ali Jinnah, visited Hyderabad and the nizam several times. Again, as a reaction and to counteract such activities, Arya Samaj launched the *Shuddhi* (purification) movement to re-convert Hindus who had become Muslims.

It was no surprise therefore that the struggle for Indian independence was also a struggle within India between Hindus and Muslims, and that, as an independent Muslim state, Hyderabad was to play an important role. As the supreme and independent ruler of Hyderabad, the nizam sought to enter into a treaty between two equals—his own Nizam State and the Indian Union. While India and Pakistan celebrated their independence on 15 August 1947, the Majlis Ittihad-ul-Muslimin staged celebrations in Hyderabad, claiming that Hyderabad had also become independent, freeing itself from foreign domination, and leaving the nizam as the ruler.

In the opinion of the Majlis and its leader, Qasim Razvi, the Indian Union was a separate entity with which the Hyderabad State had nothing to do. Against this, the Hyderabad State Congress reacted by saying that the right to decide the relationship with the Indian Union belonged to the people, not to the nizam, and urged the population to resist any attempt to impose an autocratic, Muslim regime in isolation from the rest of India. Congress argued for an immediate accession to India and the introduction of responsible government. Except for a few feudal lords who supported the Majlis' call for an independent Hyderabad, most of the Hindus wanted to join India. However, it was against the Communists that the supporters of the nizam first became engaged.

While the nizam's government was bogged down with the problems of religious conflict and political turmoil, the Communists attempted to bring down the state. The Marxists, with support in the villages in the northern districts of Hyderabad State, began agitating against the landlords and protested the nizam's protection of the feudal lords and the bourgeoisie, demanding the right of land ownership for cultivators. To suppress the Communist-led revolt, government forces used the *Razakars*, volunteers in the most militant wing of Majlis-Iittehad-ul-Muslimin. It was estimated that the number of *Razakars* employed ranged between 30,000 and 50,000, and that they were armed with only 3,000 to 4,000 muzzle-loaders and a few 12-bores and sporting rifles (Bawa 1992: 265).

In 1947, the Majlis-Ittihad-ul Muslimin enlisted 900,000 members in Hyderabad, out of the total Muslim population of 2,200,000. They also supported the atrocities carried out by the *Razakars* and the police, allegedly against innocent Hindus suspected of participating in Communist terrorist activities, working as informants for the Communists, or simply supporting the Communists. But the state government's callous attitude towards the killing of innocent Hindus and atrocities by the police and the *Razakars* was also criticized by some Muslims. But the *Razakar* fanatics branded their critics as traitors and called for their execution. Qasim Razvi became increasingly arrogant, announcing on the radio that Hyderabad was a Muslim state and that its army would even march to Delhi and hoist the Asaf Jahi flag on the

Lal Quila, or Red Fort. He even announced on 8 April 1948 that the nizam would annex disputed areas of India.

The crisis ended with the Indian takeover of Hyderabad. The "Standstill Agreement," drafted in October 1947, was broken by both sides, again and again, and finally, the Indian Union decided to use military force against the nizam. While Pakistan was still recovering from the death of the country's founder, Mohammad Ali Jinnah, India launched Operation Polo on 13 September 1948. India classified the military operation as a police action.

Within five days, the Southern Command of the Indian Military had attacked Hyderabad from five directions. The nizam's forces had no alternative but to surrender to the Indian Military. The surrender ceremony took place outside Hyderabad, on 18 September. The government placed Mir Laik Ali, the prime minister, and Qasim Razvi, the leader of Majlis, under house arrest; both managed to escape to Pakistan. Several other Muslim leaders were arrested and imprisoned as a precautionary measure, to prevent a larger Muslim insurrection.

With Muslim power crushed, the Hindus immediately started their retaliation. In the days between the actual invasion and the establishment of martial law, thousands of Muslims in Hyderabad city and in villages were slaughtered, uprooted, burned, raped and terrorised by Hindu fanatics. Properties were also expropriated. Eventually, order was restored. J.N. Choudhary was made Military Governor of Hyderabad and continued in this position till the end of 1949, when an intermediate civil administration was put in place.

General elections were held in 1952 and won by the still popular Congress Party, which then formed a state government. But the violent events of the preceding years were to have a strong impact, including the relocation of large numbers of people. Many, including noblemen, bureaucrats and the wealthy, who were pro-*Razakar*, had fled to Pakistan to avoid revenge, and many destitute Muslims in rural villages escaped to Hyderabad and took refuge among the large Muslim community there.

It is difficult to have a clear picture about the role of the Hadramis during these tragic events, but certainly they were also caught up by the drama. Major-General Syed Ahmed el Edross states in his autobiography that the Arabs took no part in the *Razakar* movement. In fact, he says, the *Razakars* raided the house of the Arab lecturer Saif bin Hussain Al-Qaity of the Osmania University, burning his furniture and library. The incident happened because the house was wanted as the *Razakar* headquarters and the lecturer had refused to vacate it (el Edross 1994: 115). V.K. Bawa, on the other hand, writes: "There were also Arabs (*chaoosh*) in different parts of the State who were part of the Razakar phenomenon, although not always uniformed" (Bawa 1992: 265).

The uncertainty about the role of the Arabs also relates to the position of Major-General Syed Ahmed el Edross himself and the part he played during the "police action." The issue is whether he, as commander-in-chief of the army, did what was necessary to defend Hyderabad, or whether he was actually in league with the Indians (see Omar Khalidi's discussion, 1994: 212). He was arrested and held for some months after the successful escape of the nizam's prime minister.

But it is a fact that the dismantling of the nizam's army after its defeat had already begun under the supervision of Syed Ahmed el Edross. As he himself wrote:

> The repatriation of Pathans started and they were sent back to Pakistan. The Arabs were dispatched to Arabia via Bombay. The Moplas returned to the Malabar coast. The Muslim refugees that had come into Hyderabd from Bejar and other adjoining areas were all repatriated. The few British officers in Hyderabad at the time were sent to the United Kingdom with all their assets. (el Edroos 1994: 144–45)

Omar Khalidi notes that "immediately after the collapse of Hyderabadi resistance, many thousands of Muslims were deported out of India, on the charge of being foreigners (non-*mulki*)." According to official records, 200 Pathans were deported to Afghanistan. Similarly, 489 Arabs were paid all their dues and repatriated to the Western Protectorate, Aden. But Khalidi notes that, according to the versions of those deported, as many as 3,000 Hadramis were expelled from Hyderabad (Omar Khalidi 1988: 207). General Edross himself left for Bangalore, where his mother's family lived.

From "barracks" to "Barkas"—the story of a township

For the Hadramis who remained in Hyderabad, life continued under new circumstances. Although some Hadrami families still lived in the Walled City as before, they were few and "invisible" compared to the large number of Hadramis living in the township of Barkas. Barkas would therefore be a better place to seek information on the Hadrami fortunes in post-nizam Hyderabad. To go to Barkas one passes through the Walled City and continue for some five to six kilometres towards the southwest. As one passes the Falknuma Palace (one of the palaces used by nizams) and crosses the railway bridge, one finds a newly constructed mosque on the left, suggesting that Muslims live in the area.

On the right stands the Chandrayangutta, a small hillock on which is located a Hindu temple and a number of small houses. After passing the Chandrayangutta crossroads and, on taking the road south, one enters Barkas and comes first to the Chandrayangutta ("Gutta") marketplace with its crowded shops, hotels, banks, and other establishments. There are Hadrami shops, displaying Arabic writing and a drawing of the Sahin bird on their doors. Inside the shops, plates bearing neatly written Quranic verses are hung on the walls. Some of the men wear colorful *lungis* with white *topis* on their heads and women are hidden beneath black *burqas*.

There are shops selling cloth; restaurants (serving food including beef, mutton, and chicken); tea stalls; air travel agents; and private commercial telephone establishments (national and international), all run by people of Hadrami descent. Beyond the market is the residential area where the Hadramis live. The Arabic identity of the population of Barkas is evident in the name plates displayed at the entrance of each house. Date palm trees rise above the compounds. Each house has an enclosure, the entrance of which is always closed, unlike Hindu houses where the entrance is kept open. The walled enclosures connect one to the other, the houses running in a line along the neatly kept streets.

The history of Barkas relates closely to the story told above, about the nizam's army and the role Hadrami soldiers played in it. In 1875, about 400 Arab-Hadrami soldiers were settled at Maisaram Mankal, 19 kilometres south of Hyderabad. They were there as part of plans to create the Asaf Jah Regiment. In 1880, the regiment was moved close to Chandrayangutta, on land given by Bansi Raja, a Hindu nobleman in the court of the nizam. This place was called China Maisaram ("China" means small). Two barracks, an office, storeroom, hospital, quarter guard, and a room for storing weapons were constructed for the regiment. Uniforms were supplied to the soldiers and servants employed to launder them. The soldiers were also granted land for cultivation and could also build their own houses.

In this way the area came to be dominated by soldiers. Soon, China Maisaram became known as Barkas, a local usage of the English term "barracks." The soldiers were supplied every month with rations—rice, wheat, *dal*, ghee, vegetables—and firewood. In case of the death of a soldier, his children were recruited into the regiment; if they were still minors, they were enrolled into the Line Boys Regiment. The nizam also provided two schools that gave classes up to fourth standard: one for boys and one for girls. The teachers of these schools were taken from the regiment itself. The Hadramis in those days, however, showed little interest in education.

Given their military skills, the Hadramis easily found employment outside the army, as guards at palaces, post offices, public gardens, railway stations, and banks. It should also be mentioned that groups of people of African descent also belong to this story. They are the so-called *Siddis*, descendants of African slaves who live in many Indian cities, including Hyderabad, where they are called *Chaush*, a term for a unit in the nizam's army. Many "Hadramis" stress that the Chaush are not from their group. They contend that those of African descent have taken advantage of the privileged status granted to the Arabs, and obtained jobs by claiming Arab status and by changing their original names into Arabic ones. In this way they also obtained houses in Barkas, and, according to some, such "false Arabs" make up a significant part of the Barkas population.

Until one or two decades ago, Barkas was the southwestern edge of the city. In recent years, non-Arabs have migrated to the southern and eastern edges of Barkas and formed new neighborhoods, including Salala, Ballaguda, and Babanagar. Some Hadramis also moved to these places, seeking larger accommodation for growing families. But Barkas has continued to have its own identity, even as its population has steadily increased. As mentioned earlier, Barkas had a modest beginning with the 400 soldiers who arrived in the 1870s. But those numbers quickly increased to 1,200 as the nizam developed his army. In 1981, Ward No.18, or the Arab Zone (Census 1981), had a population of 110,002. Not knowing the exact number of Hadramis, we can conclude that there has been an enormous in-migration of people belonging to groups other than the original Arab settlers. This has made Barkas a socially complex area, with many different groups living there, as is so common in contemporary Hayderabad.

From the Army to the "informal sector"

When the government abolished the *jagirdari* system in 1949 and dissolved the nizam's army, the bottom fell out of the Hadrami economy in Barkas and elsewhere in Hyderabad. Most of the people had no marketable skills or the financial resources required to establish their own businesses. Many of the Hadramis ended up in the informal economy that developed in Hyderabad. We get a glimpse into this informal sector in a study by Naidu from 1990, in which the focus is not on Hadramis as such but on the broader category of "Muslims."

Naidu found people engaged in daily wage manual labor (*hamali*); unskilled self-employment like vending, hawking, and rickshaw pulling; craftwork (weaving and *chappal* making); and work as cleaners, tea boys in hotels, and hired auto-rickshaw drivers. Based on her survey, Naidu offered the following distribution of the general employment categories (rounded figures, including both Hindus and Muslims): Category I – big business (jewelers, wholesale traders, managerial jobs); II – privately practicing and government-employed professionals; III – nongazetted officials and clerks, agriculturalists, retired government officials; IV – skilled, semi-skilled self-employed workers (informal sector); V – contract, daily workers (rickshaw pulling, produce selling).

Without going into details (see Naidu 1990, chapter five) there does not seem to be a big difference between Hindu and Muslim employment patterns, although differences were detected in two of the occupational categories. The proportion of Hindus is higher than Muslims in the occupation category I, due to the predominance of the Marwaris who are engaged in big business. On the other hand, Muslims dominate category III, which is a category of people with a history relating to earlier government services and current employment in informal sector activities and also migration to the Gulf countries.

Looking at our information from Hadrami informants in Barkas, we see a similar development. After retiring from the military service, some Hadramis started small business ventures, like selling fruit, running a stationery shop, food stores and the like which were later taken over by their sons. Some cultivated vegetable and fruit on the land granted to them, for which there was a good market in the city. One man also started up a dairy operation. The following three cases based on my interviews in Barkas give a picture of the changes that took place following the end of military careers.

The ancestors of one family came to the Deccan more than five generations ago. A jagir was granted to them at Kohir in Medak district. The grandfather of the informant was appointed as a police officer and his son was employed with the nizam as a civil supplies officer. When he retired, his three sons had sufficient income from their jagir and started a transport business. But in 1970, two of their lorries were burnt down by agitators of the Hindi Movement. This resulted in heavy losses and necessitated selling most of their land and starting the business again. One son continued the business but went to Ahmedabad, while another joined the film industry in Bombay, but he also incurred a loss due to problems in making a film. This person shifted to work as a property dealer and estate marketer, an option which was possible because of contacts with people in the Gulf countries and also some in Hyderabad. He now works as an agent in property sales. The third son started up the transport business again.

In the second case, the original migrant came to Hyderabad to work in the military of the nizam, but one of his descendants (the father of the informant) got involved in the business of oil seeds and worked as a commission agent of clothing. One of his sons continued the same business and later established a trading company that exported handicrafts made of bamboo, palm leaves, and hand-woven garments. The company received a national excellence award in 1975. Another son showed much interest in football. Though initially he joined the police force of the nizam, he left the job and joined the football clubs Muhammadan Sporting Club and Mohan Bhagan in Calcutta. Then he went to Yemen as a football coach, got further training as a coach in Germany, and worked in Yemen and Abu Dhabi for some time but returned to India some years ago.

In the last case, an immigrant started a small business after coming to Hyderabad, but the income was not enough to maintain all of his entire family. So one of his sons enlisted in the nizam's army and, at the same time, started a cycle shop that bought, sold, and repaired bicycles. In the military he obtained a good position as Subedar and earned a good salary, which he invested in a taxi. One of his sons was trained as a mechanic and also started a cloth business. Two sons are now auto mechanics: one eventually went to the Gulf to make a living as a driver-cum-mechanic, while the other has continued running his cloth business in Barkas.

The three examples give us only a glimpse of the variety of careers and adaptive strategies in which the Hadramis became involved after the fall of the nizam. A survey among the Hadramis shows that a majority are engaged in business. But there are also poor, unemployed people. Significantly, many families report that they have adult children working in Gulf countries who send remittances home. Some also get small pensions, either from the Nizam's Trust or the state government, which are insufficient to live on.

The government publication *Special Report of Hyderabad City* (1981) describes the economic position of Arabs living in Barkas in the following way:

> A good number of the Arabs have been employed in the Nizam's Private estate after the abolition of the military forces of the Nizam on an average pay of Rs. 25 to each individual. And few of the Arabs entered bank services also. Fruit selling and fan, bag, basket and mat-making have been adopted as subsidiary occupations by several of the Arabs whose income otherwise was meagre. Among fruits guava, figs and *jamoon* are very important as they are abundantly grown in Maisaram which is inhabited mostly by the Arabs. There is not a single house where a guava tree is not to be found either in the front yard or the back yard of their houses. They bring baskets full of guavas on their cycles and sell them either at Mozam Jahi Market or at Gulzar House. About 85% of the Arabs are engaged in this business. Besides, a few of them have opened "Lungi shops" at Pathergatti and Maisaram. During Ramzan month they generally sell dates at evening time in front each mosque of the city. Fans, baskets and bags are made of palm leaves and are sold at Mir Alam Mandi and at Gulzar House.(Census 1981: 81)

A list of Hadrami occupations, provided by the Yemeni Association of India (Al Jamaiatul Yamania Bil Hind), shows a similar variation. The information pertains to 96 households spread over different parts of Hyderabad. It is not collected in any systematic way, and should not be taken to give anything but a general impression. A majority (44) of Hadramis are engaged in business. It can also be noted that very few have what might be called a white-collar job or have received higher education. The major occupations of the households were as follows: business 44, drivers 23, agriculturalists 20, pensioner 8, driver 6, tailor 5, mechanic 4, typist 3, engineer 3, government service 2, police 2, rickshaw puller 2, electrician 2. Some occupations were only represented by one single person, such as plumber, bicycle repairist, at-tender, journalist, Imam, teacher, welder.

Khanazad

Before we proceed, let us examine the employment of Hadramis in the nizam's private estate after the fall of the regime in 1948. The last nizam was the head of one of the world's most wealthy dynasties. In the years following the police action, the government of India entered an agreement with the nizam to make payments to him and his dependants as partial compensation for the annexation of properties by the government of India. The nizam was guaran-teed an annual privy purse of Rs. 5,500,000 (tax-free); a further Rs. 2,500,000 was to be paid every year for the upkeep of his palaces and an additional Rs. 2,500,000 to replace income that had previously been received from the Sarf-e-Khas estates.

The nizam's heirs and *jagirdars* were also paid compensation for the loss of their properties. However, in view of the uncertainty that faced his family, heirs and dependants, the nizam decided to liquidate part of his wealth and transform it into a series of trusts. He created altogether thirty-two trusts of which the Khanazad Institution is important for the present study.

In recognition of the faithful service of his soldiers, the nizam decided to help some young children from these families, both boys and girls, some of whom were Hadramis from Barkas. These were called *khanazad*, meaning "sons of the house," and were treated like adopted children. The parents of these boys and girls agreed to the arrangement and gave their consent in writ-ing. The Khanazad Institution was established in 1952 by official declarations in *Shiraz*, an official publication, and in the *Nizam Gazette* notification.

The people we found who had been involved with the *khanazad* all lived in King Kothi, near the center of the city and the area where the last nizam, Mir Osman Ali Khan, lived. The *khanazad* played a special role for the nizam, and were granted favors, including accommodation, education in Persian, Arabic, and English, and lessons in royal etiquette. The nizam assumed per-sonal responsibility for the *khanazad*. However, after the death of Nizam Mir Osman Ali Khan on 24 February 1967, the *khanazads* became a symbol of an earlier era. More importantly, the largesse they had depended on was also of the past. They had earlier received pocket money of Rs. 100 a month, while the nizam covered all their day-to-day costs. Without the nizam's support, and with prices for basic goods rising, the *khanazads* were in trouble.

They pleaded for more money, but the trustees of the Khanazad Institute refused. The *khanazad* then formed an association to lobby for their interests. This association was headed by Yousuf Ali Khan, who was also in charge of the Langer Khana mess that supplied food to all the *khanazad*. He was considered to be in a position to best represent their grievances to the Nizam's Trust and Prince Mukarram Jah, who had followed his father, the nizam, as family head. But Yousuf Ali Khan was murdered in 1968 by unidentified assailants, and the remaining *khanazad* never managed to develop any organizational strength to win their demands.

The Khanazad Institute was dissolved in 1980, which led to the division of the remaining funds. Forty percent of the money went to Prince Mukarram Jah, and 60 percent was distributed by the *khanazad* among themselves, each member receiving about Rs. 35,000. A special problem for the *khanazad* was the legal ownership of the houses they had been living in. In January 1987, the government of Andhra Pradesh issued an order to vacate the houses occupied by some *khanazad* on the grounds that they did not have a legal basis for their possession of the houses.

This was true, as the nizam in his time had only permitted them to live in the houses by an oral order or *hiba*. The *khanazad* took it to court and won a decision giving them legal possession of their houses. This of course helped the individuals who were directly involved, but they represented only a tiny minority of Hadramis. Of far greater importance to their future economic welfare was the sudden oil boom and labor shortage in neighboring Saudi Arabia and the Gulf in the 1970s.

Migration to the Gulf

Opportunities for employment, combined with a liberalization of passport policies by the Janata government of 1977, enabled mass migration from India. Again referring to Naidu's study, most migrant laborers in her survey were employed in construction; others were mechanics, tailors, cooks, and drivers. There were some white-collar jobs for clerks, but fewer positions for professionals, like doctors and engineers. In Naidu's findings, a majority of the Gulf migrants got their jobs through friends and relatives. Many also found employment through agents in Hyderabad. This was in spite of the fact that the use of agents was considered risky (the job might not exist or the agent could turn out to be a fraud). Others acquired employment through direct contacts with employers, while a few found work through the government of India.

Although the remittances were too low to affect the general socioeconomic status of people in Hyderabad, Naidu notes visible economic results for the individuals involved, in improved housing and more elaborate weddings and funerals. There were also cultural effects, including the spread of Arabic styles of dress, increased usage of the Arabic language and a higher incidence of *purdah* among women.

Regarding the Hadramis and their involvement in labor migration to the Gulf, the "local historian" Osman Baosman writes:

[E]xcept a few (*khanazad*), several others had been facing economic problems such as (1) they do not get government jobs, (2) they do not have savings to start any business and (3) they do not have an experience of doing business. Thank God. In spite of all these problems people of Barkas are living peacefully. Some of them have gone to Yemen, Saudi Arabia and other Gulf countries for earning their livelihood. Because of this emigration, some economic problems are being mitigated from the remittances of those emigrated. (Baosman n.d.: 48)

Baosman himself went to Aden in 1962 to work in a college and did not return to Barkas until 1984.

In a survey that we undertook among the Hadramis, twenty-four out of forty-seven families interviewed reported migration to the Gulf, the most common destinations mentioned being Dubai and Saudi Arabia. There was also a clear pattern showing that it was the generation in their twenties and thirties in the 1970s that most commonly migrated, thus giving migration a clear generational pattern. In her survey, Naidu (1990) reports that 12 percent of the sample households in the old city of Hyderabad had family members in Gulf countries and that one in every two or three households in Barkas has a member in the Gulf; in Barkas, the State Road Transport Corporation had to arrange special buses from Barkas to the airport to handle the large number of travellers (1990: 96). She also found that the occupations pursued in the Gulf countries showed "low occupational status and high job uncertainty."

Although the remittances sent home by these migrants were of low monetary value, the income had a major impact on the economic situation of individual households. Naidu writes:

According to our survey, barely 2 percent of the beneficiary households used this money productively, either investing it in business or purchasing land. Eleven per cent saved their income from the Gulf in banks to meet marriage or similar expenses in the future; 55 percent used it to meet household expenses and buy luxury goods; while 32 percent spent it to renovate and repair their homes. (Naidu 1990: 97)

Usama Khalidi also noted the same. He writes:

Back in Hyderabad, families at all economic levels were rolling in the money (of Gulf). Some neighbourhoods, such as Barkas, were luckier than others in their share of the new affluence. In their economic behaviour, the newly affluent were not as prudent as they should have been, and spent their money on lavish ceremonies, consumer luxuries and in other generally unproductive ways. Families remodelled and improved their properties, bought television sets and arranged the marriages of their sons and daughters in grand style. (quoted in O. Khalidi 1988: 195–96)

Being Hadrami in Hyderabad

The maintenance of everyday Hadrami identities in Barkas in Hyderabad happens through many processes. One such process is through the staging of different traditional practices on the occasions of birth, marriage, and death, as well as an adherence to culinary varieties, tastes, and preferences in dress, music, dance, and so on. All of these cultural traits or practices differentiate the Hadramis from other groups, and Hadramis themselves use them as diacritical marks of their identity and exclusivity.

However, without going into great detail, it is clear that the Hadramis are strongly influenced by the local traditions of the local Deccani Muslims, and also by the Hindus, the major population surrounding them. The educational system has pulled the Hadramis towards integration with other local groups based on the dominant integrative policies of the state. Before 1947 there were only two schools in Barkas, one for boys and one for girls. Teaching in both was conducted in Urdu, the state language. This means that Hadramis became fluent in Urdu, and only in rare cases were able to maintain their Arabic language skills. This was different from the earlier situation in which the Hadrami soldiers learnt Urdu in order to interact within the nizam's state system, but through constant migrations and new arrivals from Hadramaut, the possibility to maintain Arabic as well was better.

With the Indian takeover in 1948, Arabic also became secondary to both Telugu and English, as well as Hindi. This all meant that Arabic disappeared as a language actively spoken by many Hadramis, and today only a minority of people of Hadrami descent in Hyderabad have a command of Arabic beyond prayers and religious sayings. In the late 1990s, when our study was carried out, there were seven schools teaching in English language recognised by the state government, some of which took students up to tenth class. There was one government-run Urdu high school for girls, and two private junior colleges, one for girls and one for boys.

The provision of schools has improved the educational level of the inhabitants, and high school education as well as university enrollment is now common. Boys were encouraged by their parents to pursue their educations in both Urdu and English beyond high school, but girls were until very recently kept at home, the reason being that the parents did not want to send the girls far away into the city for college studies. But this also changed with the establishment of a junior college exclusively for girls in Barkas itself.

The spread of modern education then has helped make Hadrami children more into Hyderabadis than Hadramis. But the situation varies among families. Some families have been better able to maintain their use of the Arabic language and also have clearer memories of their family pasts in Hadramaut than others. Such a development is partly related to the events following the military crackdown in 1948. Many Hadramis were sent back home after the police action while others remained: There are some links between families that left and those that stayed in Hyderabad.

Labor migration to the Gulf has even made it easier for individuals to visit their relatives who reside in the ancient homeland. If such direct contact does not occur, others communicate by letter writing and by telephone. But such contacts with Hadramaut have been greatly reduced over the years, and in most of the cases the people we spoke to said that they had long ago lost contact with their relatives. But even if such direct and real links have disappeared, other links are being recreated through processes of imagination. Revitilization of identities based on the imagining of links to the homeland is of course common in most diasporic communities, and the Hadramis in Hyderabad are no exception.

Labor migration to the Gulf and Saudi Arabia has of course brought people geographically closer to their homeland, and into situations in which they have met fellow migrants who have themselves come from Hadramaut. Such encounters, and the stories told by people who actually live in Hadramaut, have provided Hadrami migrants with a sort of memory about the homeland that they were in danger of losing. At home, in Barkas, the establishment of various types of organizations have also produced a new awareness about historical links to Arabia. There are many examples of committees and boards functioning for the well-being of Barkas residents that also help to create an awareness about who they are. The organizations of relevance to the Hadramis may promote an Islamic identity, an Arab identity, or a Yemeni identity.

Examples of such organizations in Barkas are Sabeel-ul-Khair, the Masjid Committee, Arab Educational Board, Khair Supplying Committee, Jamaitul Khairia, Football Association, Youth Association, Shabab Committee, and Jamait-ul-Yamania Bil Hind. The Sabeel-ul-Khair has been run with contributions from residents, and has positions such as president, secretary, and treasurer, who are elected every three years. It has established Madarse Huffaz (for memorizing the Koran) and Madarse Khair-ul-Uloom, for teaching Arabic. The Masjid Committee looks after the affairs of the two Masjids in Barkas while an elected board runs the Arabic school, Madarse Khair-ul-Uloom.

Jamait-Al-Hadramia Bil Hind was established in 1967 to provide Arabic education, but in the course of time its scope was expanded. In 1981 it was registered as Al-Jamaiatul Yamania Bil Hind with three-year terms of office for a president, vice-president, secretary, and treasurer. It runs an Arabic school in Barkas and helps Hadramis get identification certificates from the Embassy of Yemen at New Delhi for those who want to visit or permanently return to Yemen or other Gulf countries (Baosman n.d.: 59–60).

The organization has sought support from Yemen for people in the diaspora. At one point, a formal request was made to the Yemeni government for the provision of Yemeni Arabic newspapers and Arabic teachers. The Jamait-Al-Hadramia Bil Hind asked Yemen to open a consulate office in Bombay to facilitate relations between Indo-Yemenis and Yemenis. As well, it was felt that the Yemeni government should find work for qualified Yemeni Indians in the Gulf and that it should provide funding to the Barkas Welfare Association. It was not known whether the Yemen government replied to the requests in the affirmative.

Regardless, the organization has attempted to connect Hadramis of Barkas and Hyderabad with Yemen and other Gulf countries. Those who want to visit Gulf states can register with the Al-Jamaitul Hadrami Bil Hind and apply for an identification certificate which is used to speed up visa applications.

Contemporary Hadrami identities—the Hindu-Muslim divide

The general status of the Hadrami group in contemporary Hyderabad seems to be ambivalent. Certainly, the Hadramis try to combine their various possible identities in different ways. Added to the notion of Hadrami identities is the complex ethnic and cultural pattern of Hyderabad. In the Census of India report of 1981, the following groups are mentioned: Arabs in Barkas, of which the Hadramis are part; various Hindu groups coming from Rajasthan (Marwadi zone from Marwar region in Rajasthan, consisting of Jodhpur, Udaipur, Jaipur, and Bikaneer); the Kayasth and Khatri castes; Maharashrians (Maratha zone); Muslim groups consisting of Shi'as and Sunnis (categorised locally into Sayeds, Shaikh, Mughal, and Pathan); Bohoras, most of whom are Ismailis; a population relating to former eunuchs (Eunuch zone); smaller groups of Hindus like Pardhi (Pardhi zone), Joshi (Jotishi zone), and Lodha; Parsis who are Zoroastrians; Christians of various denominations; and, finally, an increasing number of immigrants of Telegu-speaking Hindus from elsewhere in Andhra Pradesh state, many coming from the coastal zone in the east.

Two basic types of identities stand out as particularly important for the Hadramis in their general adaptation as a Muslim group in Hyderabad. This is the basic division in Indian society between the Hindu and Muslim population. This national division has shaped the situation of the Hadramis, from being part of local elite groups during the Muslim dynasties before Indian

Independence, to becoming part of a marginalized Muslim and Arab population during the decades after 1947.

The Hadramis have sought to develop peaceful relationships with their Hindu neighbors in Barkas as well as elsewhere. But communal riots continue to flare up from time to time in Hyderabad and such periods of unrest must also affect the Hadramis. The situation relates also to national politics. As we know, the national situation has been characterized by a movement away from the secular model represented by the Congress Party at the time of Indian independence, towards communalist polarization, represented in politics by the Hindu BJP and Muslim Majlis parties (see, for example, van der Veer 1994; van der Veer and Lehman, eds. 1999). This development also characterizes Hyderabad politics in the post-1948 period.

After the Police Action, there was a gradual loss of the influence by the Congress Party, particularly after Nehru's death in 1964, which led to a weakening of secularism. Efforts to integrate Hindus and Muslims within the same political umbrella had not succeeded. Instead, religion became a political factor of increasing importance, with fundamentalist parties promoting so-called communalism. There was also an upsurge in the number of regional parties. We see both developments in Andhra Pradesh.

The period of the 1950s and into the 1960s was one in which the Congress Party dominated politics, winning Hyderabad seats in national elections from 1952 to 1984. This was also a period in which Congress was trying to build a secular state in which Hindus and the remaining Indian Muslims could live together. The establishment in 1957 of Andhra Pradesh as a new state also led to political splits along religious lines.

It was decided that the Telugu language would become the dominant language of Andhra Pradesh, replacing Urdu. As Urdu was the language of Muslims, of the former ruling elite and linked to Pakistan, it immediately became a political issue (see for example, Omar Khalidi ed, 1988, for the importance of Urdu as a factor in politics during the 1984, 1989, and 1991 elections). Similarly, issues like Muslim personal law, family planning in Muslim areas (as they have higher rates of population increase), and conversions (Hindus converting to Islam) were all increasingly important and controversial. For instance, in 1990 a regulation forbade conversion to Islam (or Christianity) by civil servants of "scheduled caste" origin.

But there were also sites of conflict that were not related to Hindu-Muslim relations. Internal regionalism developed between Andhra, Rayalasima, and Telangana, while caste differences appeared in politics among Kammas, Reddis, and a large population of "scheduled castes" and tribes. All of these developments were reflected in politics. A later consequence of the political situation was the 1982 creation of the Telugu Desam party by N.T. Rama Rao and the victory of the party in the 1983 state election. The party held state power until 1989, losing to the Congress Party, and then won it back in 1994. Extreme Hindu parties also emerged in this period, including Jan Sangh (since the 1967 election), and later the Bharatiya Janata Party (BJP), both of which came to play a major role in Hyderabad.

On the Muslim side, 1957 saw the revival of the Majlis al-Ittihad-ul-Muslimin. The party challenged the Congress Party in local municipal elections after 1960 and state elections after 1967. In 1985, a Majlis candidate won a seat in Parliament, defending it in 1989. A large part of the Muslim vote backed the Majlis, but the 1949 establishment of constituencies was a setback for the party. The new constituencies included a mix of Hindu and Muslim populations, which made it more difficult for Majlis to tap into its supporters (prior to 1949, Muslims and other minorities were represented by separate seats). Majlis went into alliances with other parties, both "scheduled castes" and tribes (see Omar Khalidi ed, 1988: 186ff for a case study on elections to the Lok Sabha, or lower house of Indian Parliament).

Today, this party has split into two, with the main Majlis Party following the traditional leader, Sultan Salauddin Owaisi, and his son, Asaduddin Owaisi, and one breakaway faction, Majlis Bachao Tehrik (MBT), headed by Owaisi's earlier close associate, Amanulla Khan, both competing for the Muslim vote. Muslims, including Hadramis, also participate in activities organized by Muslim organizations such as *Jamaat-i-Islami*, founded in 1941 by Maududi, and Tabliqi Jamaat, founded by Mohamed Ilyas in the 1920s. Both organizations were popular, and the annual meetings in Barkas in Hyderabad were attended by thousands (Usama Khalidi 1988: 195).

For the Hadramis, the situation must have been complicated. They are Muslims, but also Arab "outsiders." Having served the nizam, they represent a group which must tread carefully through what is a volatile political landscape. Residents of Barkas have had to protect themselves during communal tensions and to develop strategies to maintain a peaceful existence. This problem has been handled at two levels: at the political level, and at the local community level. At the political level, they have been dependent on local Muslim politicians.

These politicians take up issues with senior bureaucrats and administrators and provide links through which demands for material support can be furthered. But it also involves the Hadramis in political conflicts relating to party politics. Politics and elections can be violent affairs, and Hyderabad has had its share of communal riots, riots that have only worsened as the focus on religion in politics has increased. The 1980 elections in Hyderabad left five people dead and sixty-two injured; elections to the Andhra Pradesh State Assembly in January 1983 left eleven people dead and seventy-four injured; two years later, nine were killed and many more injured.

In 1990, the BJP president, L.K. Advani staged a *rathyatra* (Hindi chariot procession) that sparked unrest in which Muslims were killed. Although the violence may appear random and spontaneous, both Hindu and Muslim organizations provide physical training for their members at "gymnasiums" (*akhara* in Hindi, *taleemkhanas* in Urdu). This training is said to produce "wrestlers" (*pehlwan*) and "rowdies" (*goonda*), both of are active during times of violence. Such "gymnasiums" have existed since the 1930s. Earlier riots (the first large-scale riot in Hyderabad was in April 1938) strengthened the belief on both sides that their supporters needed to know martial arts and show physical strength (Roosa 1998).

The violence is also perpetuated by the transference of anger about earlier events onto new generations. The youth are told about historical atrocities and the bloody partition of the country. The feeling of enmity and the heightened sense of religious identification are therefore related to the ways in which earlier instances of violence are narrated and dramatized, thus producing a "meeting of muscles and morals" (Kakar 1996: 82). Such communal violence between Muslims and Hindus is also related to their respective places of religious worship—mosques and temples. The locations of such mosques and temples and the respect, or lack of, shown by non-followers can spark wider conflicts. Some of Hyderabad's major religious processions routinely pass these sites. Insulting behavior or outright vandalism sometimes occurs.

This is particularly the case for *Bonalu* (for lower-class Hindus in July) and *Ghanesh* (all Hindus in September) and the *Muharram* (for Shi'a Muslims). The character of the two Hindu processions has changed markedly since the late 1970s. What were once small, local events are now used by Hindi fundamentalists to mobilize huge crowds of Hindus from all over Hyderabad and beyond. As the processions move through Muslim residential areas, rioting is not uncommon. In some years, the *Ghanesh* and the *Muharram* have coincided (1983 and 1985), leading to some of the worst Hindu-Muslim clashes. A new Muslim procession, *Pankha*, has also been established, starting just three days before the *Ghanesh* and further adding to the tension.

At the local level, attempts are made to solve such issues in a peaceful manner. People know that violence may be started by political activists who have an interest in keeping the communal conflicts alive, in order to demonstrate the inability of their adversaries to maintain law and order. The destruction of the Babri Masjid Mosque at Ayodhya in 1992 ignited communal clashes between Hindus and Muslims in Bombay, Ahmedabad, Surat, and Calcutta. More than a thousand people were killed in Bombay alone (van der Veer 1994).

It is important to note that Hyderabad has not experienced any major riots. Islamic organizations there were reported to have shown restraint in the period immediately following the Ayodhya crisis. It is also important to note that religious organizations such as the Muslim *dargas*, and religious ceremonies such as the *urs*, bring members of the different religions together in peaceful celebration. We should also note the importance of local organizations such as the Barkas Welfare Association. During the communal riots, the association helped provide security for all the residents in Barkas. Leading members of the association have met with the police and civil authorities during times of unrest. When excesses are seen to have been committed by riot police, the association seeks help from higher officials and demands investigations into such incidents.

Muslim schools are also now seen as problematic. A headline in *The Times of India* (13 July 2004) reads, "Patriotism to be taught in some Madrasas." The story reported that patriotism is to be taught in *madrasas* in order to change the perception that Muslim schools are "anti-nationalist indoctrination camps for young and impressionable minds." There are more than 20,000 students in *madrasas* in Hyderabad, according to *The Times of India*, and several of the schools are counted among the ten leading *madrasas* in the country. Students in these schools will now be taught lessons on what Islam says about the concept of motherland, the role of *madrasas* in the freedom movement, and the contribution of various Muslims in post-independence India, all to show that Indian Muslims are as "Indian" as anyone else.

CHAPTER THREE

✻ Hadramis in Sudan
A Red Sea Tale

I first met Ahmed Abu Bakr Bajabr in Mukalla, in the southern part of Yemen on the Gulf of Aden, in 1994. Or rather, he met me. He had heard me
speaking Arabic with someone in a government office, noticed my Sudanese
accent and came over to find out what strange incident had given a *khawajah*
such an accent. As Ahmed indeed was from Sudan, he came to represent a
special case for me, too. It turned out that he was visiting from Port Sudan,
trying to establish a poultry farm in the area, which was his way of joining
the economic boom going on in Mukalla at the time. Hadramis abroad, particularly from Saudi Arabia and the Gulf, had started to invest heavily both
in businesses and house construction after the Yemeni unification in 1990.
My first meeting with Ahmed Bajabr took place in an office dealing with
land sales connected to the investment boom. The boom was to last until the
1995 civil war. The outbreak of fighting ended the optimistic forecasts about
unification held by Hadramis in the diaspora. But that is another story. We
shall first return to Ahmed and his life story.

Ahmed Abu Bakr Bajabr was born in Andel, near Hureida, Hadramaut, in
about 1934. His father died when he was two years old. He has three sisters,
two living in Andel, and one in Mukalla. As the eldest, he was expected to
contribute to the family's income. His father had been a farmer, with small
means, so there was not much for Ahmed to do in Andel. He attended Islamic school before leaving some time around 1945, at the age of eleven, with
an uncle called FaBr. They traveled by *sambouk* from Mukalla to Jeddah, Saudi
Arabia, staying there for six months before taking another *sambouk* to Sudan.
They landed at the Red Sea port of Suakin, where they were involved in
trade. They later moved inland, to Aroma, in the Gash Delta near Kassala,
where Ahmed received further schooling.

Ahmed was not the first Bajabr to settle in Sudan. Another FaBr Mohamed Omer Bajabr had been the first of his family to leave Andel for Sudan
in 1925. He established himself as a trader in Suakin, but later returned to
Hadramawt, where he died. Mohamed Omer married both in Hadramaut and
in Sudan (in Sudan he had two wives, one from the Hadrami community and

one from a local family in Kassala). His sons also married girls in Hadramaut as well as in Sudan (in Port Sudan and Aroma), which meant that when Ahmed arrived in Suakin he already had relatives in Sudan.

Other Hadrami families had come to Sudan before the Bajabrs. Names such as Al Amoudi, Ba Hayder, Bin Said and BaGouffa were common. They had all come from Wadi Du'an. These early settlers lived in Suakin, along with Turks, Saudis, North Yemenis and a few Yemeni. According to Ahmed, other people were involved as carriers (*atala*) and as fishermen. But the Hadramis stuck to their traditional vocation-trade. Some of this trade was to Jeddah, Saudi Arabia, when it was still a small town. They traded palm products and oil. Some Hadramis from Suakin went south to Eritrea and to the border town of Aqiq. There they traded in agricultural products and animals, which also brought many of them into close contact with the Beni Amer, the dominant group in the area.

While living in Aroma, Ahmed married a Beni Amer girl whose father was from Eritrea. Their first son went to school in England and eventually married there with a girl from Wales. The son is no longer alive, but the wife and daughter visit Port Sudan from England where they live. The second son, Badr Ahmed Bajabr, is involved in his father's business. I met the two together in Mukalla, when the son was visiting from his base in Sana'a. Then, Ahmed has two daughters in Saudi Arabia, and one who lives in Sudan.

Ahmed has had a number of occupations. From 1949 to 1952 he was a trader; in 1952 he established a hotel, Funduq al Felah, in Omdurman, running it until the 1960s; at one point in the 1950s, he went to Jeddah but, finding he did not like it, returned to Sudan; in 1971 he established a Funduq al Felah in Port Sudan, which he ran until 1984; later, he set up the Funduq al Riadh. He also traded in a part of Port Sudan called *Hai el-Arab*, where he had an office and a *hosh* of 1,000 square metres where he kept his main trade items, *hadid* and *akshab* (iron and wood). In 1979 he went to Saudi Arabia and stayed in Jeddah for three years. When he returned to Sudan, he worked in agriculture in Gereif (*mazrah*). Although he still travels, Ahmed's base is in Port Sudan, where he owns two houses and some land.

His involvement in Yemen goes back to the late 1980s, when the ambassadors of North Yemen and South Yemen came to Port Sudan to discuss possibilities for opening trade between Sudan and the then two separate countries. Ahmed got a Yemeni passport and opened a food shop in Sana'a. After unity in 1990, he went to Aden and Mukalla, and in the late 1990s he was trying to get land to establish a chicken feed production. One of his workers in Mukalla is another Sudanese Hadrami, by the name of Hamoudi. He is one of the six sons of Abdalla al Mahamoudi, a tribesman from Wadi Hamoudi near Mukalla. Abdalla had driven lorries between Tokar and Port Sudan and knew the area well. Other relatives from the same family had gone to Kenya and Somalia. Ahmed's five brothers were also living in Mukalla. One became a millionaire in the overheated land market that followed unification.

Movement across the Red Sea

Ahmed's account of his time in Sudan is representative of the experience of a number of Hadramis whom I later came to meet in Mukalla, Port Sudan, and Khartoum. The migration to Sudan began during a period of profound change, not only in the Red Sea region but southwards, along the Swahili coast. A significant economic development was the opening of the Suez Canal. It was also a time of political competition between the regional powers of Egypt and Ethiopia and European colonial powers, including Britain, France, Italy, and Germany. In this section, two developments will be focused upon: British and Italian activities in Somalia involving the Omani Sultanate of Zanzibar; and the British and Egyptian competition in the Red Sea that led to Britain's colonization of Egypt in 1884 and Sudan in 1898.

Let us start in the northern end of the area, along the Red Sea and in the two coastal towns of Suakin, in Sudan, and Massawa, in Ethiopia. It was here that Khedive Islamil Pasha of Egypt (1863–1879), inspired by his grandfather, Mohamed Ali, dreamed of creating an African empire. The proximity of the three trading centers of Suakin, Massawa, and Jeddah linked Africa to the Hijaz and the Muslim pilgrimage. From the time of the suppression of the Wahhabi revolt, Muhamed Ali had been interested in these towns. Egypt gained control of the towns in 1811, and Muhamed Ali named his son, Ahmad Tusun Pasha, governor of the Vilayet of Jeddah.

In 1827, after the Wahhabi revolt had been crushed in Arabia, the towns reverted to Ottoman Turkish rule, but were left for Egypt to dominate during the lifetime of Muhamed Ali. Mohamed Ali became involved in the Yemeni coffee trade, and set up a monopoly in the 1830s. He had already occupied Sudan in 1821 and, with his Syrian campaigns beginning from 1831, Mohamed Ali was seen as a ruler of importance. Britain watched these developments with concern. The regional developments certainly played a role in its decision to occupy Aden in 1837. From Aden the British could also keep an eye on Ethiopia, especially the important trading town of Massawa.

But Muhamed Ali died in 1849 and his two successors, Abbas (1849–1854) and Sa'id (1854–1863), were not particularly interested in developing his expansionist policies in Africa. This changed when Ismail Pasha became the ruler of Egypt in 1863. He wanted both to create an empire like that of his grandfather, Mohamed Ali, and also to safeguard the territories won earlier in the Nile Valley (Talhami 1979). After Egyptian control was secured, a series of administrative reforms and experiments were begun. Administrative structures shifted between organizing Suakin, Kassala, and Massawa into one province under the control of Khartoum or leaving each with its own governor, answering to Cairo.

Soon they were developing plans for transport links, telegraph lines, and water works. The region suffered from a lack of health services, schools, mosques, and basic housing, so new systems of taxation and local administration were introduced. The senior administrators, Mumtaz and Munziger, operated with considerable independence, but sometimes conflicted with their superiors in Cairo, as they did with the local population over the payment of taxes and forced labor. Economic development was also promoted. Increased production of cotton and *dura* was a priority in areas that could be irrigated. The cultivation of such cash crops were introduced to areas such as the Tokar Delta , Gash and, in the south, Aqiq. Cotton was a priority in order to exploit international market shortages caused by the American Civil War.

Mining was another activity, as was salt, which was shipped to Jeddah to be resold to Indian boats. Minerals were also sought. To better reach markets, improved transport between Sudan and Egypt became another priority. Work began on the Aswan-Khartoum railway link (against the Berber-Suakin link), and British engineers were brought in to improve river transport through the Nile cataracts. With costs mounting, Egypt began to borrow heavily from foreign sources.

Plans to develop the ports of Massawa and Suakin were brought to a halt by Egypt's war with Ethiopia in 1875–1876. Egypt's defeat created discontent among senior officers and further strained the already weak economy. The defeat also brought Britain more actively into the regional politics of the Red Sea, both as an arbitrator after the Egyptian-Ethiopian war and as a direct actor in Sudan.

A show of European power was seen as a way to end what was viewed in Europe as "African," "Muslim," and/or "Turkish" chaos. And, due to Egypt's debts, Britain became more directly involved in Egyptian affairs. Ismail was deposed and Mohamed Tawfiq took over. A nationalist initiative by Urabi Pasha and other Circassian officers was also contained. With the Mahdist Revolution in Sudan and the British takeover of Egypt and Sudan, the region was increasingly run by the British. Suakin, regarded as the only Egyptian territory that had escaped Mahdist control, was no exception (Talhami 1979).

It is during this time of general unrest and foreign occupation that we find the early migration of Hadramis (Ewald and Clarence-Smith 1997). The Hadramis came from the inland of Hadramaut, particularly Wadi Du'an, and traveled to Aden, and the Red Sea ports of Jeddah and Suakin, as well as to Cairo. With the development of railway tracks and roads, the interior was now open to trade. The migrants also went to Ethiopia, Somalia, and Kenya. Shipping was an important activity. We have seen the interests of the Hadramis in Singapore in the pilgrimage traffic, and the same traffic was also important also for Red Sea shipping, not by steamships but by dhows. Trade in slaves was also common; slaves were also commonly used as crew on the dhows. Trade in coffee to Egypt was important, as was the arms trade to Djibouti.

Less important trade items included millet and sesame from Somalia to Hadramaut (Alpers 1983) and hides, millet, and camels out of Massawa. Moneylending was also common, in which the Hadramis competed with Indians. By 1930, Hadramis had invested heavily in property. They were also involved in the politics of the Sharif of Mecca and served as soldiers under various leaders, a career that was also common in Hyderabad. Their religious impact was not as big as in Asia, and the Shafi'e law schools of Islam, to which they belonged, was less common in these areas.

Suakin, the first center

Suakin illustrates the common characteristics of a coastal Red Sea town, in its economy, social organization, and the role of religion. Suakin is also a special case, possibly having ancient religious relations with Hadramaut (Hofheinz 1996). Suakin was built on a coral island, separated from the mainland, or *Al-Geif*, by a narrow channel. The difference between the island and the mainland was not only one of geography, but also of the social and cultural character of its inhabitants. The island was an Indian Ocean merchant town with houses made of limestone.

The development of new buildings was slow until the building boom of the 1860s and 1870s, led by the policies of Khedive Ismail. Apart from the government *diwan*, the town of Suakin included two mosques, some warehouses, and coffee houses. There were few houses on the mainland, as the area was mostly inhabited by the Beja people who traditionally lived in semipermanent huts or shelters. There was a mosque as early as 1822, according to Burckhardt (1822/1978). While mainland culture was dominated by the Beja, the island's inhabitants represented Arabic culture, speaking Arabic and dressing like *hijazis*. The mainlanders spoke Ti-Bedawyet and wore traditional clothing.

The two population groups stood out—the townspeople and the Beja. But each group was heterogeneous. On the island there were "Turks," which included people from everywhere in the Ottoman Empire; and "Banyans," a term used for a group of non-Muslim Indians engaged in trade with India and also moneylending. The group included merchant castes from northern and western India (Sind and Gujarat), most of whom were Hindu but who could also be Jain. Finally, there were also local elite religious groups like the Beja Hasanab and the Artega.

On the mainland, meanwhile, the inhabitants were Hadariba and Beja (Bishariyyin, Amarar and Hadendowa, collectively known as Sawakini). The Hadariba were related to religious elites among the Beja dating from pre-Islamic times and who claimed ancestry from Hadramaut. It is unclear at what time this occurred, indicating a lack of a clear genealogy, and perhaps also that the term Hadariba is more of an ethnic label for people who advanced claims about Hadrami descent in general.

The Artega (or "patricians") were the political leaders, comprising five families from which the *amir al-Hadariba* (prince of Hadariba) was chosen. They claimed ancestry from Hadrami *ashraf* through Mohammad BaSaffar, who is said to have immigrated from Hadramaut. Mohammed was related to Mohamad b. al-Hanafiyya (637–700/1), a son of Ali b. Ali Talib (not from Fatima but from Khawla, a prisoner/slave), who was the first Alid to be declared a *mahdi*. Some Kurds were there, descendants from earlier Ottoman soldiers, prisoners, and exiles who remained after the Ottoman occupation of the town in the sixteenth century. There were also pilgrims from West Africa (*takarir*) and slaves. There were Shafi'e mosques (dominated by the Shafi'e law school) controlled by Hasanab, and also government (Ottoman) mosques which were dominated by the Hanefi law school. The Eastern Sudanese hinterland, however, was generally dominated by the Maliki law school.

The Hasanab, among whom muftis were chosen, trace descent through Ibrahim b. Ismail b. Ahmad, back to Ahmad b. Ujayl, a *shafi'e faqi* who lived north of Zebid, in the area around which the town Beyt al-Faqi developed. The Ashraf claim descent from Sharif Muhammad, who is believed to have arrived in Suakin sometime between the mid fifteenth and early seventeenth centuries.

In the early nineteenth century most of the trade from Suakin went to Arabia, with sorghum (*dura*) being the most important export item. The grain came from Kassala-Gedaref (Butana) and the Gash, but some also came from agricultural areas along the Nile. The Beja brought animal products, mats, *dom* fruit, *nabaq,* camels, and a few cattle. Fishermen provided fish and some pearls. Slaves and gold made up the luxury goods, together with ivory, tobacco, incense, gum arabic, ostrich feathers and eggs, horses, ebony, and musk. Cloth (*dammur*) was also traded. Indian goods were among the imports, including textiles, spices, perfumes, ornaments, and rice. From Jeddah, traders imported household utensils, dates, onions, sugar, coffee, tobacco, iron, and steel. All imported goods went through customs in Suakin.

Burckhardt, who was in Suakin in the 1820s, confirms this. He estimated the population on the island to be around 3,000, with an additional 5,000 on the mainland. He noted the apparent wealth of the Hadarba, Suakin's renowned trading community, and pointed out that they owed their success to their blood ties with the people of the Arabian seashore. Hadarba agents operated in Jeddah, Khartoum, Berber and Kassala. From Jeddah, they kept in touch with India. They traded with the Nubian centers of Sennar and Shendi, acquiring slaves, gold, tobacco, incense, and ostrich feathers for export.

From Kassala they bought butter, which they carried in a liquid state (*semn*), and *dura,* the grain which had a market in Arabia. The town also provided waterskins and other leather products. Mats were acquired from various Beja groups, while the famous racing camels were obtained from the Bishariyyin, one of the groups within the Beja confederation. Imports from India, shipped through Jeddah, included women's dresses and ornaments, Indian sugar, coffee, dates, and iron. The iron was used to made knives and swords treasured by the Beja. These goods were brought across the Red Sea by small boats run by Arabs. Sudanese goods came on the Berber-Suakin caravans, but also from Khartoum via Kassala. As the slave trade diminished, gum Arabic from the Kordofan region of western Sudan rose as a new important export crop.

By 1867 the main trade items were gum Arabic, ivory, and hides. Trade from Massawa was affected by instability in Ethiopia caused by Amhara disturbances. Because of this, new opportunities arose for Sudanese *jellabah* traders from Matemma in the Berber province in Gallabat, near Gondar. There, Ethiopian (including Galla, Tigrean, and Amhara) traders brought civet, coffee, mules, horses, cattle, ivory, and gold in exchange for the *jellabah*'s coarse cotton cloth (*damour*), mirrors, swords, spearheads, beads, and salt, products of which many were of Indian origin. There was an extensive ethnic division over which items were traded by whom. Grain, for instance, was transported by the Hadendowa and marketed by Hadariba. They were also involved in the caravan trade with Sennar and Shendi/Berber. The trade in so-called luxury goods was in the hands of Arabs. Because of these distinctions, changes in trade fortunes would affect different traders differently. This was also true for shipping: sailors on the ships were mainly Somali, while the captains were often Yemeni.

For a time, Suakin became once again an important center of trade. The town had suffered from the earlier changes in sea routes to India. In the seventeenth and eighteenth centuries, it had become a backwater for the trans-oceanic trade. It had, however, retained its position in the Arabian trade, particularly relating to Jeddah, but also to Hudeidha and Mukha. Because of the shifting trade patterns, the island's population declined in the eighteenth century. In 1822, Burckhard reported that there were some 3,000 people living there. At the same time, the numbers of people living on the mainland increased. On the mainland, according the same Burckhard, the inhabitants were put at some 5,000 (ibid.). In 1853, Munzinger put the numbers at 10,000 on the mainland and some 6,000 to 8,000 in Suakin town. In 1905, Suakin's last year as Sudan's major port, the island had about 300 registered properties (with 490 houses), compared to 300 on the mainland (Rhoden 1970). Although large according to Sudanese standards, other Red Sea ports, including Yemen's Mukha, were larger.

To the south of Suakin, Massawa was the most important African Red Sea port. Being close to Hudeida and Aden in Yemen, and also the closest Ethiopian port to Jeddah, Massawa linked the traditional trade routes between these areas. It became the main entry point for Indian goods imported into Sudan (particularly cotton) and for the export of goods from Sudan (including ivory). At the same time, a substantial portion of Ethiopian trade went to Hudeida and Luhaia in Yemen. Being the outlet for the rich Galla and Sidama territories, from which slaves were collected, also gave the town an edge. But after 1857, when slavery was outlawed in the Ottoman empire, trade goods were mainly musk horns, hides, ivory, gum Arabic, butter, and wax.

But Massawa never rivaled Jeddah for Red Sea trade, and Ethiopian insecurity limited its role in African trade. European firms were present for only short periods and never became fully established there. But everyone with commercial interests had an agent in Massawa. Apart from European representatives, there were Hadramis and Banyan Indians who maintained trade links with Egypt and Indian respectively. There were also Ethiopan traders and Egyptians. Only the small island port of Aqiq, which catered to encampments of Beni Amer tribesmen on the coast, could be considered a rival to the ports of Suakin and Massawa.

Suakin was linked up with the inland region of Kassala. Founded as an Egyptian garrison town in 1840, Kassala is an oasis of alluvial soil. The existence of the seasonal River Gash allowed for the cultivation of a variety of crops. Particularly, the Gash delta had possibilities. Local subsistence cultivators did not exploit the commercial possibilities of the area, and only after Egyptians introduced cotton cultivation did the economic potential become more developed.

The coastal area itself was inhabited by pastoral nomads, including various Beja tribes, who were involved in the caravan trade. Along the coast, to the south into Eritrea, were the Beni Amer, a group of mixed Beja and Tigre descent. The Beni Amer have an aristocratic ruling class and claim Arab Hadramouti origin. The Beni Amer were Islamized by Funj holy men, but only with the Khatmiyya did they really become Muslims. The Artega moved to Tokar and developed various types of relationships to the dominant group there, the Beni Amir. In the same way as in Gash, the Egyptians encouraged the expansion of cultivation in Khor Baraka in Tokar, and Hadramis were involved in the development of the Tokar irrigation scheme. Other Beja tribes are the Hadendowa and the Bishariyyin and the Hadramis maintained relationships with both of them. They met the Hadendowa in the Red Sea area, but also in the Gash area, and in Aroma, the central town there. The Bishariyyin resided in the northern part of the Red Sea Hills, and were used as laborers in Hadrami mining operations, as well as supplying the Hadrami traders with racing camels, as mentioned above.

The Hadrami diaspora in Sudan

The history of the Hadramis in Sudan really takes off in the first half of the twentieth century. At that time Sudan was being administered by the British and Port Sudan had become the dominant city in eastern Sudan, replacing Suakin. As Sudan's major port, Port Sudan had become the region's biggest market and was now of crucial importance to the capital, Khartoum, and the nation as a whole. It was also a gateway to the east, into the Red Sea and Gulf of Aden, and hence, to the Indian Ocean (Perkin 1993).

After it was determined that Suakin, the ancient urban center on the western shore of the Red Sea, was no longer a suitable harbor for twentieth-century Sudan, the development of Port Sudan became a major concern for British colonial rule. The story of the port begins in 1904, when it was founded by the British at Shaikh Barghuth, the burial place of a Muslim saint. The site of the new city was chosen because of the area's suitability as a harbor that could handle the type of shipping prevalent at the turn of the twentieth century. Once established, the population of Port Sudan quickly grew.

Among its varied population were Sudanese, Egyptians, Saudi Arabians, Ethiopians, Syrians, Persians, Somalis, Eritreans, Indians, Italians, and Greeks, in addition to the British themselves. The British allocated land according to race and class, with first-class plots allocated to commercial elites of European origin, down to the *daims* (undeveloped areas) for the local Beja people. Over the decades, accommodation of the growing Beja population has been a constant challenge for city planners.

The development of Port Sudan became an increasing drain on the region's marginal resources. The problem of providing services to the city's inhabitants continues to this day. Drinkable water is a major problem, water being transported from Khor Arba'at. The increasing demand for wood to serve fuel needs is another. The use of irrigation to grow vegetables and fruit for the city dwellers is a third. Labor shortages, particularly in the port, have also plagued Port Sudan throughout its history. Unable to draw sufficient labor from the resident population, Port Sudan has imported workers from outside, mainly Upper Egypt and Yemen. Ali Yahia al Yamani, who arrived in Sudan from Aden in 1906, worked as a recruitment agent. The agents were powerful people, and Ali was one of the most successful well into the 1930s. In the 1920s, Sudanese agents challenged his control of the labor market and tried to enlist the support of the British to employ more Sudanese laborers, in competition with the Yemenis brought to Port Sudan by Ali. The British were reluctant, however, as the local labor supply among the Beja pastoralists fluctuated with the climate in their home areas.

During droughts they willingly came forward, but in years of sufficient rainfall they abandoned Port Sudan for their pastures. An initiative to bring in laborers from western Sudan also triggered British concern, as the solution would mix groups from western and eastern Sudan. The two regions made up the core areas of support for northern Sudan's two major religious movements and political parties: the Ansar supported the Umma Party, while the Khatmiyya supported the Democratic Unionists Party (DUP). The colonial authorities were worried that bringing the two groups together could cause political unrest. Attempts to solve the labor issue in Port Sudan thus related to international relationships across the Red Sea and to Egypt, as well as to basic national concerns within Sudan itself.

These labor issues related as much to Northern Yemenis as to Hadramis. Hadramis, as Ahmed Bajabr said, were involved in trade. But they were certainly part of the picture in Port Sudan and eastern Sudan. Judging from sources from the 1930s, there were important Hadrami settlements only in eastern Sudan. At Port Sudan there was an important Hadrami merchant (of the Safi family) who had offices in Port Sudan and Suakin. The acting commissioner stated, in reply to a request from Harold Ingrams, resident advisor to the Quaity sultan, that colonies of Hadramis could be found at Port Sudan, Suakin, and Tokar, with small groups at Halaib, Aqiq, and Karora. A total of 742 residents were reported, their distribution being as follows: Port Sudan (180), Suakin (228), Tokar (294), Halaib (4), Aqiq (30), and Karora (6).

The Hadramis in Sudan at that time were of two categories. The first category were those who were permanently settled, had been in the region since the era of the port of Suakin, and had practically severed their connections with Hadramaut. The second category was made up of visitors who would normally spend about three years in Sudan between visits of about a year's duration to their homes. The division between the categories was said to be roughly half and half. In the towns, the Hadramis were primarily shopkeepers or shop assistants. A few made their living as cooks, bakers, and laborers, and in the Tokar Delta many had taken up cultivation. There does not appear to have been a Hadrami community of any size in the interior of Sudan. Only one person was reported to be permanently settled in Khartoum (running a cafe) and two in Omdurman.

The British estimated that about a third of the Hadramis in Sudan had severed their connections with Hadramaut but had not assimilated to any noticeable degree with the local population. The settled Hadramis principally married among themselves, although the "visitors" occasionally married local inhabitants, principally the women of the Beni Amer. The majority either had wives in Hadramaut or remained single. The British noted a surprisingly large number of bachelors, none of the thirty residents of Aqiq being married. Commercial relations with Hadramaut were at that time said to be negligible if not nonexistent.

A survey carried out in the 1990s (with Samia al Naqar al Hadi) gives a general impression that Hadramis in Sudan had become integrated and achieved considerable economic and social success. Hadramis had also moved into central Sudanese towns, become involved in a broader variety of occupations and employed marriage strategies both among themselves and with Sudanese that allow for a steady increase in numbers of the "Hadrami" community. This is in contrast with the somewhat static situation depicted by the British commissioner six decades previously. There have also been changes in the extent of marriage into Sudanese society and the level of social ties among the Hadramis themselves. Generally, however, the Hadramis show a history of integration, of involvement in the economic development of Sudan, including schemes for irrigated agriculture and mechanized farming.

Government investment in the Red Sea area from the time of the colonial period consisted mainly of sponsoring two agricultural schemes (Gash and Tokar). A number of mines were also opened in the Red Sea Hills, though these did not prove profitable. The railway was constructed in the 1920s, and a tarmac road linking Port Sudan with the interior was built in the 1970s. Hadramis have been part of all these developments. The rail and road lines opened up new opportunities in the transport and service sector, including the running of hotels and restaurants. But the region has lacked substantial job opportunities, due to the small scale of investment and a general lack of technical skills.

The Gash and Tokar agricultural schemes have been of more importance to the Hadramis. In some cases, Hadramis directly invested in the schemes and also supplied basic necessities to the various groups of people who flocked to the areas for employment. This history represents the major part of Ahmed Bajabr's story with which this chapter began. The family histories collected confirm this pattern on a more general level. Hadramis came to Sudan through Suakin and later Port Sudan, then farmed in places like Tokar and Gash, where first the Egyptians and later the British developed irrigated cotton farming. They invested in hotels and provided services to the expanding urban areas of Port Sudan, Omdurman, and Khartoum. Their children were sent to Sudanese schools and universities, and later went on to become highly respected professionals in their adopted country. Marriages were both within the Hadrami group but also with various Sudanese families. The early operators in Tokar married Beni Amer women while more established families later married into families from the Nile Valley.

Hadrami identity in Sudan seems to be without problems, and the maintenance of this identity has not led to conflict with other types of identity. They have integrated into the culture of eastern Sudan, while also influencing it through their prestige as Shafi'i muslims and their history of Islamic teaching in Hadramaut.

Some have joined Sufi movements in eastern Sudan, particularly the Khatmiyya. Furthermore, developments initiated by the British during the period of Anglo-Egyptian Sudan, as well as by various governments in independent Sudan seem to have provided platforms on which the Hadramis could build careers in trade, in the professions, and as leaders. During the time of the British administration, some were even prominent in the anti-colonial movement, including Bakhreeba, a trade union leader in the Gezira Tenants Union.

In the 1990s, after the unification of the two Yemens, contact between Hadrami in Sudan and Hadramaut also increased. Several Hadrami families, or individual family members, actually returned to Hadramaut to work, start businesses and to build their lives there.

Education and links between Sudan and Hadramaut

Sudan and Hadramaut developed a special relationship through the field of education. It came about as part of British efforts to develop modern education in the Quaity Sultanate. Traditional schooling in Hadramaut was in the form of Islamic education, which involves children, boys that is, being sent to school to learn the Koran and some Arabic. This type of Islamic school was long established in Hadramaut, and we have seen how diasporic families living in Singapore played an active role in their development. Such schools were supported by wealthy families, including that of Sayyid Abu Bakr bin Sheikh Al Kaf of Tarim, Sheikh Mohamad Said Marta of Henin and the La'ajam family of Shibam, as well as Muslim organizations. Texts written by earlier generations of Hadrami Sayyid families were used throughout the diaspora, but the effects of modernization in the twentieth century helped establish alternative forms of education.

These developments were also felt in Hadramaut. The syllabus of the schools was taken from the Arabic schools in Java and in Egypt and aimed at teaching the Arabic language. Arabic newsletters came to Hadramaut from the East Indies, Egypt and other Arab countries, although Egyptian newspapers and magazines dominated. A substantial amount of time was still spent learning the Koran. The importance families put on this type of knowledge is shown by the fact that many families withdrew their children from schools after they had memorized the most important parts of the Koran. Such schools exist until today in the area, and students from Southeast Asia are once again traveling to Tarim and to Shihir for a Muslim education.

However, the Bedouin people of the plains to the north and south of Wadi Hadramaut (Al Jol) did not have any schools. Nor were the British colonialists particularly interested in promoting Islamic schools. They wanted to establish an alternative to Muslim schools, based on Western ideals of learning. Modern education of this type started within the Quaity Sultanate in the 1930s. There were some seven schools, attended by around 1,200 boys, located in major towns and villages (in Mukalla and Shihir) on the coast, and in the interior (in Tarim, Seiyun, and Shibam). These schools existed alongside the religious schools (*rubat*). Various ethnic communities also had their own schools. There was a considerable Indian community in the area in the 1930s (due to the special links between India and south Yemen described in earlier chapters); the community ran a school for Indian pupils under an Indian headmaster. There was also a Gujarati school in Mukalla serving the Indian community (thirty pupils), whereas the Indian community in Shihir had a private teacher.

The start of direct British involvement in education was begun in the late 1930s by V.L. Griffiths, principal of the Bakht-er-Ruda College in Sudan. The British made surveys of local views on modern education, and used an education expert to report on the best way to go about this task. In 1938, the expert, Griffith, found that people wanted modern subjects like geography and history, and also English. The motive for this, as reported by Griffith, was the need to compete with Javanese Hadramis in trade. Griffith's view, and the British policy, advocated education for the leading families as a strategy to provide national leaders capable of taking over the running of the Quaity and Kathiri from the various foreigners who occupied central positions in these states.

In the colonial terminology of the day, the "target group" for the modern schools were members of the some 90 town-based commercial families of importance, members of the about 250 leading agricultural families, the 95 leading religious families and the children in the families of over 70 Bedouin chiefs. These educated members would then replace about 150 government employees in the Quaity and Kathiri states. The need for agricultural development was also used as an argument for providing a more Westernized education, as was the general notion that educated people would make better citizens (Griffith 1938).

It is at this point that Sudan became involved in the development of education in Hadramaut. Realizing that the basic weakness in Hadramaut was the shortage of local teachers and teacher training, as well as the absence of a general education culture, the British introduced their experiences in Sudan as a model for primary education. Furthermore, due to the well-established education system in Sudan, students were sent to Sudan for secondary schooling and professional training. The first student was a man called BaShamal. Sent

to Sudan in 1943, he was later to play a central role in South Yemen's education system. Sudan thus became the country to which many of the Hadramis
went for further studies, forging close links between the two countries. With
time, Sudanese teachers were also recruited to Hadramaut to teach in local
schools.

From the British side, this choice was based on the similarities between
the two countries in climate and development, although Aden, the Western
Protectorate and Somaliland were closer geographically. At the elementary
school level, this also implied that Sudan's elementary syllabi and textbooks
should be used as a base, with an extra year to secure sufficient time to include
the religious training that was considered necessary. For secondary education, two schools were opened, in Mukalla and in Seiyun, based on the Sudan Intermediate School Certificate, with studies in religion, Islamic history,
Arabic, and English. Sudan was also chosen as the site of teacher training for
an interim period while local courses were developed. The teacher training
was based on the Sudanese school at Bakht-er-Ruda, a school developed by
the same Griffith who had written the report on education in Hadramaut. In
the meantime, Sudanese teachers were also given preference as teachers in
Hadramaut because they were Muslims and knew Arabic.

This collaboration was to have a great impact on relations between the
two areas. The first Sudanese teacher sent to develop the Hadramaut education system was Al-Shaykh al-Qaddal, who arrived in the late 1930s. He first
worked as director of education, pioneering Sudan's involvement in education. He was soon promoted to first secretary and later became prime minister
of Quaity state, remaining in Hadramaut until 1957. His son, the historian
Muhamed Said al-Qaddal, married a woman from a Hadrami family living
in Sudan, the BaAbbouds. At the time of my field visits to Hadramaut, Muhamed Said al-Qaddal was a teacher at the Mukalla branch of the University
of Aden. Although the reason for his stay in Hadramaut this time was for
political reasons (he was expelled from Sudan by the Islamist regime), he was
in a way continuing his family's history of promoting education among the
Hadramis.

The BaAbboud family into which Muhamed Said married also played
a role in building relations between Hadramaut and Sudan in the field of
education. As a sort of government agent, the head of the family, Ahmed
BaAbboud, was a contact point for Hadrami students who traveled to Sudan,
advancing scholarship money to them and keeping his house in Omdurman
open for Hadrami students. BaAbboud went to Mukalla regularly to be repaid his expenses from the government there. This repayment was in Pound
Sterling, a currency he later used to exchange money for the northern Yemenis who worked in Sudan. They were paid in Sudanese pounds but wanted
to change their savings into British pounds. The whole operation thus falls

neatly into a circular flow of financial services that the Hadramis were such experts at exploiting.

The links between the two education systems also facilitated good relations between Sudanese Hadarma and people of their homeland, and between Sudanese Hadrama and Sudanese nationals. Several such individuals have played important roles in Sudanese history, showing their integration into that community. Hadramis who had stayed in the Sudan were also accepted at home in Hadramaut, and when they returned home from their stay in the diaspora they did not encounter the cultural tensions experienced by the Hadramis coming from India, Southeast Asia, and East Africa.

The collaboration between Sudan and Hadramaut continued until the end of the 1960s, when the emerging socialist regime in independent South Yemen shifted its higher education contacts to Eastern Europe. An education conference was convened in Aden in 1975, which officially established a Marxist base for education in South Yemen. This, together with the sending of students to East Bloc countries, saw South Yemen adopt a new, more politicized education program and ended its contact with Western-style education.

In 1990, the two Yemens united, and schools in South Yemen adopted the North Yemeni education system. Prior to the 1994 civil war, there was a debate in Yemen about the degree to which schools and curricula should be Islamized. In a historical irony, Sudan was once again a major player. This time Hassan el Turabi and his Islamist regime in Khartoum were strong supporters of the Islamists in Yemen, represented by the Islah Party, in their call for an Islamized curriculum. Secular education was defended by the Socialist Party and, with the support of the ruling Congress Party, Islah was defeated in the vote.

A new type of Hadrami? A new type of diaspora?

Finally, let us look at some developments in Sudan in which the Hadrami diaspora has made its influence felt. I am thinking here about the presence in Sudan during the 1990s of Osama Bin Laden. Bin Laden lived in Sudan at the time when I first met Ahmad Bajabr in Mukalla. But whereas Ahmad represented a Hadrami of the traditional type living in Sudan, dealing with his challenges and concerns as a small trader, Osama Bin Laden was a financial tycoon, with a fortune built upon his father's successful enterprises in Saudi Arabia. His career as a global jihadist certainly made him a more famous representative of the diasporic world of which Ahmad was part. Osama himself is a Hadrami born in the diaspora, namely in Saudi Arabia. His family comes from Wadi Du'an, one of the branches of the main Wadi Hadramaut. His father moved to Saudi Arabia in the 1950s, where Usama was born in 1957.

As the world's most famous "terrorist," Osama Bin Laden's life is of course surrounded by myth and speculation, and I shall not engage in further myth-making here. But it is possible to isolate certain features of Bin Laden's ac-tivities that show how he, as a person, and his activities represent a different type of "diaspora" than that of Ahmed. While Ahmed Bajabr is the typical representative of a historical Hadrami diaspora in Sudan, the story of Osama begins in the same diasporic world, but develops into the global, Muslim di-aspora that we have seen unfold since the 1970s. This type of global, Islamic diaspora is increasingly defined in opposition to the Western world, which is interpreted as U.S. imperial culture and Israeli aggression. But this develop-ment also has links to recent history in Sudan and the Horn of Africa (e.g., de Waal 2004). We need, therefore, a discussion of those specific contexts in which Osama's activities should be placed in order to provide a comparative view of this diaspora, compared to the diaspora of Ahmed Bajabr and the other Hadramis also discussed in this chapter.

The migration of the Bin Laden family signifies the most recent historical wave of Hadrami migration, to Saudi Arabia and the Gulf. Many of the fami-lies that ended up in Sudan followed the same route. Osama's father devel-oped links to the royal family in Saudi Arabia and built himself an economic empire in the construction business. In this the Bin Laden family was a very successful, but not atypical, example of Hadrami adaptations in Saudi Arabia. But here Osama's life story takes a significant turn and must be interpreted against regional and global political events.

Israel, the United States, and the West make up one important context. From an initial restoration of Arab self-respect through the Yom Kippur war in 1973, the effects of the oil boom of the 1970s brought wealth to the con-servative oil countries, allowing for the import of the latest technologies, but also increased travels to the West, for leisure and education, as well as a local lifestyle that many interpreted as a threat to Islam. This situation led to many types of tensions and reactions. In Saudi Arabia, the assassination of King Faisal by a "Westernized" prince is part of this picture. Anwar Sadat's sign-ing of the U.S.-brokered Camp David Peace Accords with Israel in 1978 was proof of the same. These developments were debated among young people in the Middle East, also in the Saudi universities where Osama studied.

But there were other political developments that helped form the life of Osama bin Laden and others of his generation. Khomeini's Iranian revolu-tion is one Islamic reaction to what went on in the Middle East during the 1970s. The seizure of the Grand Mosque in Mecca in 1979 in order to "save Islam" was another. Another shock came when the Soviet Union invaded Afghanistan, putting Muslims under Communist rule. And this event was actually what made Osama Bin Laden go to Afghanistan, to volunteer in the Afghan *jihad* against the Soviet invaders. This was also a period during which he maintained close links to the Royal House in Riyadh. But as we know, this was to change: He lost his Saudi citizenship after falling out with his father's old friends.

It is at this point that Sudan becomes of direct importance to our story. Sudan had only recently, in 1989, been taken over by a new regime based on the Islamist groups surrounding the strongman Hassan el Turabi. Radical Islamist policies were pursued in the early part of the 1990s, ideologically inspired policies taking the place of more realistic, pragmatic positions. It was a period in which the regime called for a *jihad* against non-Muslim rebels in southern Sudan, and both non-Muslim and Muslims in the Nuba Mountains. The regime also put in place Islamist social policy through "the comprehensive call" program (*al da'wa al shamla*).

The same ideological bent influenced Sudan's foreign policies. Turabi declared Sudan's support for Iraq and Saddam Hussein in 1991, following Iraq's occupation of Kuwait. This was of course a position that did not go down well in Riyadh, and when the Saudi Royal House broke its relations with Osama, he and Turabi shared a common enemy. But the alliance was pragmatic. In Khartoum, Islamist policies were already in place with the new regime, and new visa regulations in 1990 opened up the country for Arab Islamists. But Osama certainly fitted into the wider agenda of Turabi's policies, an agenda in which Turabi sought to consolidate his position as a leading figure within the Islamists' camp. Osama could operate as part of Turabi's "universal framework for the Islamic movement," based on organizations such as the Islamic Arab Peoples' Conference (IAPC) and Popular International Organisation (PIO).

Meanwhile, Osama also followed his own agenda. During this period there had been a shift in Osama's thinking, away from a localized anti-Soviet resistance in Afghanistan towards an increased emphasis on Islamic resistance both against the West and Westernized Muslim regimes such as the one in Riyadh. With Osama now residing in Sudan, the international group of "Afghans" who had fought with him in Afghanistan had a place to go, and they could further develop their organization around their leader. Through the combination of Turabi's policies and Osama bin Laden's intentions, Sudan became further entangled in the type of Islamist policies that to an increasing degree also involved violence and terrorism. Osama's personal role was partly as a big trader involved in legal trade, but also as a person involved in *mujahideen* training camps in the country.

This combination of personal wealth and direct involvement in political and military activities gives a special profile to Osama bin Laden's development in the 1990s. His personal wealth, of course, made him particularly important. One example is the role he played in the period following the collapse of the Bank of Credit and Commerce International (BCCI) in 1991.

The collapse of the bank not only created an international financial scandal, but also threatened to reveal important financial structures of the militant Islamist groups since many of them had used BCCI for money laundering and the financing of clandestine operations. After the collapse of the bank, there was a need to rebuild a financial system for Islamic organizations. Turabi gave Osama Bin Laden the job of doing this in the part of the financial system with which Turabi was linked.

Within Sudan's security and military-commercial complex, Osama found allies who controlled considerable wealth, and who also shared his vision. These networks operated together in Somalia in 1992, some to spread Islam in Africa, some to stem U.S. imperial intentions in the Horn of Africa. Whatever the reasons, in 1993 the United States put Sudan on its list of states that sponsored terrorism, a move inspired both by events in Somalia and also the 1993 bombing of the World Trade Center involving Islamists linked to Khartoum.

In June 1995, an attempt was made on the life of the Egyptian president, Hosni Mubarak, in Addis Ababa. Given the Sudanese regime's hostility towards Mubarak, the regime was quickly named as a suspect behind the assassination attempt. Sudan's support for Islamist opposition groups in the region had angered neighboring countries and further exposed Sudan's links to international terrorism. The situation was serious, and the regime in Khartoum sought to first appease Washington, Egypt's strongest ally, by offering Osama to the United States, to show that Khartoum was not harboring terrorists. When the United States declined, the regime expelled Osama from Sudan in March 1996, allowing him to return to Afghanistan, together with many of his followers. But the regime's political crisis continued and could easily have ended with a total collapse had it not been for the regional consequences of the war that broke out between Eritrea and Ethiopia in 1998.

We shall not speculate to what extent Sudan's Islamist regime or Osama bin Laden were involved in the terrorist attacks on U.S. embassies, naval ships, and airlines. The U.S. government certainly thought there were links and directly punished both Afghanistan and Sudan with missile attacks after the 1998 bombings of U.S. embassies in Kenya and Tanzania. Nor shall we speculate on possible links between Hadramaut and Yemen and the terrorist attack on tourists in December 1998 in Abyan, Yemen, or the 2000 suicide attack on the U.S. navy destroyer the *USS Cole* outside Aden, carried out by individuals who were said to have come from Wadi Du'an.

Both Afghanistan and Sudan were counted among the key enemies that had to be dealt with in the U.S. counterterrorism strategy of the 1990s. The September 11, 2001 attack on the World Trade Center took away possible doubts the United States might have had. The attack brought the terrorist war home and made clear that there was an international network of militant

Islamists, among whom Bin Laden was playing a central role. Both Osama bin Laden and Al Qa'ida became household names in the West. Bin Laden was by then in Afghanistan and there was little doubt that Al Qa'ida-type organizations were mushrooming, and that there had developed various links between militant groups, Islamic NGOs, and some national governments.

The Afghan guerrillas had of course played a direct military role in Afghanistan, but were also active in Pakistan and Kashmir. Islamic NGOs had played central roles in Somalia, the Balkans, and Chechnya. Similar developments occurred in Europe, most dramatically illustrated by the 2004 Madrid bombings. Links to militant groups in the Philippines and Indonesia were also established and made visible through the 2005 Bali bombings. At the time of writing, Islamic groups operating in Iraq make up the most recent example of a globalized Muslim diaspora in a deadly battle with an imperial enemy.

It is this contemporary reality that is of interest in our discussion here. It is interesting because it shows the ways in which several historical trends have come together to form a new, globalized diaspora, formed on an ideology that puts emphasis on the unity of all Muslims around the concept of *umma* (meaning "community" or "nation"), the idea that the *umma* is threatened by non-Muslims and must be defended or must defend itself, and the concept that in this defense all means are allowed. Whatever role Osama bin Laden has played in this development, he did not come to the role merely because he is a Hadrami and belongs to the traditional Hadrami diaspora. Rather, Osama's career shows that the Hadrami diaspora is part of a broader religious diaspora of Muslims. This religious diaspora has, throughout history, produced individuals who stand out as leaders and spokesmen for the *umma*, some arguing for peaceful coexistence with non-Muslims, others encouraging violence.

Osama's story is also part of this particular development, and his life can be seen as part of that long tradition of continuous Muslim commentary on the wider world, and on events in that world. Such radical Islamic commentaries may be directed at the Western world or at moderate Muslim forces that are criticized for not conforming to the stricter tenets of Islamic belief. Times and places of *jihads* and violent acts certainly vary but the themes and rhetoric used to justify them show clear continuities based on a long historical relationship among Muslim communities of which the Hadramis are a part, and Western colonial and imperial forces.

Unfortunately, this history is too often told from a Western perspective, a perspective that tends to ignore important characteristics of the Muslim communities involved. One bias is the representation of all Muslims as terrorists, thus placing people like the simple trader Ahmed Bajabr and the Al-Qaeda leader Osama bin Laden in the same group of anti-Western Muslims. It is a central argument in this chapter that this is not the case. In spite of the differences, however, both individuals do belong to a religious and a cultural tradition that unites them. It is this shared belonging to tradition we have to grasp if we want to understand how Muslims, who are as appalled by the violence as anybody else, also seem somehow to "sympathize" with what these groups are trying to do.

Conclusion

The discussion in this chapter shows several interesting aspects of Hadrami adaptation in the diaspora. In Sudan we see that a shared Arabic language and Muslim culture enabled the Hadramis to easily adapt to life in northern Sudan. We see that they are accepted and respected by Sudanese for their contributions to what is represented as a Sudanese national culture. Our account thus seems to show a harmonious diaspora-homeland relationship. A long history of direct Sudanese involvement in the development of modern education in Hadramaut, with many Hadramis studying in Sudan and many Sudanese teachers living in Hadramaut, further adds strength to these ties.

But the story of Osama bin Laden also opens up a different aspect of the Hadrami diaspora, as part of a Muslim diaspora in which links between the various diasporic communities are more important than links to the homeland, representing relations not only focused on the maintenance of specific types of diasporic identities, or to promote a religious mission or trade interests, but also political links that are forged in opposition to forces that are seen by some as threats to the diaspora itself. In principle, little is new in this. Similar relations can be seen in different historical periods. But it is important to show how the various links connect at particular historical moments and shape the overall development of the diaspora itself.

We have seen that through the case of Osama bin Laden and Hassan el Turabi, Sudan came to play an important role in these complex interrelationships. Through the Sudanese example we also see that the links between diaspora and the nation state are not unidirectional, nor can they always be portrayed as forces opposed to each other. The alliance between Hassan el Turabi and Osama bin Laden represents an example of a type of diaspora-nation-state interaction that at a certain time was characterized by shared pragmatic interests, but that over time caused both parties to pursue strategies that made them drift apart. There was no shared ideological platform between the two to keep the alliance together.

Turabi was following policies that might be inspired by international Islamism but were shaped in a basic way by his position in Sudanese politics. Many local and national concerns that were crucial to Turabi's choice of action were of little importance to bin Laden. When such national interests called for recognition of U.S. counterterrorist policies, Osama's days in Sudan were numbered. And when competing factions within the Sudanese regime found that Turabi's politics were a threat to more pragmatic positions, Turabi himself was sidelined in a Sudanese power struggle in 2000.

Osama, for his part, could never be bogged down by the interests of any one nation state. He continued his increasingly global quest for a Muslim response to his enemies, in particular, by mobilizing his *mujahidiin*. In this battle Sudan no longer played a significant part. Peace negotiations aimed at ending the North-South civil war and a growing international presence in the country made it unlikely that what went on in the country during the 1990s could happen again, at least in the near future. But Osama's influence continues, perhaps in person, and most certainly symbolically. If we look only at the violent implications of Osama's acts he probably stands alone in Hadrami history, but if we see him as a case representing Muslim responses to the Western world, he fits into a pattern in which there have been many Muslims, and also some Hadramis, before him (e.g., Bang 2003; Ho 2004). They all represent individual cases of reaction and resistance that can only be understood if the dynamics of the diaspora are understood. Some of these dynamics relate to specific times and places; others are not localized in the same way. But they all belong to a history of migration that helped reshape local as well as global geographies.

A history of migration resulted in the emergence of diasporic communities that were tied together not only by ethnic origin but also by religious belonging. The religious dimensions have given the diaspora a global perspective that at certain historical moments has collided with another globalizing tendency—the spread of Western capitalism and political ambitions. Diaspora has been pitched against empire, and the contemporary form of this conflict is but one example of a long tradition. But the details of this conflict belong to a later chapter.

CHAPTER FOUR

❀ Ethiopia

The Problem of Being "Arab," "Somali," "Capitalist," and "Terrorist"

The story of Hadramis in Ethiopia begins in the capital, Addis Ababa. Dr. Getachew Kassa, at the Institute of Ethiopian Studies, introduced me to several Hadrami families in Addis. It was through him that I got in touch with Awad Saeed, the then leader of the Yemeni Association in Ethiopia. Tragically, Awad died only a short time after our first meeting. Before his death, however, we met many times at his house in the huge Merkato market district, considered the largest open-air market in Africa. It serves as a meeting point for Hadramis in Addis. People come here to do business, or to take part in *qat*-chewing sessions. It was at these social gatherings that I took part in discussions about the lives of Hadramis in Ethiopia. These discussions were the starting point for uncovering the following story of Hadrami adaptations in Ethiopia.

Hadramis in Ethiopia: A broad history

The history of Hadramis in Ethiopia is, of course, linked to developments in the Red Sea region, as discussed in chapter three. The nineteenth century saw a growing international interest in both Ethiopia and Somalia, collectively known as the Horn of Africa. The decline of the Ottoman Empire in the eighteenth century had greatly affected trade in the Red Sea and the Horn. We have already heard about the rise to power of Muhamad Ali in Egypt, and his subsequent expansionist activities in search of ivory, gold, and slaves. The opening of the Suez Canal in 1869 had also renewed Europe's interests in Red Sea region and the Gulf of Aden.

The rise of Omani power in Zanzibar in the early nineteenth century had brought a new dynamic to trade in the region, with cloves and sesame being shipped from Zanzibar while slaves, ivory, and gum copal were transported from the African interior. This trade brought American, European, and Indian merchants, as well as Arabs, to the Benaadir (Somali Coast) and the Swahili coast. Somali towns traded in ivory, aromatic woods, animal skins, and grain.

A similar situation developed on the northern Somali coast, where the British bought supplies of live animals and meat from Somalia for their soldiers stationed in nearby Aden. Due to the volume of the trade, Omanis in Zanzibar claimed control of the Somali ports. By the second half of the nineteenth century, however, Omani power had weakened and they were increasingly dependent on British support. Links between Zanzibar and the Benaadir coast for trade in slaves, salt, and dried shark meat dated from antiquity. But Omani attempts to gain political control soon brought unrest: Under pressure from the British, the Omanis leased out Benaadir to the Italians. The Italians were chosen since they were considered less of a threat than the French, who were then building a railway from Djibouti to Addis, or the Germans, then the colonial power in Tanganiyka (Hess 1966).

Egypt was also part of this imperial game. In 1867 the Khedive Ismail made a claim to Berbera, and in 1875 Egyptian forces took possession of Zeila, occupying Harar, setting up an administration that lasted for ten years. The plan was probably to continue to the Somali coast, thus challenging the European powers that were already active in the area (Hill 1959). Egypt was eager to keep Italy out of the Ethiopian port of Assab, where the Italians wanted to establish a station where their steamships could load coal for their onward journeys. To keep the Italians out, Egypt worked to make alliances with coastal populations and secure areas under Ottoman control. The British interpreted this as an Egyptian attempt to control all of the northeast African coast—from Suez to Cape Guardafui, on the most northeasterly tip of Somalia—and joined forces with the Italians in order to prevent such an expansion of Egyptian control. In Ethiopia, meanwhile, Italy succeeded in obtaining control of Assab in 1882 and also made claims for Massawa. The killing of Italian explorers provided one excuse for action, and in 1885 Italy took over the administration of Massawa and in 1888 declared a protectorate over Zula, thirty miles to the south.

The Ethiopians on their side also had interests in the area, and Emperor Menelik occupied Harar, taking it from the Egyptians. Ethiopia also occupied Dirre and Liban in present-day southern Ethiopia, conquering Borana and establishing an administrative post in Arero. From their conquered territories, the Ethiopians raided into neighboring areas from their military camps (*katamas*). They attacked Luuq in 1896, and devastated the countryside in Somalia. The European powers accepted several of the Ethiopian advances in treaties of 1894 and 1908, hoping that Ethiopia would "police" the interior for them.

Toward the end of the century the situation in the region had become increasingly volatile. The Ethiopian military activities created a security problem for the caravans. The abolition of slavery had disrupted agricultural production and tribal conflicts over land had displaced large numbers of people. Into this situation Islamic *tariqas* began organizing resistance against the colonial powers, receiving support from pastoralists who were losing pasture areas due to the unrest. The activities of Sayyid Muhammed Abdullah Hassan, the famous "Mad Mullah," leader of Somali anti-colonial resistance, actually started in southern Somalia and later expanded his activities to the north against the British and Italians (Abdi Sheikh-Abdi 1993).

The case of Sayyid Mohammed shows that Islam was a rallying point for resistance. The resistance made Italian attempts at establishing a protectorate, for instance through the establishment of the Royal Italian East African Company, more difficult. As a result, from the 1890s and well into the twentieth century, Italians controlled only the coastal towns and adjacent territory, making treatises with local mercantile elites. In 1895, Ugo Ferrandi established a garrison at Luuq, in southwestern Somalia, to discourage Ethiopian expansion in the region. Well into the twentieth century, Luuq remained the only inland stronghold of the Italians. Only in the 1920s, under Mussolini's Fascist regime, were the areas in southern Somalia really controlled by the colonial power.

Following the southern caravan trail

In nineteenth-century Somalia, colonial and international powers controlled the towns, while the countryside was under the control of Somali pastoralist groups. But the two systems were linked by trade. We find Hadramis present in both systems, but here we focus on Hadrami relations in the rural areas with inland Somali pastoralists.

The trade route between the Banaadir coast and southern Ethiopia was one of three major nineteenth-century caravan routes in the Horn of Africa. The other two were the caravan trade of Zanzibari merchants (Arab and Swahili merchants active on the East African coast and the interiors of Tanganyika and Kenya), and that of Sudanese *jellabah* merchants who pushed southwards from Khartoum, beyond the *sudd* areas of southern Sudan, and into Uganda and Kenya. The western and southern provinces of Ethiopia were included in each of these trade routes and provided the region's luxury goods—gold, ivory, musk, precious skins, and spices. The caravan routes not only distributed goods and wealth. Merchants were also major agents in the processes of Islamization and the spread of trade languages as lingua franca around East Africa, including Arabic, Swahili, Somali, and Boran (Abir 1968).

Caravan trade into the interior passed through the towns of Luuq, Baydhabo and Baardhere. These towns were strategically placed on the caravan routes from the coast towards the interior. This caravan trade was not new, and probably dates back to the end of the period of the Ajuuraan dynasty in the late seventeenth century, when the Rahanwiin clans controlled the territory between the rivers.

Luuq was referred to as *"Timbuctu nella occidentale,"* the traders being mostly Somali, and known locally as *sofara*. From the coast to Luuq a caravan took some ten to fifteen days. Groups such as Gasr Gudda, Elai and Garre engaged in this trade, as did coastal Somali and Arab traders. A population of traders from Merca, Brava, and Mogadishu resided there, and there were men, camels, and caravan equipment for sale or hire. The trading system was highly organized, with the Sultan setting regulations and levying taxes. Contracts were common:

> Sherif Abubekr of Merka, a resident trader, presents to the Italian <u>Residente</u> of Lugh in company of Omar Mali Muti of Brava and a trader in Borana, an agreement stating that the first wants from the second, three months from the date of this agreement, that is on January 12, 1897, one and one half frasilas of babulaia ivory. Omar Mali Muti confirms that he has received from Sherif Abubekr the value of the ivory in cloth valued at $ 110.00, and has received on consignment $ 10.00, and is obliged to pay the remainder by the above date. (quoted in Dalleo 1975: 51 fn. 1)

Journeys into the interior were risky due to tribal unrest. Traders bought ghee and hides from the pastoralists and sold luxury goods from the coast (ivory, slaves, gums, and coffee). This inland trade was segmented with a lot of smaller niches occupied by members of different clans, moving with small caravans towards the coast. But there was also an inland, regional trade in animals, grain, and salt. Ferrandi, the Italian Resident in Luuq (1895–1897), provides detailed information on this. The Italians tried to establish market courts and a legal system to deal with the trade. Their influence, however, did not go beyond the town limits.

The trade links continued from here towards Ethiopia, where the Borana and Oromo pastoralists constituted a market. A Catholic missionary, Leon des Avancheres, claimed in 1858 that there was a route in use between the ancient Somali port city of Brawa, southeast of Mogadishu, and Kaffa, in southwestern Ethiopia. The British traveler C.P. Beke, who was in the areas in the 1840s, also confirmed links between southern Ethiopia and the Indian Ocean, and later, in 1897, Donaldson Smith wrote:

> For years the Somalis from the coast towns near the mouth of the Juba have been accustomed to trade with the Boran for ivory, and it is from these traders that many of the reports concerning the Boran and their country have reached the ears of European residents on the coast. (Abir 1968: 112–14)

Two major routes linked the upper Juba with southern Ethiopia. Caravans from Luuq traveled along the Daua before striking out for Dirre and Liban. Those from Bardera usually halted at El Wak before moving further north. Once in Borana, places like Ascebo or Cercale served as meeting points where traders, nomads and agriculturalists gathered to exchange goods. People living along these trade routes also controlled the caravans. These were the Arjuan, the Gurre, and the Gasr Gudda. Caravans moved by night and rested by day, and were rather small. The actual travel time was only some twenty days, but the conducting of trade along the way took time, and a round trip was said to take about six months.

Arriving in Borana, the traders were dependent on their hosts. The traders paid in cloth, brass wire, and tobacco. Blocks of salt (*amoleh*) were also used as currency (Abir 1965,1970). In return the trader got a hut, milk, and animals for the return journey. It is unclear whether this system penetrated beyond the Borana lands to the areas of the Konso, Rendille, and Samburo, or whether it stopped there. However, an early traveler, Donaldson Smith, in 1897 reported that the Borana did trade with the Konsos and the Galla to the north, and with the Amaro and Kaffa to the west (quoted in Pankhurst 1965; see also Pankhurst 1968). But Donaldson Smith, along with British officials Baird and Zaphiro, and Kluckhohn (1962), argued that trade links with Somalia were the most important ones.

To operate in these faraway areas one needed an *abbaan*, or host/protector. Such persons might also be middlemen in the trade (*dallals*) themselves, having regular contact with trading houses on the Somali coast (see Abir 1965 for a general discussion about this system in northern Ethiopia). Respected religious leaders could also provide such protection. One consequence of this system was that foreign traders could be excluded, as was the case throughout the nineteenth century.

Inland trade was in Somali hands until the 1890s and even later, in contrast to the early trading posts further south along the coast, which remained under Somali control only until the 1830s and 1840s. Only Hadrami Arabs were on good terms with the inland Somalis and seemed to have established a foothold in the caravan trade before other foreign groups (including the Ibadi Omanis from Zanzibar). Similarly, trade drew people from northern Somaliland, such as the Harti of the Darood. Figures provided by Cassanelli (1982) show that the goods being traded changed from exports of ivory, woods, gums, and myrrh in the 1840s to *dura*, sesame, and cotton by the 1890s, most of it exported to southern Arabia. Traditional caravan goods were replaced by agricultural products from the Juba-Shebelle plantation economy.

In the nineteenth century, Muslim communities in southern Ethiopia became more settled. In this century we also see Islamic principalities emerge in southern Ethiopia, and Islamic learned men and sufi saints began to establish religious centers. The Egyptian occupation of Harar brought Muslim scholars from Cairo to spread Islam among the neighboring Oromo people from 1875 to 1885, and the activities of the Mahdi in Sudan also helped radicalize Muslims in the region. The traders we discuss here were also part of these developments.

However, such developments within areas dominated by Muslims were counteracted by the success of Menelik II in conquering areas in southern Ethiopia (Erlich 1994). In spite of the spread of Christianity in these areas as a result of the conquests, Muslims were allowed to practice their faith. But the era of a "politicized Islam" was over, and even the activities of Iyasu, Menelik's grandson, who built his strategy on Ottoman support and links to the *jihad* of the Mad Mullah in Somalia, could not change this. Eventually, Haile Selassie emerged as emperor in 1930 (Erlich ibid.) and ended Jimma's autonomy in 1934, as part of his centralization policies. At the same time, Selassie also granted constitutional equality to all religions. The rise of pan-Arabism and President Nasser's attempts in Egypt to stir Muslim sentiments later encouraged the reappearance of a politicized Islamic identity. In 1962, Egypt sent troops to Yemen, asserting its interests in the Red Sea region. Somali independence in 1960 created tension on the Ethiopian-Somali border area and Ethiopia, sensitive to regional political developments and remembering the *jihads* of Ahmad Gregn, began to turn more actively towards other African nations.

By the end of the twentieth century, regional trade systems had changed in character. With the emergence of nation states the ancient caravan trade had disappeared, being replaced by a new type of trade in which traders sold their products in local shops (*dukas*). Traders in southern Ethiopia shifted their interests northwards, towards Addis Ababa, and lessened their investment in Benaadir. Trade links were not entirely severed, however, and even today merchants in southern Ethiopia are part of the East African trade network.

The abolition of slavery greatly affected agricultural industries. The production of cotton and the making of *tobe* Banaadir, used as a medium of exchange and highly lucrative as a trade item, suffered. With the disappearance of slave labor and the importation of cheap, U.S.-made cloth (*tobe 'mericani*, and *marduf*), the local cotton market disappeared. Nor could Somali traders compete with Indian and Arab trading houses that had entered the region, particularly from the 1880s onwards, when the Somali economy was already weakened by drought and rinderpest. These factors also affected the Boranan and Oromo pastoralist groups in the interior who constituted the main market for cloth. As things worsened, Somali traders were forced to borrow money from the foreign traders and, over time, many reverted to pastoralism. In this way, Arab traders gained a foothold in the cattle market and strengthened their hold on the trade of agricultural products.

By 1882, a new trading point at Goobweyn, just north of Kismayo, included 200 Arabs traders and 150 Zanzibari soldiers (Menkhaus 1996: 140). By 1908, a regular trade route to Borana from Kismayo had been established. Hadramis were involved in this route. The trade from Borana to Kismayo was in ivory, hides, coffee, rhinoceros horns, ostrich feathers, wax, rubber, and salt (Pankhurst 1965), whereas cloth was brought from Kismayo to Borana (Menkhaus 1989: 210–11). As a consequence of this trade, every village along the Jubba River had from one to ten Arab shops. Places like Jamaame, Jelib, and Alexandra became known as Arab and Indian towns (including ex-*askaris*). The merchants operated local, kin-based trade networks, but also extended the trade through relatives in Mombasa, Zanzibar, and Saudi Arabia (Menkhaus ibid.: 212). In addition to buying and selling, the traders lent money to local people, cultivated cash crops like fruit, rather than staples, and ran camel-driven sesame mills.

Trade along the river was important enough to attract the British Emperor Navigation Company European, which operated a steamboat as far north as Baardheere (Bardera City), when the river was high. Italian steamboats were also present. The number of imported trade items found in local markets had also grown, including white cotton cloth from the United States, colored cloth from Australia and Germany, kerosene from the United States and Russia and matches from Sweden. Hides and cotton were exported to Italy and Germany, fins and dried fish to China, and cotton to Great Britain. Grain was also traded, mostly regionally rather than for export, and included the coastal towns. The various currencies used testified to the increased rate of commercialization. The Maria Theresa Thaler (the silver bullion coin named after named after the Empress of Austria, Hungary), rupees, British Sterling and lire were all used. Ferrari reports that Arab traders gladly accepted checks from Italian citizens in rupees drawn on the National Bank of India in Mombasa, Kenya (Menkhaus ibid.: 214ff).

But another change was also taking place. This was the shift of trade away from the Benaadir coast and the Upper Juba and Shebelle River areas, and towards the interior, particularly into northern Kenya. This was due to the British colonial policy of stabilization in those areas (Dalleo 1975). As I mentioned in the introduction, Arab traders operated in these areas, both from northern Sudan and from Zanzibar and the more southerly East African coast (Abir 1968). Some traveled with Swahili-speakers up the Tana River from Lamu to trade with the Pokomo and the Akamba. But the Arabs were vulnerable outside their home areas: only through marriage could relationships be forged with local populations. Prior to the British, Arab caravans also operated in northern Kenya, purchasing camels from nomads near Kismayo, using Somali herders to tend them, and then moving the livestock to Moyale and El Wak on the Ethiopian-Kenyan border.

The journey was taken in two legs, one from the coast to Wajir, northeastern Kenya, which took ten to seventeen days, and the second from Wajir to the border town of Moyale, taking five days. The entire journey was shorter than the one from Luuq to Borana. Cloth was the main medium of exchange, including *tobe* Benaadir from Mogadishu, colored cloth from India, but mostly the *tobe 'merican* or *marduf* from the United States. Because cash was scarce outside the main towns, goats and rifle cartridges were used as payment. As Arab trade increased, the town of Wajir became increasingly connected to the southeastern Somali coastal town of Kismayo, and the Tana more linked to Lamu; the Juba-Shebelle region reverted to something of a backwater.

Thus, by the late nineteenth and early twentieth centuries, traders operating in what is today northern Kenya were drawn into the Borana-Luuq-Benaadir sphere and eventually came to dominate it. Trade centers developed on the periphery, with Moyale becoming a center for Borana trade in the early 1900s. Goods and livestock were sent to Nairobi via Marsabit, or to Kismayo via Wajir. Even Lamu became integrated in the trade networks. The position of Luuq was weakened, and from 1910 to 1920, trade shifted even further into Kenya as traders set up their *dukas* in newly established British administrative stations and nomads sought goods there. Wajir, Serenli, Bura, Sankuri, Garissa, and Mandera all grew in size and importance, and the Kenyan cities of Nairobi and Kismayo challenged the trading power of the Benaadir coastal towns.

These changes were parallel to British attempts to establish colonial order in northeastern Kenya. In 1909, the British established the Northern Frontier District. Britain wanted to divert trade to the areas (Kismayo) under its control. As one administrator complained in 1907: "Nearly all the produce of Borana and the south (cattle, goats, camels, goatskins, ivory, rhino horn, ostrich feathers, salt and a few horses and mules) is exported to Lugh and Bardera" (P. Zaphiro, quoted in Dalleo 1975: 101). One effect of this shift of trader routes was to increase Borana cattle trade to the Rift Valley, down to Moyale and on to Marsabit. Moyale was at the time a mixed town, with Arab, Indian, Somali, Boran, Gurre, Sakuye, Ajuran, Burji, and Konso inhabitants. With the decline of caravan trade, they sought new sources of revenue, particularly by establishing *dukas*.

Methods of transport were also changing and trucks became important investments. Arabs, Indians, and northern Somali groups like the Herti and Isaaq replaced the southern Somali traders, becoming merchants, middlemen, transporters, hawkers, and caravaneers. The poaching of wild game also became a lucrative trade, with hides and meat being sold to traders on the coast, at Brava, Kismayo, and Lamu. *Duka* owners financed hunting expeditions and exploited the trade in rhino horns and leopard skins that was formerly the sole preserve of Somali pastoralists. Such trade also included members from the southern groups, such as Kikuyu, Meru, Emu, and Kemba traders. Trade in tea, sugar, and cloth, as well as the intoxicant *miraa* or *qat* (grown in Meru) was important. The towns of Wajir, Garissa, Isiolo, and Marsabit all flourished as regional trade grew.

Inland caravan traffic slowed while *duka* trade began to dominate. In small urban centers, however, *dukas* saw only petty trade with colonial administrators and troops, selling tea, sugar, cloth, and canned goods. Nomads brought livestock, hides, milk, and ghee. But the changing trade patterns brought Arab, Indian, and Somali traders into northern Kenya in growing numbers; the number of Arabs in the Northern Frontier District was only fourteen in 1921 and had increased to 418 by 1949 (Dalleo ibid.: 132).

Arabs and Indians did retail trade while Somalis sold animals and smuggled ivory. Arabs from Mukalla in Hadramaut are reported to have worked out of Moyale, Wajir, and Garissa (Dalleo ibid.: 137–38). Goans from India operated from Boranaland. Although the British tried to limit the number of shops per trader, many expanded their businesses, installing relatives in their new shops. Development was bringing a new kind of trade. Roads favored trucks, and cash favored traders. And the source of trade goods shifted from Benaadir to Kenya. These developments also led groups of Borana, who had come from their southern Ethiopian homelands of Dirre and Liban, to settle in northern Kenya. Many of them converted to Islam and joined the Somalis in anti-British activities. Traditional, non-Muslim Borana, however, tended to seek protection from the same government (Baxter 1969).

Back in Somalia, the economic situation had also changed. Throughout the 1920s, Italian colonialists expanded their control over the interior. They entered into the agricultural economy by taking control of cultivable land along the Shebelle and Juba rivers. Agricultural surveys started around 1910, and based on these, cultivation was started in the 1920s and organized by Societa' agricola italo-somalia (SAIS), drawing labor from the local population. Cotton, sugar cane, maize, bananas, and coconuts were the main crops cultivated. With this, the coastal economy started to change. By providing roads and transport, the Italians eroded the coast's monopoly over inland trade and opened up the coastal markets to goods coming from the inland.

New traders came in, including the Hadrami trader Ibn Quer, who bought most of the *dura* around Baidhabo for export. The Italians also replaced Hadrami and Eritrean garrison soldiers with local, Somali ones. Preparations in 1935 for the Italian invasion of Ethiopia also brought Somalis into the towns, affecting the position of the town traders. The large military buildup also meant that Italians for the first time could control the local population through the conscription of local labor, the *kolonya* system, and expropriate land for Italian settlers. Banana plantations were established to supply the export market, taking cultivable land out of food production thus negatively affecting local food supplies. War-time rule worsened the crisis until the ouster of the Italians from East Africa in 1941, when the British Military Administration reverted the land to food production, particularly through the Juba Scheme.

Somali nationalism emerged during and after the war and had a major impact on Arab-Hadrami traders. New political parties were established, including the Somali Youth Club, established in 1943. In 1948 this organization became the Somali Youth League, which called for the deportation of Arabs (Dalleo 1975: 298). In 1948, anti-Arab riots in Mogadishu saw eight Arabs killed and twenty-six injured. The Arabs joined with non-Somali forces in Xisbia and formed Jeriat el Arabia to present a united front against the growing Somali hostility towards Arabs and to protect Arab businesses and trade (Ibid.: 301). It should be said, however, that the Southern-based Somali parties such as Jumiya (Patriotic Benefit Union, founded in 1943), followed by Xisba (1947), were open to all groups, including Arabs.

From 1950 to 1969, commercial agriculture was further developed and education and social services improved. Small trade continued to be dominated by Arabs until the early 1960s. At Somalia's independence in 1960, anti-Arab sentiments increased and some of the Arab trading community began to leave. The anti-Arab sentiments were also affected by the 1964 revolution in Zanzibar and the massacre of thousands of Arab Zanzibaris. These events inflamed tensions between Arabs and Africans throughout entire East Africa. One effect of this departure of Arab merchants was the opening up of trade to local people.

Through Zeyla and Berbera to Dire Dawa

Dire Dawa was founded in 1902 after the construction of the Addis Ababa-Djibouti Railway. Located some 473 kilometers east of Addis Ababa and some 509 kilometers south of Djibouti, Dire Dawa is today the second largest city in Ethiopia, having a population of some 250,000 people (according to the 1994 census). The building of the railway led to the collapse of the historic coastal trading towns of Zeyla and Berbera in the Gulf of Aden, and towns along the inland trade routes, including Jeldessa and Harar. Settlements along the railway line began to grow as trade links with Djibouti were developed. Hadramis in Dire Dawa were involved in import and export trade, as well as retail trade and the running of hotels. They dominated the local markets until the 1960s, when they were replaced by Hadere, Oromo, and Gurage traders.

Samson Abebe Bezabeh (2004; see also 2008) reports from a field study on the Hadramis in Dire Dawa that the most successful Yemeni trader families in that town included Salah Deban, Ababakar Ba Maeruf, Abdulkadire Salime Ba

Shenfer, and the Hashimi family. The first three families were coffee exporters while the fourth owned the Hashimi Hotel and a sweetshop called "Hashimi Pastry." The Ba Shenfer family continues to live in Dire Dawa and exports coffee through the family-run firm, Ba Shenfer Trading PLC. The other two families—the Salah Deban and Ba Maeuruf—left the country in the 1960s.

Also drawing on the thesis by Samson Abebe, it was clear that Hadramis from Dire Dawa were involved in the important *qat* trade between Aden and the Hararge region in Ethiopia. This trade was organized in a company with two major branches, the Aden branch of the company, which was licensed to import *qat* from Ethiopia, and the Ethiopian based branch, which was licensed to export. This monopoly was broken during the 1960s when small Ethiopian traders organized against the monopoly enjoyed by the "foreign" traders and managed to influence the government to end the monopoly system. The government wanted to maintain this important trade, but broke the domination by the Hadrami and Yemeni Arabs by allowing in Armenian traders. This move secured the continuation of the trade but signaled the end of "Arab" dominance by engaging members of a group that was considered more "loyal" to the Ethiopian state.

Historically, though, the Hadrami and Yemeni Arabs had been engaged in the public sector, in close relationships with various Ethiopian regimes (Bezabeh 2008). Salim Aqile Ba Ubad originally came from the town of Shibam in Hadramaut. He entered eastern Ethiopia through the port of Zayla and settled in the town of Jeldesa, where he was a trader. Later on, he was employed by the Imperial government as customs officer in Jeldessa town. During the Italian occupation, from 1936 to 1941, Salim served as an Islamic judge or *qadi*, making rulings according to Islamic law or *sharia*, in the government court. Others of Hadrami descent served as religious leaders. The first three imams of the largest mosque in Dire Dawa, Masjid Juma, were Yemeni clerics, namely, Ahmed Seif Alkabrie, Ashaikh Abdurahman Ba Makhrama, and Hag Umar Ahmed Seif Alkabrie.

Yemeni Muslim clerics were also engaged in Islamic teaching and healing practices, including Seyid Abedela Al-Watie, whose tomb is found inside the Muslim cemetery in Dire Dawa, which bears his name. In the past, Muslims visited his tomb to perform religious rituals on the on fifteenth day of the Islamic month of Rajab. Most of those who took part in this festival were Yemeni or other Arab migrants living in Dire Dawa. Non-Arab Muslims belonging to different ethnic groups in Dire Dawa also participated.

From Somalia to Borana and Bale

As in Dire Dawa in the east, both Hadramis and North Yemenis can be found among the trading families in Borana in southern Ethiopia. A survey conducted by Dr. Getachew Kassa shows that immigrant families came to such southern trading towns as Suftu, Negelle, and Moyale in the Borana administrative districts of Liban and Moyale. The same groups are also in the Bale region. Most of those interviewed in the survey came to Borana and Bale because of trade opportunities. The pattern of adaptation is similar for all of the families. Their fathers and grandfathers were born and raised in Somalia, and they continue to have close ties to the country, which explains in part their lack of contact with Hadramis in Addis Ababa. After reaching Borana, immigrant Yemenis (including Hadramis) initially lived with local contacts who gave them food and shelter.

In addition to the local market, Borana offered cross-border trading (both legal and contraband). Most of the local pastoralists had no apparent interest in taking part in this thriving caravan trade. Because of this, Somalis and Hadramis quickly controlled the trade. Later, with the development of roads and the introduction of lorries, Hadramis also went into the transport business, running garages and servicing vehicles. Family members worked as mechanics, drivers, and technicians (watch and radio repairs), and some opened petrol stations. There were other ways of making quick money, like the smuggling of people from Ethiopia into Kenya during volatile periods of, first, colonial rule and later, the Soviet-backed Derg.

"Eritrean Arabism," "Greater Somalia-ism," and "Ethiopian Socialism"

Hadrami fortunes in Ethiopia changed dramatically from the 1950s to the 1970s. Returning to the thesis of Samson Abebe, Samson claims there were three main developments behind change. First, the Hadramis were negatively affected by the development of "Arabism" in Eritrea and the conflict between the Eritrean Liberation Front (ELF) and the Haile Selassie regime; second, Siad Barre's call for a "Greater Somalia" and the Ogaden War with Ethiopia saw Hadramis identified as "enemies"; third, the 1974 overthrow of Haile Selassie, and the development of Ethiopian socialism placed Hadrami traders as capitalists, i.e. among the economic enemies of the regime. Let us have a quick look at all three of these factors in the diminishing fortunes of the Hadramis.

In the post-World War II period, with the end of Italy's occupation of Ethiopia, Britain sought to join the lowlands of Eritrea with its colony in Sudan. At the same time, the United States was showing interest in Eritrea because of its potential as a military base. To promote their interests the Americans maintained good relations with Emperor Haile Selassie. In return, the United States government supported Ethiopia's policy towards Eritrea at the United Nations Security Council, with the result that the federation of Eritrea with Ethiopia was accepted by the General Assembly on 17 December 1952.

However, the federal arrangement with Eritrea, which was supposed to be based on a democratic constitution, was soon undermined by Ethiopia's repressive measures. As a result, Eritrea's federal status lasted only ten years. In 1962 the Ethiopian regime changed the name of the Eritrean "government" to "administration" and officially included Eritrea as one of the fourteen provinces (Ellingson 1978: 614–19). As a response, Eritrean groups began to organize armed resistance through various independence movements. In the early years of the resistance, the ELF, based in the western lowlands of Eritrea, was the most prominent (Ellingson 1978: 614–19).

Right from the start, the ELF received outside support for its campaign to end Ethiopian domination. Egypt was at the forefront as the then leaders of Egypt had an ambitious plan to form a greater Egypt, bringing the Nile countries under its control. Under Nasser, Egypt assisted exiled Eritreans in establishing the ELF in July 1960. The Egyptian government gave the ELF an office in Cairo and continued its support until 1963 (Erlich 1994: 130–31). Other interest groups in the Arab world also supported the ELF, but had a rather broader agenda than the Egyptian focus on the Nile waters. This broader vision focused on the Arabization of Eritrea, aimed at giving Arab powers control over the strategic Red Sea area. The main actor in this game was Syria's Baathist regime (Erlich 1995: 130–31) which, in 1952, "had defined the Arab homeland as constituting that area which extends beyond the Taurus mountain the Gulf of Basra, the Arabian sea, the Ethiopian mountains … the Atlantic ocean and the Mediterranean sea and constituting one single complete unity in which no part therefore my be alienated" (Ibid.: 152).

In July 1963, with the regime's support, the ELF opened an office in Damascus. Syria provided military support and training at an academy in Aleppo, famous for its connections to guerrilla movements (Ibid.: 152–53). In response, the United States and Israel, increased their military and economic support for the imperial Ethiopian government in a bid to suppress the ELF (Lyons 1986: 59–60; Sheim 1988: 29).

Another pressing issue also emerged during this period, this time from the eastern part of Ethiopia. That was Somalia's claim to the Ogaden, a region that was incorporated into Ethiopia during the southern expansion of Emperor Menelik. After World War II the British government sought to join the Ogaden territory to its colony in northern Somalia (Bahru 2002: 180–82), but the plan was not realized, and in 1954 Ethiopia restored its rule over the disputed area. This action was not well received by the Somalis, particularly the national party and the Somali Youth League (SYL), both of which supported a nationalistic vision of Greater Somalia. Under this vision, all the lands inhabited by Somalis were to be brought together under one sovereign state. This eventually led to the 1977–1978 war between Ethiopia and Somalia, known as the Ogaden War.

The 1960s and 1970s were marked by internal and external conflict and the downfall of the Haile Selassie regime. Following the overthrow of the dynasty, the military junta, known as the Derg, took power and adopted socialism. The Derg nationalized all lands and quickly changed its Cold War alliance from the United States to the Soviet Union (Bahru 2002: 229–48).

Cold War politics aside, our concern here is with the effect these developments had on Hadramis and Yemenis living in Ethiopia. The result was tragic for members of these groups. As Arabs, they were linked to the Eritrean problem and particularly the Syrian support of the ELF. A dramatic expression of this occurred following the ELF's bombing of an Ethiopian Airways jet at Frankfurt Airport, West Germany, in 1969. Within days of the bombing, large demonstrations were staged throughout Ethiopia, including Dire Dawa. The public opposed the bombing of the plane and denounced the Syrian government and other Arab nations backing the ELF. Demonstrators accused Arab citizens living in Ethiopia of supporting the ELF forces and called on the government to expel them from the country.

As Yemenis their situation was further aggravated by the fact that during the 1960s the Ethiopian government felt generally threatened by the developments in Yemen itself. Egypt had actively supported the republicans who toppled the Imam in 1962, and who in return supported Nasser's pan-Arabism. Radical forces kept attacking the British in South Yemen, and with the British withdrawal in 1967 the road was open for a communist regime. Thus, the Ethiopians felt surrounded by radical regimes which constituted both ideological challenges and also made claims to areas within the Red Sea region.

At the time, the Yemeni community distanced itself from these developments and instead tried to signal its loyalty to Ethiopia. They joined demonstrations in Addis Ababa, Dessie, and Dire Dawa, as well as in Asmara, the Ethiopian-controlled capital of Eritrea. Their leaders also met with Emperor Haile Selassie in a bid to defuse the rising anti-Arab sentiment. However, none of this seems to have changed the negative attitude of local people toward Arabs. In spite of the expressions of solidarity, Yemeni Arabs were harassed and abused by local people who continued to insist on their expulsion. Eventually, the imperial government passed a decree demanding that all Arab citizens leave Ethiopia.

Hadramis also suffered from the worsening climate in the Ethiopian relationships with Somalia. Because they had a long history of intermarriage with Somalis, Hadramis were considered sympathetic to the Somali claim on the Ogaden. They were accused of spying for Somalia on Ethiopian military movements. The Ogaden War also led to major interruptions in the economic activities of most Yemenis. In Borana, Hadramis were imprisoned as alleged supporters of both the general Somali government policy and also of the activities of anti-government Somali groups. But Yemenis dealing in the border area of Somalia and Ethiopia also suffered on the Somali side. Many were robbed on the road by armed Somali fighters and their lorries destroyed by land mines. With unrest worsening and the security situation becoming dangerous, Yemenis began to limit their trade to their urban shops only, or they abandoned their shops in the border towns altogether and moved to safer areas, in both Ethiopia and Kenya.

Finally, as traders involved in the commercial sector, Hadramis were labeled as "capitalists" and "feudal enemies" of the socialist Derg regime that took power in Ethiopia in 1974. Many had houses and other property confiscated and those who were seen as collaborators with anti-government forces were persecuted. This was the case both for Yemenis and Hadramis. In Borana, specific families were considered as supporters of anti-government groups that were still in favor of the toppled Haile Selassie regime. They were accused of having smuggled out wanted individuals (government officials and their children) and also to have helped Falashas (Ethiopian Jews) cross the border into Kenya. Some Yemenis suspected of being involved in the smuggling of people were killed by the Derg while others managed to escape to Kenya and Djibouti.

In addition to their political problems, the Yemenis have in recent years faced new economic challenges. For decades, Yemenis were the dominant actors in the livestock trade, contraband, shop-keeping, and transport. By the 1990s, however, other ethnic groups were challenging the Yemeni hold over regional commerce, especially Somalis, Tigrayans, Gurage, and Werji. In addition to the competition, Yemeni business was made more difficult by tighter customs controls over local trade, and instability in the border regions due to the collapse of the Somali state.

The issue of identity among Yemeni families in Ethiopia

The events that occurred between the late 1950s and 1970s have of course influenced the identity of Yemenis living in Ethiopia, as well as intra-ethnic relations. As a start of such a discussion of Hadrami identities in Ethiopia, let us return to Awad Saeed's house in Merkato and recall what he told me about the Yemeni Community Association in Addis Ababa. Awad was generally positive about the future of the Yemenis in Ethiopia and saw the Yemeni Association as an important part of that future. Unfortunately, it seems that the optimistic tone struck by Awad seems not to be well founded. Let us illustrate by a few examples, including, first, the school that the association is running.

The Yemeni Community Association is responsible for the running of the Yemeni Community School in Addis, which used to educate children of Yemeni families as well as children of other Arab communities in Addis Ababa, up to grade 12. Children in this school were given religious and Arabic-language instruction, in addition to classes in Yemeni and Arab culture and history. It is important to note, however, that the school also used to follow the Ethiopian syllabus and that the school also taught mathematics and other subjects in Amharic. This divided system made it possible for the students to learn about their own Arab and Islamic heritage and at the same time adapt to an Ethiopian educational system and eventually also to the labor market.

However, some five years ago the Ethiopian government forbade the teaching of any religion in Ethiopian schools, and in order to protect the teaching of Islam, the Yemeni school chose to close down the teaching related to the Ethiopian curriculum. Instead of working as an integrating factor, education thus became a symbol of how "different" the Arab families were, also underlining the diasporic situation the Hadramis and Yemenis found themselves in. This led many families to re-evaluate their position vis-à-vis the school. With the increased and only focus on the Arabic part of the curriculum and on Islam, many families opted to send their children to other schools, where they could get more English teaching and also be more in line with the requirements of the Ethiopian school system. This change also led to a reduction of donations to the school, and today the school is facing a crisis both in terms of student recruitment and in funding.

Also when it comes to the association itself, Awad's dreams seem not to be fulfilled. Established in 1942, the association's head office is still located in the Merkato area. From the time of its creation, the association has served as a principal bridge between Yemeni families living in Ethiopia and those at home, both in the Yemen Arab Republic (YAR) and the People's Democratic Republic of Yemen (PDRY). In Awad's time, scholarships were provided to young Yemeni-Ethiopian girls and boys to study in Yemen and other Arab countries, and the association announced job opportunities in Yemen and in the region. To benefit from this, applicants had to acquire legal documents showing that they were Ethiopian Yemenis, and the association facilitated the process of obtaining Yemen national identity cards from the Yemeni Embassy in Addis Ababa. Acquiring Yemeni papers also made travel to countries like Saudi Arabia and the other Gulf States less difficult. As a token of its special relationship to Yemen, the association every year received four air tickets from the government of Yemen, which the association handed out to Ethiopian Yemeni nationals who could not pay their air ticket expenses to Yemen or other Arab countries. Through the association's activities, Hadramis could stay informed about Yemen, and keep in touch with the wider Yemeni community in Addis.

However, this facilitating role is also changing now. The association is still there, but weakened. The social functions have more or less stopped and the relationships to Yemen seem to be handled more on an individual level rather than through the officials of the association. And, as noted above, its role within the field of education is diminishing.

Its role as a link to other Yemeni and Hadrami communities within Ethiopia is also reduced. Although being centered in Addis, branch offices of the association were opened in Jimaa, Dire Dawa, and Harar, and the association used to work for the interests of Yemeni families in Ethiopia. For instance, as noted above, during the Ogaden War between Ethiopia and Somalia in 1977–1978, many Yemeni families lost their property and were displaced. In some of these cases, the association sought donations from the Yemeni community, especially businessmen. Some of those who were displaced by the war were given passports, air tickets, airport and visa fees, and pocket money. Today, no such links exist. When Yemenis come to Addis they do not go to the association but make use of their individual networks to obtain what they came for.

But let us be fair to Awad Saeed. He also saw the problems coming. Although convinced that the Yemeni association would help create an awareness about identity and place of origin that had an effect on how Hadramis understand their own history, he also realized that the political and social climate in Ethiopia could challenge the work of the association. In this sense Awad showed himself to be a realist. In our conversations at his house he admitted that contact between the association and Hadramis living in the regions outside Addis Ababa was weak. And this fact, said Awad, would lead to a difference in the experiences of Hadramis and Yemenis living in eastern and southern Ethiopia from the experiences of people living in the Ethiopian capital.

And this is indeed what has emerged as a pattern. Isolated and more directly affected by border tensions and anti-Arab sentiment, many Hadramis have left Ethiopia and migrated to other countries. Many found new opportunities in the booming oil economies of Saudi Arabia and the Gulf. For those who stayed behind, the option was to take Ethiopian citizenship and move away from the traditional "Arab" population centers, to relocate to other parts of the country where they could blend in with local groups, presenting themselves as Oromo and Somali rather than as Arab.

As far as economic adaptations are concerned, the younger generation of Hadramis have traditionally followed in the footsteps of their fathers, continuing businesses and forms of trade begun by those who came before. With the current political and security problems, however, there is not much room for newcomers to enter the trading systems in Ethiopia. Because of this, young people are pursuing different paths. Modern, Westernized education is crucial in this respect. Young Yemenis attend Ethiopian schools and are employed in the government and private-sector businesses, and also with nongovernmental organizations inside and outside Ethiopia. Traveling abroad in pursuit of better opportunities is also a new trend for the young generation of Hadramis in Ethiopia. The migrants have gone many places: to Kenya, Yemen, Kuwait, and Saudi Arabia, but also to Canada, Australia, Holland, Malaysia, and India. In these places migrants are either finding work or attending colleges and universities.

The migration of family members to other countries for work has had an impact on the general economic status of their families back home. Remittances are invested in better housing, new businesses, and more elaborate styles of weddings and funerals. The cultural impact of migration to Saudi Arabia and the Gulf is also clear, with the spread of Arabic styles of dress and the increased popularity of the Arabic language, as well as increased *purdah* among women. These trends are also seen among people who have not migrated, thus indicating a stronger public appearance of Islam in the region.

The issue of Yemeni identity is, however, still a tricky one for the Hadramis living in the regions. In spite of some economic success through migration, the identity of these migrant groups is problematic. The Yemenis have experienced several decades of settlement and interaction with diverse Ethiopian ethnic groups. The consequence has been the creation of identities characterized by ambivalence. Most people are of mixed origin, or *kelles*, as it is known locally in Amharic. They may have lived among the Cushitic-speaking Muslim pastoralists, such as the Somali, Garri, Borana, and Arssi. They have married into Somali families as well as Oromo ones (Borana and Shewa). And they live in communities in which people from north Yemen are also present; marriages between those from the north and those from the south have also occurred.

Several informants argue that such mixed communities might be considered "inferior" by the more "proper" Yemeni community in the larger Ethiopian cities, especially Addis Ababa. Given such attitudes, we can expect the Hadrami diaspora in Ethiopia to be internally differentiated. One group is made up of people who follow the type of strategies represented by the Yemeni Association in Addis Ababa, seeking a more organized and institutional relationship to Yemen, for business reasons as well as educational reasons. Members of this group will have an interest in maintaining a public Hadrami identity as long as it will serve their economic interests. At the same time they are businessmen who will also maintain their relationships with the Ethiopian elites, promoting the economic interests of both. If need be, the same people can blend in with this Ethiopian elite. A quick trip around Addis to visit the offices of successful Yemeni businessmen gives precisely this impression.

The other group is made up of small traders who have adapted to their local situations and taken up local identities. For them, however, there is no way back to a Hadrami identity. What they are faced with is not a balancing act in which there are different choices available. For them this is a real process of assimilation. Historically, Yemenis in general and Hadramis in particular have related to Muslim groups such as the Somali and the Oromo. They are Muslims, but may vary in the degree to which religion plays a part in their lives. Some people engage in local funeral associations (*idir*) or credit associations (*iqub*) thereby embracing local cultures, others not. Particularly women engage in local associations run by other ethnic groups, thus connecting to the local culture and community.

The process of assimilation that is to be expected from this is counteracted by new opportunities to travel to Yemen and also by labor migration to the Arabian peninsula. Through exposure to other Hadramis in the wider region, a new awareness about "homeland" has developed. But more important than a new notion of a homeland is a new and more intense feeling of being Muslim, which also means being affected by the ongoing rise of Islamic fundamentalism in the Horn of Africa. We have seen how Sudan became a laboratory for political Islam in the 1990s, and the same goes for the rest of the Horn of Africa region. One important result of the migration of Ethiopian Yemenis and Hadramis to Saudi Arabia and the Gulf is the spread of Wahhabi ideology, often by way of engagement in Muslim welfare-oriented organizations. In the current climate, dominated by the war on terrorism, it almost goes without saying that these organizations are not seen as humanitarian agencies but rather as covers for the planning and carrying out of terrorist acts on behalf of al-Qaida. Again, history is important. Links to Somalia are obvious, where Islamism also took off after the collapse of the Somali state and the international intervention in the early 1990s. Regional nationalist movements and guerrilla warfare against Ethiopia's Derg also created Muslim resistance, represented, for instance, by the Islamic Front for the Liberation of Oromia (IFLO). The Islamist regime in Khartoum supported the IFLO against the Ethiopia government, which was itself providing military bases to southern Sudanese rebels at war with the northern Sudanese government in Khartoum.

Through the decades, we see a regional pattern in which countries, governments, and opposition groups interact and form alliances that may quickly change, creating a rather chaotic situation. Eritrea, Sudan, Ethiopia, Djibouti, Somalia, and Egypt are as ever locked into localized battles for territory, power, and resources—battles in which the global power of the United States plays a key role (see e.g. de Waal 2004). For the Ethiopian Yemenis and Hadramis, a major consequence of these developments is that they are regarded as potential terrorists. Thus, the label "terrorist" has been added to the earlier stigmatizing labels of "Arab," "Somali," and "capitalist."

But, what we see today, at the time of this writing, is that the Ethiopian government is changing its tactics vis-à-vis the Muslims, probably due to the Ethiopian engagements in Somalia where Ethiopian troops are fighting the local Somali fundamentalists. Back home in Ethiopia there are indications that the Ethiopian regime is pulling in the Muslims in order to demonstrate that they are not against Muslims as such, only the terrorist regime in Somalia. This public show of concern for Muslims immediately creates uncertainties among Ethiopia's Christian majority, who are asking themselves whether the regime itself is turning Muslim. We don't know where these current developments will end, but one thing seems for sure: The various balancing acts that the Yemenis in general, and the Hadramis in particular, have been engaged in seem to continue, and in the future we might expect new labels to appear following those of Arab, Somali, capitalist, and terrorist.

Identities in the Making

CHAPTER FIVE

Maintaining a Hadrami Identity in the Diaspora

Hadrami collective identities

This chapter discusses the maintenance of different Hadrami identities in the various diasporic communities. We have seen that the reproduction of Hadrami identity is ongoing. But "Hadrami" is not the only collective identity. Hadramis can also be characterized as "Arabs," thus also being grouped with people of non-Hadrami origin but of Arab descent. And today we also see the emerging label of "Yemeni," actualized by the unification of North and South Yemen. But we also know that in many cases these ethnic identities are irrelevant, as earlier Hadrami migrants intermarried with local people and their descendants embraced the indigenous ethnic identity. For all Hadramis, however, regardless of their residence, their identity as "Muslim" is shared.

Part one showed different variations in the ways the identities can be played out. In Singapore, the ethnic landscape is organized along the "CIMO" model—"Chinese, Indians, Malays, and others." Hadramis are within the category of "others" and are not differentiated within the publicly recognized system. Each category is further divided but these divisions are not likely to have much relevance to Hadramis. This changes, however, when an individual Hadrami creates a special relationship, for instance through marriage, and thus enters the social world of that particular category.

The choice that Hadrami Arabs are faced with in Singapore is between maintaining an identity as Arab and Muslim, or as Muslim only, in which case they might be officially categorized as Malay. Many Hadrami men have married Malay women and effectively become Malay. Because Singapore's official language is English, pupils must "choose" a second language from Chinese, Indian, and Malay. Their choice is taken to indicate the students' "mother tongue." Hadramis tend to choose Malay, further adding to their inclusion in the Malay category of the official Singaporean ethnic structure.

In Hyderabad in India, the identities of Hadrami, Arab, and Yemeni were all used. In addition, a "Hyderabadi" identity distinguishes those born in Hyderabad from those born in Hadramaut itself. "Deccani" is also used, but this is a broader term used for Muslims in southern India. Other important variants are Hindu versus Muslim and Arab, as opposed to other Muslims in southern India, whether Indian–Afghans, Pathans, Bohoras, or Nawwayats, etc. Within the Muslim identity there is also a divide between the Sunni and Shi'a paths who worship separately and between whom there are often troubles during the celebration of the Shi'a *muharram* festival. Within the Sunni community, there is a separation between the Sunni of the Shafi'e school, to which Hadramis belong, and the Hanefi school, which is adhered to most Muslims in northern India. Hadramis are also followers of various Sufi sects, the two dominant ones being the Qadiriyya and the Chisti.

In Sudan, Hadrami identity is set against that of the local Sudanese living in the northeast of the country (Beni Amer, Hadendowa, and other Beja), Sudanese from elsewhere in Sudan, and the small but powerful European community (including the British administration during the colonial period, as well as Greeks, Armenians, and Lebanese). There are also Indians (*hunud, banyan*), Abyssinians (*habashi*), and Yemenis. Religious identities differentiate people in eastern Sudan who follow Shafi'e Sunni Islam, the rest of Sudan being Maliki. Hadramis are themselves Shafi'e, and thus could forge links to the inhabitants of their host region. They also joined the Khatmiyya *tariqa*, the dominant Sufi sect in the region. In terms of language, the use of Arabic for daily speech eased matters, as did the Sudanese schooling system, having been the model for education in Hadramaut since the 1940s.

In Ethiopia, Hadramis and Yemenis are often considered Oromo or Somali, which is the ethnicity of their mothers and grandmothers, their male ancestors having married locally. This means that in Ethiopia their more fluid identity makes them part of a climate of tension between ethnic and religious groups. A case from Singapore may provide us with further insights into the dynamics surrounding the issue of identity.

A debate in Singapore, 1992

The issue of identity can come up in various contexts, and should be seen on the background of specific contexts. In order to show how debates over identities can unfold I shall use a case from Singapore. The chain of events of this case started in 1992 with a TV program called "Family Portrait" which presented Hadramis in Singapore as "Malays of Arab descent." This was followed by an article in the *Strait Times* headlined, "The Arab Dilemma: Are Arabs here Malay?" The responses were not slow in coming. Nonsense, said some Arabs, "We are Singaporean Arabs, full stop!" (*Asiaweek*, 31 July 1992). But others said that it was certainly true that most Arabs living in Singapore lived as Malays, though some commented on the presence of Arabic culture at community events, including weddings.

A Muslim Malay MP entered the fray, commenting that there was nothing wrong with wanting to be considered an Arab. Historically, Arabs brought Islam to southeast Asia and spread the faith. The Malay politician stressed that what is important is that all people are Singaporean and that bridges can be built between communities. And a voice from the National University of Singapore asked what reasons there may be why Arabs were depicted as Malays. Are "they" (those who insist they should be seen as Malays) afraid Arabs should again rise to the former glory of the early Hadrami families in the city, for example the "big four" we presented in chapter one—al Junaid, al Kaf, al Saqqaf, bin Taleb? Families who at the height of their influence owned a lot of property and who controlled a big part of business in the city. Maybe, the man from NUS continued, it was because Arabs do better than Malays in schools, thus being able to challenge the Chinese hegemony in the city state? But, according to the university man, the real problem is not the question of what identity Arabs have, but rather the quality of the leadership of the Arab community in Singapore. The old guard is considered out of touch, and younger people don't care.

The debate also continues within the Hadrami community itself. As the magazine *Al–Mahjar* commented:

> It was never the case that all Arabs were wealthy. Bluntly speaking: Our fore-fathers are the precursors of the Bangladeshi and Thai workers of today, forced to eke out a living in a foreign country because of the pathetic state of their economy in their country of origin. The past is all that is left to us, and the wealth is not earned, it is inherited. (al-Mahjar 1997, vol. 2, no. 1)

But such a view of the Hadrami migration history, that they were only part of the army of cheap laborers being exploited in a colonial economy, is immediately objected to in the next issue of the magazine: "We came as entrepreneurs, we worked hard and succeeded. It was the government's land acquisition that bungled the Arab lifestyle," wrote a bin Talib, a relative of the Yemeni consul in Singapore whom we met in chapter one.

But the controversy did not only appear in *al-Mahjar* magazine. In 1995, the Arab Association organized a conference in which this issue was the main topic. The idea of a conference came from a position paper, "A Vision for the Future," written by Ameen Ali Talib, Helmi Talib, and Khaled Talib. In the paper the writers complained about the lack of organized Arab response to questions about their identity. The conference was called "Singapore Arabs in the 21st Century," and the discussions confirmed the views expressed in the position paper, that the key issue facing the Arab community in Singapore was the ongoing crisis of identity. This identity crisis stemmed from a lack of attention to their traditions, the loss of Arabic as a working language, the falling interest in religious studies, the lack of appeal of Al Wehda for the younger generation and poorly developed economic ties with the Arab world. One necessary condition for improving the situation would be to improve the education of Arab Singaporeans.

To improve people's identification with Arab culture, the authors introduced the idea of *assabiyya,* a concept introduced by the Arab sociologist Ibn Khaldoun in his book *Al Muqaddimah* for the type of natural solidarity that the author saw among the Arab Beduin tribes. This internal solidarity, claimed Ibn Khaldoun, disappeared in the context of city life, thus eroding the feeling of unity among the Arab tribes. This feeling of unity, if restored among Arabs, claimed the authors, could be as effective as the Chinese family networks, known as *guang xi,* which they saw had played a role in the development of the Chinese economic hegemony. The strategy would be a more active Arab Association which assumed a higher profile in national events and in the press. Scholarships to Islamic schools should be offered to improve Muslim knowledge among young people. And they recommended the establishment of venture capital companies to support businesses seeking to expand in the region, to improve relations between Southeast Asia and the Middle East, and to improve networking.

Defining a Hadrami identity

The complex picture in Singapore, as well as the three other places noted above, implies a complicated identity game, one in which Hadramis can present themselves as Hadramis against a host of "others." In general terms, Hadramis play out identities that are appropriate to the context they are in, which again is defined by who the significant "others" are, and what the interaction is about. But after generations in the diaspora and intermarriage with local women, there are fewer phenotypical differences between Hadramis and local populations. Ethnic relations are therefore not easily expressed in racial terms.

In such a situation, diacritical signs other than the biological ones emerge, and such signs are more negotiable than representations of race. Arabic language is such a sign when the individuals speak Arabic. Integration into local communities and national education systems have led to the disappearance of Arabic as a spoken language. Dress could be used as a sign, but wearing Hadrami clothes is a thing Hadramis do in private settings—in their homes and while visiting each other. It is not so much a public sign any more. Nor is Hadrami food, or general cultural expressions like songs and dances, evident in the public arena as Hadrami boundary markers. These signs or markers all belong to situations that are clearly defined as Hadami events, like weddings and other celebrations.

Hence, such cultural markers are relevant for the display of cultural origin within the group, but they do not serve as public markers that show Hadramis as being different from other groups. Their neighbors will of course know who they are, and be able to point them out from other groups. But no specific type of behavior has emerged as a boundary marker to establish who is a proper Hadrami and who is not. Thus, an observer with no prior knowledge will in many cases find it difficult to see any difference between a person of Hadrami descent and those of non-Hadrami descent. The absence of such ethnic characteristics also leaves Hadramis in the diaspora with a choice. They can choose to "disappear" into the local population and reappear as Muslims of Indian, Malay, Somali, or Sudanese descent. But this might also constitute a problem to some.

The debates in Singapore over the extent to which those of Hadrami origin are Arab or Malay show that the balancing act Hadramis perform in order to take part in the Singaporean nation state might be problematic in the sense that non-Hadramis stop seeing them as Arabs and classify them as Malay Muslims, a classification which many object to. Similar dynamics may be at play in Hyderabad, although there are also people who are eager to appear as Hadrami Arabs when they go to the Middle East as labor migrants, obtaining Hadrami identity cards from community organizations to improve their chances of finding work in Saudi Arabia and the Gulf countries. In this case an Arab identity, with a known descent from Hadramaut, can facilitate adaptational strategies that would be close to Indian Muslims. But pursuing such strategies in a different continent would not bring immediate consequences for the local Hadrami strategies in Hyderabad, nor would local identity games as Indian Muslims constitute a threat to the strategies the migrants can pursue in the various labor markets in the Gulf. Understanding Hadrami identities is thus a complex affair that requires an understanding of the organizing features of Hadrami identity processes.

Localising factors: Hadrami family and kinship

The starting point for such an analysis is to understand what type of experiences a Hadrami migrant faces and in what way such experiences will decide the person's feeling of identity. One of the earliest discussions of Hadramis abroad was in the book by Professor Van den Berg, published in 1886. Focussing on Hadramis in Indonesia he wrote that when a Hadrami needs help he seeks someone from his family or his tribe. There is a tendency to find people in the same place coming from the same area or river valley (*wadi*) in

Hadramaut. Van den Berg found that in the Indian Archipelago, people came from the main Wadi Hadramaut, between Tarim and Shibam. Ingrams found much the same pattern in 1936. Emigrants to Java were from the Al Kathir, though inhabitants from Tarim and Wadi Hajarein (particularly the towns of Badra and Haura) and the tribes of Nahd and Ja'ada are also represented. The Singaporean communities come from Tarim, Seyun, and Shibam and the Nahd tribesmen.

In East Africa, people are of the Tamimi and BaHadeira tribes and from those of Hajr. Zanzibar has connections with the town of Shihr. Around the Red Sea, in Egypt, Jeddah, Abyssinia, and Sudan, the migrants were from Dua'an. With the practice of marrying local women, and with a patrilineal descent system, children became members of the father's kinship group. And when children married, such marriages were also arranged with the group membership of the involved parties in mind. Hadrami marriages thus are a critical factor in reproducing kinship groups as distinct social categories. It is of importance, therefore, to elicit information on how people conceptualize who an appropriate or acceptable spouse is.

The material collected in the four places discussed in part one indicates a similar pattern. The early migrants might have been married in Hadramaut before they left the homeland, but wives were rarely brought with them when they traveled. As Muslims they could have four wives, so there were few restrictions on marrying again in the diaspora. And the material shows that this is what male Hadrami migrants did. The choice of marriage partners in the various diasporic communities depended on the "availability" of proper candidates. Again, the prevailing conditions for migration played a part. In Singapore, young women were brought from Hadramaut in order to meet the demand for "proper" wives.

By the early part of the twentieth century, however, rules controlling migration were tightened and young women, or even girls, from Hadramaut could no longer move easily to Singapore. Because of this, men married from within the established Hadrami community or outside, with local Malay Muslim women. The same pattern was reported in Hyderabad and Ethiopia. This led then to a situation in which Hadrami offspring, while over time maintaining a Hadrami cultural identity, increasingly came to physically resemble the local Malay, Indian, Somali, and Ethiopian populations. Sudan was a special case, since the populations Hadramis encountered there were rather closer, in physical appearance, to their Arab background.

When the various nation states began to introduce nationalistic policies, resident populations were forced to choose between a national identity and a non-national one. Because of the prevalence of marriage to non-Hadramis, the assimilation process in physical terms had already moved quite far. Hadramis could easily blend into the local populations, having assimilated into local cultures as well as sharing physical features with the national populations. This continuous process of assimilation was of concern to those individuals in Hadrami communities who sought to reproduce Hadrami culture and identity.

A focus on marriage strategies foreshadows discussions in chapter six, where I discuss how Hadrami groups generally claim a superior social status: Marrying from within the group becomes an important way to maintain that identity. Marriage was thus not only an important factor in defining external boundaries within a host population. It was also important for the maintenance of internal boundaries for various types of Hadrami identity. In the case of Hadramis, there is thus the additional point that there are several social categories within the larger group itself. Marriages between members of these social categories have been rare, and the institution of *kafa'a* marriage (marriage *within* a group) is still of importance. In spite of a general tendency to marry within the group, it is also a fact that when marriages outside the group do happen, the implication for the identities of the involved parties show clear gender dimensions. A man can marry outside his group without much difficulty as the children of such a marriage will still belong to the father's descent line. The problem occurs when a woman from one of the higher groups is to marry a man from a group of lesser standing. According to the patrilineal genealogical reckoning, the children of such a marriage will belong to a lower category. This fact sometimes leads to spinsterhood for women of the higher status if no man of the "right" category comes forward. The same type of thinking is applied to marriages from outside the Hadrami group itself. Just such a case, represented by the Alawi-Irshadi controversy, will be a major focus in the next chapter.

The Alewi-Irshadi controversy started in Indonesia in the early years of the twentieth century, with an Indian Muslim who wanted to marry a Hadrami woman of Sada descent. Muslim scholars were asked to make a ruling, or *fatwa*, on the matter. The Sada scholars argued that the marriage had to be evaluated within the *kafa'a* tradition, and that therefore a Sada girl should not be married outside the Sada group. The ruling was countered by more liberal Muslim scholars, particularly a Sudanese by the name of Ahmad Surketti. He argued that what defined the group within which *kafa'a* marriage could take place was being a Muslim. Hence the Indian Muslim man could marry the Sada woman and it would still be a *kafa'a* marriage as the bride was also a Muslim.

The importance of marriage partners shows how Hadrami identity relates to the local level of family life and the in-groups that define this level. This long tradition has continued into the present day. The French anthropologist Sylvaine Camelin, who did fieldwork in Shihir on the Hadramaut coast, reports that by the 1990s, people were arguing that marriages between groups do take place, and that traditional marriages within the groups belong to the past (personal communication). But when she tried to find specific cases she was always referred to one single case, that of a Sada girl who had married "down" during the socialist period. The couple moved to Aden and never lived in Shihir. Apart from this case there seemed to be no marriages of this sort, further strengthening the impression of marriage being a significant field for the maintenance of social status, in Hadramaut as well as in the diaspora. The limited statistics on marriage collected for this study indicate an overwhelming majority of traditional marriages.

The same view is given in interviews in which men's notions of the "ideal wife" are sought out. The answers relate to the woman's willingness to perform certain duties, normally followed by statements that this is the reason why they prefer their own women, not women outside the group. It is interesting, however, that this works both ways. In Hadramaut, people prefer someone from their home village, whereas in Hyderabad for instance, the local girl from Hyderabad with a Hadrami background is preferred before one from the homeland. This obviously relates to linguistic competence as Hadramis in Hyderabad are not well versed in Arabic, and bringing women from Hadramaut is seen as difficult. The significance of close relatives is also expressed in economic life. The most basic solidarity is found between brothers and relatives within the same sublineages. This is also the basic reference point when a person travels to migrant areas in the diaspora or comes from the diaspora.

Hadrami identities and gender

But the reproduction of a category is not the same as the reproduction of the cultural content of that category. To get at the content, and thus also move closer to the experience of the individuals involved, we need to see how carrying a specific Hadrami identity within the diasporic community can be combined with being part of the various "local cultures" in places such as Hyderabad, Singapore, Sudan, and Ethiopia. In order to understand Hadrami culture as experience, we need to understand the way Hadrami culture is gendered. Hadrami men carry a tradition as "cosmopolitans," traveling and marrying into the local communities in which they have settled. Women are "locals" who maintain local cultures (*adat wa taqalid*) and at the same time are a part of Hadrami cosmopolitanism. The effect of this has been a reproduction of specific Hadrami group identities that at the same time produces individual Hadrami identities with very different cultural content.

Growing up in Malaysia and growing up in Tanzania are different things. I have spoken to men who are brothers, sharing the same father but having different mothers from each of the two countries, who will meet each other perhaps once during their lifetimes, and required several interpreters, one from Malay to English, one from Swahili to English, to communicate. Historically, it is under such circumstances that the "local" level of the "Hadrami model" has been played out. Mothers raise children, cook food, and select clothing, take the children with them to visit neighbors and friends—in short, they socialize new generations into the local traditions.

If neighborhoods are made up of only Hadramis, such processes are defined as Hadrami. But if neighborhoods are mixed, this process of reproducing local tradition is more "multicultural" and exposes children to families from other cultural groups. Over time the experience of boys and girls would move in different directions. Girls would remain local, constrained by strict rules of seclusion, eventually marrying a man who was defined as an acceptable spouse according to the principles outlined above. Such a spouse could come from Hadramaut, from Hadrami communities elsewhere in the Indian Ocean, or the local Hadrami community. But since it is the men who move, the wife will continue to primarily relate to the local situation. Upon entering adulthood, a man has more choices.

He could, in principle, marry outside the Hadrami group. Given the situation within Hadrami groups, however, the boy would also be directed towards a "proper" spouse. But the man would not necessarily remain local. As an adult, he would start to join the more cosmopolitan circles of Hadrami men, participating in the public arenas in which local Hadramis meet with newly arrived Hadramis, or he could himself travel to other diasporic communities, or even travel to Hadramaut, where he could engage in trade, receive a religious education, or just visit. Maybe he has been to Hadramaut already, together with his father, and he might have spent time there with relatives, learning Arabic, perhaps attending a religious *madrasa,* and generally learning the local Hadrami ways of life in the homeland. Later, he may send his own sons on similar journeys, thus maintaining the cosmopolitan pattern.

In this way, the Hadrami man is exposed to different types of arenas than that experienced by a Hadrami woman, arenas in which public identities are displayed and evaluated by other Hadramis, as well as people from other groups. In such a situation it is likely that we might find a separate male and female Hadrami "culture," organized around very different ideals and played out in very different types of arenas. I also find it very likely that the cultural content of these two "cultures" will differ from what is found in the homeland, Hadramaut. As Hadrami individuals enter these processes in different ways, there will also be great variation in the participation of any one individual in these processes.

Such a historical pattern mirrors in interesting ways an analysis of Europeans who have taken part in the Indian Ocean trade. Focusing on the Dutch, Taylor (1983) shows how Dutch traders and officials of the Dutch East India

Company (in Dutch: *Vereenigde Oostindische Compagnie*, or VOC) were more closely linked to other Indian Ocean possessions of the Dutch than to Holland, and how the long-resident expatriate Dutch were closer in culture and everyday life to the *mestizo* (persons of mixed European and Asian ancestry) and other populations within the town than to the Dutch who came directly from Holland. The Dutch established churches and schools, just as the Muslims built mosques and *madrasas*. Linguistically, Portuguese was more common as trade language than Dutch, and the Dutch Calvinist tradition did not really penetrate the local population.

The reasons why the Dutch faced problems reproducing Dutch culture were many. Dutch traders and soldiers commonly left Holland on renewable five-year contracts and could not travel back to Holland as they pleased. Furthermore, there were not many Dutch women in the trading towns, and the men rather married the daughters of already established local families. These families were the result of mixed marriages between earlier Dutch arrivals and *mestiz* women. Marriage to the widows of deceased VOC officials was also common. Furthermore, in order to secure a Dutch future for their sons, young men were sent back to Holland, whereas young women were kept locally and married off to new arrivals from Holland.

In this way the local "Dutch" population was thus to an increasing degree being reproduced through *mestio* women, and the relationships between the men were through links as in-laws. This produced a local, colonial culture that differed radically from the one that later emerged, when the Europeans established their territorial empires. Local family ties, rather than ties to Holland, held communities together. Local cliques, not headquarters in Holland, decided what was to go on in trade. Property was also transferred within these circles of in-laws, not from father to son. Women were kept at home, apart from going to church. This segregation and restrictions on their movement was not modeled on Dutch custom, but that of the local Asian one. This was true for both Portuguese and Asians alike.

Slaves were kept in the households, and the chewing of *betel* was common. The slaves brought up the children, and children grew up not knowing Dutch but learning the many languages represented by slaves. Those who wanted their children to learn Dutch culture had to send them back to Holland. Even as Batavia (now Jakarta) developed in the eighteenth century, the distinct local culture continued, with men managing the public VOC world and women remaining within the domestic space. Only newcomers were truly "European." Race was not relevant in defining roles, as most people had been raised by the same kinds of Asian servants or slaves. Colonial society was "a medley of borrowed forms: it created is own meanings that can be understood as neither Dutch nor Asian but as Mestizo" (Taylor 1983: 68). The glue that held society together was the family system.

Women could inherit and bring wealth into a marriage. The ruling elite was preoccupied by the definition of "European." Technically, these were persons born in Europe, born in Asia to European parents (Creoles), women married to European men, legitimate children of European fathers, and illegitimate children acknowledged by a European father. But the *mestizo* culture was strange for "real" Europeans and Dutch visitors. A quote from Van den Berg on the assimilation of Hadramis is a good illustration of how a "real" European and Dutchman viewed such processes for that particular group:

> [T]he Arab families have an inevitable tendency to sink and become assimilated, in a few generations, to the native population. What first disappears is the Arab language, then the dress, and, lastly, the family name … Almost all the examples I have just given to set forth the decay of the Arab half-castes and their assimilation to the natives only refer to the Sayyids. As for the Arabs who have little culture of mind, or who have no name to keep up, it is easy to understand that the condition of their descendants is worse still. Of these Arabs of low degree I know some even who, though born in Hadramaut, think so little of their nationality that they pass themselves off as natives, in spite of the scandal such a proceeding must cause among their fellow-countrymen. … Even the European families in the Indian Archipelago have a pronounced tendency to sink **down** [emphasis in original], and the Arabs are in a very much worse plight by reason of the greater social intimacy between them and the natives. (1886)

Globalizing factors: de-territorialization and cosmopolitanism

We have seen that Hadrami men participate in public arenas in ways that Hadrami women do not. In such public arenas the issue of a public Hadrami identity becomes more important. Certainly, individual Hadramis have pursued individual adaptations and thus differ in their various experiences. At the same time, however, they have participated in organizations that have helped reproduce the cosmopolitanism already described and facilitated their adaptation to new places, as well as maintaining links back home.

This brings us to the importance of ethnic associations. In principle, such associations are organized around specific goals and headed by ethnic-political entrepreneurs who pursue specific strategies to maintain an ethnic identity. Such organizations also provide arenas in which a public identity may be developed and defined. At this level, the issue of difference between groups may be underlined in ways that is not possible at the level of an individual's domestic life.

One institutional context for this is provided by the Tariqa al-Alewi through which learning, traveling, meeting with relatives, and visiting the graves of important ancestors are basic characteristics. The following chapter addresses this organization in more detail; here it suffices to point out that the organization is a religious one, but is at the same time based on genealogical membership in the Sada group and can thus unite as well as divide the Hadramis. A classical example discussed in chapter six is the Alewi-Irshadi conflict in Indonesia. This "conflict" shows the ways the Tariqa al-Alewi can be divisive when used to promote Sada social dominance over non-Sada.

In other countries the same organization would be more neutral, primarily reflecting the religious status of the Sada, thus being an organization through which religious personalities are produced. These "personalities" may work as missionaries or religious leaders in the diaspora, teaching at religious schools and leading mosques. After their death they were buried in graves that all Hadramis could relate to through pilgrimages (e.g., Ho 2006). In this sense, the Tariqa al-Alewia enables a shared Hadrami religious identity as Shafi'e Muslims, differentiating them from non-Muslim groups as well as Muslims of the three other law-schools in Islam (Maliki, Hanefi, Hanbali) and sufi sects.

Another type of organization that has been of fundamental importance to the maintenance of Hadrami identity is the non-kin based associations that have developed both in Hadramaut and in the diaspora (Freitag 2003). One example is the Hadramaut Welfare Association, established in the early 1940s during the Qaity sultanate by the then first secretary, Gaddal. This was during a famine period, and the association sought to help starving people living inland from Wadi Hadramaut. Today, Hadrami communities around the world have many welfare organizations of this type, many of which were formed after World War II amid emerging nationalism among newly independent states.

In Hadramaut, this was also inspired by its independence from India, which had formerly administered the territories. In 1947 the Nationalist Party was formed in Hadramaut. It was not conventionally "nationalistic" in any ideological sense but rather a tool used by the Sultan in the local politics between the Qaity and Kathiri states (see al-Qaddal 1997). The same year also saw the formation of the Hadrami League and the Committee for the Union of Hadramaut, in Hadramaut itself, and the National Hadrami Committee in Asmara, Eritrea. They represented a national awakening and functioned as intellectual organizations and religious and literary societies, at home and in the diaspora, with the important aim of overcoming sectarian loyalties among Hadramis and establishing an overall Hadrami identity.

An important source of inspiration for these organizations were the cultural societies already established in Java in the first part of the twentieth century, as well as the emerging Arab nationalism (see Bujra 1971 for an account of how the northern Yemeni revolution of 1962, overthrowing the Imam's regime, was received in Hureidha in Hadramaut). This is not the place to evaluate the political significance of these organizations, nor to discuss their rather vague and idealistic aims. My point is to show that after World War II the introduction of such organizations created new kinds of links, and spurred dialogue between the homeland and the diaspora aimed at supporting a Hadrami ethnic identity.

Many of these organizations continue to be active today. Particularly the Welfare Associations, which have branches in Hadramaut, Aden, Sanaa, and Riyadh and many other places. The association still works for the good of the people, supporting local health clinics and other services. Although co-operating with the government, the association is careful to point out that it does not represent the government and does not engage in party politics.

Similar organizations are found in the diaspora, as we saw in Part One. Here we also see the interrelationship between the various identities of "Hadrami," "Arab," and "Yemeni," identities that of course relate to the general position of Hadramis in their various diasporic communities. This reminds us that the dynamics at this public level of Hadrami social organization have different implications than the individual identity of Hadramis as it is defined by membership in local kinship groups. At that level we see an internal differentiation in which the choice of marriage partners constitutes a boundary-making process vis-à-vis other Hadrami kinship groups.

On the level of ethnic associations, Hadramis appear in the public arenas in which the differences between a Hadrami, an Arab, and a Yemeni are not visible to members of other groups that Hadramis interact with, nor may the difference be relevant to the political authorities that decide on the allocation of resources to such organizations. Actually, it might serve Hadrami interests to leave such differences blurred. An example of this is the way many "Hadrami" associations became "Yemeni" associations at the time of unity between North and South Yemen (*Al Wahda*) in 1990. Another example is the way the Jamaitul Yamania Bil Hind in Hyderabad redefined its activities after Yemeni Unity. A similar development involving re-definition has occurred in Sudan. After Yemeni unification, people in Port Sudan formed a Dar Abna al Yemen al Kheiri which includes all Yemenis living in Sudan. They acquired a house where visiting Yemenis can stay and assist people with contacts back to Yemen. The chair of this committee is a northern Yemeni, whereas the majority of Yemenis in Sudan are Hadramis.

In Singapore, similar functions are carried out by an organization that uses "Arab" as the defining term. This is Al Wehdah, or the Arab Association, which was described in chapter one. It publishes the magazine *Al-Mahjar* (*The Diaspora*), which carries articles on issues of concern to migrants. The annual celebration of the association is a display of their Arabic and Hadrami culture. The leadership routinely travel to Yemen and Saudi Arabia to further contacts there. The increasing use of electronic technology in Singapore is interesting in a comparative perspective, as the Internet, including e-mail, helps Hadramis maintain their contacts in new ways. The Ethiopian association is similar to what has been described above.

Such differences were also affected by the unification of the two Yemens in May 1990. It was a time of major change, particularly in the People's Democratic Republic of Yemen (PDRY), to which Hadramaut belongs. Shortly after independence in 1967, the government of the PDRY initiated a series of major social reforms: The aim was to transform the country from a place where tribal and "feudal" relations of production were dominant to one that was in "transition to the national democratic state." This state was to be loosely modeled on what was then the prevailing system of the Soviet Union.

Following the bloody events of January 1986, in which violent in-fighting among the leadership of the Yemen Socialist Party broke out, leading to the downfall of the leader, Ali Nasir Muhamad, the PDRY state started to adapt to the broader changes going on around the world as the Soviet Union collapsed. As a result, many of the earlier socialist reforms were overturned in the late 1980s. In particular, legislation was passed to privatize some state assets and to provide encouragement for private investment. At the time of unification in 1990, the Supreme People's Council prepared new legislation and regulations further promoting this process.

The creation of the Republic of Yemen in May 1990 took place much faster than had been expected, taking many observers by surprise. A period of transition was decided upon before national elections were to be held in December 1992. The elections were subsequently delayed until April 1993, and ended in a coalition government of three parties, the National Congress, the Islah Party and the Yemeni Socialist Party. All through this process the momentum of privatization continued.

However, the unification process showed itself to be fragile. By January 1994, political infighting had brought the country to the verge of disintegration. President Ali Abdalla Saleh sat in Sana'a, and Vice President Ali Saleh al-Bid in Aden, each accusing the other of betraying the spirit of unity. A settlement proposing decentralization was reached in the southwestern city of Taizz, but the overall problems remains unresolved.

Civil war, in which the south unsuccessfully sought secession, broke out in 1995. Today, northern control of the south is complete, and the president and his regime work hard to promote a positive image of Yemen. This is seen in the Yemeni government's policies aimed at encouraging wealthy Yemenis and Hadramis in the diaspora to invest in their homeland. While visiting the various migrant communities, President Ali Abdalla Saleh is always the guest of the local Yemeni Association, thus giving a public stamp on the relationship between such associations and the Yemeni government.

Whatever the developments in the homeland of Yemen, the general conclusion must be that the lives of the Hadramis throughout the diaspora to an increasing degree have become tied to the internal situation of the various nation states to which they now belong. The various states have come to define identities through administrative measures and security arrangements, and by the channeling of resources to certain groups and not to others. We have seen the importance of the role of government in the lives of migrants in Singapore, India, Sudan, and Ethiopia. And in the above section we also outlined some national developments in Yemen that have affected the ways in which Yemenis in the diaspora relate to their homeland.

All of the cases underline the point that the various nation states must be studied as actors in their own right. Each state represents very different approaches to the development of ethnic policy, the consequences of which are experienced by the various ethnic groups. On a general level, our cases show that we should use caution when attempting to generalize the effects of nation states and nationalism on diasporic communities. Such effects vary a great deal, and must be related to specific developmental trajectories within each nation state, rather than assuming the effects to be common in all cases.

Which brings us to the conclusion of this section. The ethnic associations we have discussed cannot be understood as expressions of a homogeneous Hadrami culture communicated through a particular Hadrami identity. Rather, such associations are more the expressions of the interests of certain groups than that of a single Hadrami voice. Certainly, the associations aim to promote the unification of Hadrami culture, and thus to enable Hadramis to speak with one voice. At the same time, however, the associations serve the commercial interests of individuals as well as groups. They promote labor migration, which results in the sending home of remittances by individuals, and large-scale trade and investment between the diaspora and Yemen, which further enriches entrepreneurial groups. For these associations, maintaining networks with powerful groups outside Yemen is as important as supporting unifying cultural processes at home.

Betwixt and between – the *muwallad*

We have shown how identities must be seen as historical, social, political, and religious phenomena that are played out in different arenas of social life. Influences on the formation of these identities include policies on immigration, the creation of ethnic and religious associations and changing relations within and between households. Regardless of the fluctuating fortunes of either Yemen or the diaspora, the identity of "Hadrami" has been maintained. But we have also shown that the content of this identity varies from place to place, from one diasporic community to the next. An illuminating example of the fluidity of identity is the *muwallad*. Mixed marriages do occur in the diaspora, giving rise to this particular identity (sing. *muwallad;* pl. *m'walde*), which is paralleled by the Latin American *mestiz* and the Carribean Creole identity. *Muwallad* is partly a status signifying mixed origin and does not necessarily carry any particular stigma or negative inference, although it may. For example in Hyderabad, we saw in chapter two that Hadramis could hold the important position of *jamadars,* i.e., holders of land grants in the Nizam's system's feudal administrative system. Names of three such *jamadars* were mentioned by Temple (1887). They were Abdalla bin Ali, Barak Jang, and Ghalib bin Almas. Two of them came from Hadramaut but were *m'walde,* and Temple continues: "The Barak Jang was a muwallad and reputed to be a man of great influence ... I learnt that his mother came from Nagpur and his father from the Hadramaut province of Arabia" (1887: 135).

In Hadramaut itself, the term *"muwallad"* can have strong and negative connotations, as in the following saying: "Three cannot be controlled—the dog, the pig, and the *muwallad."* Such negative connotations are particularly directed at "African" Hadramis from the Swahili coast and Somalia. Words like *zift* (tar) are also used. Eng Seng Ho (1997a) argues that it problematic to be a *muwallad* in Hadramaut.. There is thus a discrepancy between the diaspora person's notion of the homeland and the reality of being in the homeland. As stated by Ho, it is puzzling that in a society where migration is of fundamental importance, the human products of such movements are persistently regarded in a negative light.

The status of the *muwallad* is significant in that it shows how people of mixed origin may entertain an idea of the homeland as a place where all the problems of the diaspora will be absent, but that this idea can be crushed through individual experiences in the homeland. The situation of Hyderabad is instructive. Hadramis from Hyderabad whom I have met have returned to Hadramaut without knowing Arabic. They speak Urdu and Telegu. Several such families have learnt enough Arabic to function, get a job, and so on. In their homes however, they speak Urdu, while their children learn Arabic in school. For those who travel back and forth to Hyderabad this allows for communication in both places.

In the local Hadrami context, such people have a lower status, which is illustrated by the following quote from an interview conducted as part of the Hyderabad survey (S. Rao 1996): "Why do you ask me to tell you about Hadramis and Hadramaut? Those fellows in Hadramaut ill-treat us, the Indian Hadrami. Tell me, in what way we are different? Have we not all come from Adam? I do not want to talk about it. Go away!" To conclude, neither the identity of a diaspora Hadrami, nor that of a *muwallad,* can be taken as fixed or as characterizing a particular history of migration. Rather, these identities must be put in the context of lived experience and understood within their historical and institutional settings. In this way, we can better reveal the ways these identities shape the diaspora existence.

Another important point is that Hadrami identity is formed by more than individual decisions, and identity maintenance shouldn't be seen as the product of isolated strategies. These strategies must be analyzed as they unfold together, and in relation to how in their totality they allow for the adaptability of Hadrami people to so many different contexts and different historical periods. What appears to be an extraordinary blend of processes of a very local character, such as making decisions about marriage and co-operation between close kin, are at the same time processes characterized by the crossing of boundaries and the handling of different cultures, all of which takes place in quite a modern and cosmopolitan way.

Back to Hadramis, one last time

Throughout this history of migration an identity as "Hadrami," "Arab," "Yemeni," and "Muslim" has been maintained, although the relative importance of the various identities has varied. What do these categories mean? Is "Hadraminess," "Arabness," and "Yemeniness" more than just some people calling themselves by those terms? Do they affect the ways Hadramis carry out their daily lives in the diaspora? And does the content of those identities affect what goes on at the ethnic boundary (i.e., are the identities are constantly being created in interaction with other groups)? Does the naming of categories include both self-ascription and ascription by others?

My argument here is that we see both self-ascription and ascription by others. Hadrami collective identities are both an aspect of a relationship with others, as well as the property of a group. The boundaries that differentiate between Hadramis and other groups do not alone make up the Hadrami identities. Internal group factors, such as kinship and family connections, must be included. It is through such links that generations are kept together and that kin and family feelings are projected onto the ways that the group identity is conceived.

We can conclude, then, that the evolving of Hadrami identities may be subject to as well as the outcome of cross-boundary relationships. But we have also seen that the social identity of the group is contested within the group itself, on grounds that also may relate to cross-boundary interaction. Religious identities show a similar processual dynamic, although the assimilation processes occurring at the ethnic level are not present when it comes to religion. People remain Muslim, even in instances where individuals no longer considered themselves to be Hadrami. But what type of Muslim a person becomes is dependent on processes that are of a similar nature to the ones we have discussed for the ethnic field.

Our discussion also shows that the identity of a diaspora Hadrami cannot be taken as fixed. Rather, these identities must be put in the context of lived experiences and understood within their historical and institutional settings in order to see how they shape diaspora existence. Hadrami identity is formed by more than just individual strategies, and identity maintenance should not be seen as an isolated strategy. These different strategies must be analyzed as they unfold together, and in relation to how they, in their totality, allow for the adaptability of Hadrami people to so many different social contexts over time and space.

What appears to be an extraordinary blend of processes of a very local character, such as making decisions about marriage and co-operation between close kin, are at the same time processes characterized by the crossing of boundaries and the negotiations between different cultures, now taking place in circumstances varying from the modern and cosmopolitan life of Singapore to that of marginal small-scale traders in southern Ethiopia. Through the ethnic process a person becomes Hadrami by belonging to certain descent groups, but also by carrying out particular activities, and by participating in certain events and specific organizations. It is not an essentialized identity. It is an embraced identity, the content of which will vary around the diaspora.

Obviously, we have to introduce a generational perspective here. First-generation migrants are people who appear to have no problem with their identity and have no lacunae in information about who they are and where they come from. They left their homeland to improve their life chances and to make money. This is different from the second generation of migrants, who have lost their direct link with the home country. They tend to define themselves more in terms of boundaries that divide them from others, and their leaders stress the importance of their culture more strongly than their fathers did. For second-generation Hadramis, the home culture becomes objectified and manifests itself in the form of moral prescriptions and rituals. They experience the dilemma of being a permanent resident in a place while remaining unintegrated in that place. Such behavior is transferred to individuals through processes of socialization as well as through participation in organizations and other arenas in which Hadrami "culture" is played out.

Hence, what we have been discussing is not a primordial Hadrami identity that has remained unchanged throughout history. The content is a product of lived realities in the context of social practice. But still there is the notion among many people that they are Hadrami. Although many of these processes are situational and are defined by specific local boundary processes among different local ethnic groups, there is also continuity through the existence of a cultural heritage that people can embrace and essentialize among themselves. The reality of this situation is experienced when Hadramis from different diaspora communities meet among themselves. Or, as has become more common since the unification of Yemen and the opening up of South Yemen following the end of the Communist period, when diasporic Hadramis travel to Yemen and meet up there.

In such cases, cultural differences among those who all call themselves "Hadrami" are heightened. These differences may relate to religious beliefs and ways of praying; personal conduct, particularly as relates to women; or physical appearances (i.e., that Malay Hadramis may look like Malays, and African Hadramis may look African). In contemporary Hadramaut, differences that are considered digressions from the norm can lead to divisions within the wider group, with some people negatively portrayed and even labeled as "bad Muslims," or the difference may be interpreted in racist terms. Many *muwallads* have experienced such stigmatization as they attempt to integrate into Yemeni society. Rather than experiencing Yemen as their homeland, they may feel they do not really belong anywhere, neither in the diaspora nor in the land of their ancestors.

CHAPTER SIX

Homeland-Diaspora Dynamics

Problematizing Diasporic Consciousness Among Sada and Non-Sada Groups

Effects of Hadrami migration

The point of departure for my discussion in this chapter is the reproduction over time of the Hadrami stratification system both at home and in the diaspora. The general system of stratification in Hadramaut is in principle similar to what we find in Yemen as a whole. The major groups are the Sada or Seiyd, people who claim descent from the Prophet Mohammed and, because of this, occupy a privileged position in the religious and social hierarchy.

Next in the hierarchy are the Mashaikh or Sheikh, who cannot show descent from the Prophet, but who are members of local lineages who through historical processes have acquired status in the region. Thirdly, the Qabail or Qabila, who are tribal groups, and fourth, the Da'fa or Da'if, among whom are traders or skilled laborers who work in the market. Continuing "downwards" there are the *akhdam* (*khaddam*) or servants who hold various positions, and those described as *abid* (slave), who are the descendants of earlier slave groups. Other terms denoting the groups in the lower parts of the hierarchy are *al masakin*, "the poor ones," or *al hirthan*, "the farmers," another word for the more common *al fellahin*.

What is important is not to reify this system but to see how the various groups have operated and created dynamics that have shaped the system as a whole and also facilitated change. Although the Sada have been considered superior, their dominance is not a given. It must be understood according to particular social developments that led to their positioning. Such positioning was affected by processes at home in Hadramaut as well as in the diaspora. At home, well-to-do Sada dominated agriculture, including the cultivation of cereals and dates. As noted by Arai (2004), Sada were less likely to migrate because of the profits they enjoyed through agriculture. One could then infer that migration was a strategy pursued only by those Sada who were not favorably placed in the system at home.

Whatever the motive, we know that there were members of the Sada group among the early migrants to the Indian Ocean, engaging in trade as well as in Islamic missionary activities. These migrating Sada related to leading groups in the areas in which they settled, and in many cases became prominent members of the wider community. This was shown in the chapter on Singapore, with family names like al-Attas, al-Kaf, al-Saqqaf, and al Juneid as examples of migrants who have flourished in their new home.

However, in all four chapters of Part One we also see that during the last century and a half the typical Hadrami migrants—traders and Islamic missionaries—were joined by new groups of migrants seeking opportunities. Ingrams (1937) estimated in 1936 that the number of Hadramis living in the diaspora at that time made up between 20 and 30 percent of the total Hadrami population at home. Many migrants stayed away for a number of years but intended to return home when they had made a fortune. Also among the resident population in Hadramaut there were many who had been abroad at some time in their lives.

The increased rate of out-migration changed perceptions about the traditional stratification system in Hadramaut. Non-Sada groups, considered of lower status than the Sada, developed new views about themselves and began to question their subordinate position in the stratification system, particularly in relationship to the Sada. As people from the lower social groups in Hadramaut began to travel and work outside Yemen, their improved opportunities and relative success led to changes in the diaspora population's notions of the social order. This brought a new dimension to Hadrami politics abroad and at home. It also had an impact on what may be termed "historical consciousness" among Hadramis.

Towards a broader understanding of social stratification

This chapter will show that the Hadrami system of social stratification cannot be depicted as in a timeless equilibrium, characterized by consensus or norm-driven practices. Nor can it be presented as a holistic system of evaluation, or a cultural system upon which political and economic relationships are automatically built (Dumont 1972). To speak about equilibrium is to lose sight of the complexities and the heterogeneous character of the field of events and relationships within which such a system of stratification operates. And it leads our thinking towards the modern/pre-modern dichotomy, which we want to avoid. What we see in the case of Hadramis is that the notion of "tradition" is by no means unproblematic, and although the various social strata exist, the role played by such a system in people's lives must be problematized.

The case of the Sada seems to be rather clear. They maintain an identity as a group, and that identity is treasured by members of the group. However, the picture is less clear with the non-Sada. Although there are several categories of non-Sada (including Mashaiyykh, Qabail, Hirthan, and Akhdam), there is a tendency in the diaspora for non-Sada categories to be redefined and lumped together under the broader category of Mashaiyykh. At the same time, the boundaries between Sada and non-Sada continue to resist change. Overall, however, the stratification system does not represent a closed order of ideology but is situated in a broader context of overlapping processes and activities. It is within such open contexts that systematization takes place, surmounting the assumed boundaries. Because of this, the system of social stratification cannot be divided into one social and one ideological side: the social and conceptual categories are aspects of the same continuity (Perlin 1994).

Rather than typologizing societies then, we should look for models that explain the dynamics in different types of societies within the same general conceptual framework. Although the ideological level is of great importance, it is not sufficient to understand a system of ideas, nor can we assume that such a system by itself will define the level of economic, political, and social organization. The starting point should be relationships among people, to see the congruence or lack of congruence between status categories and actual positions in occupational, political, religious, and economic fields.

I do not dispute that there may be overlap; that would be an empirical finding rather than a theoretical postulate. If there is no congruence, we need to explain that situation too. For instance, why do earlier notions about status and differentiation linger on in new and different contexts? The stratification groups should not be taken to be characterized by essentialized "cultures"; rather we should look at how they are organized around certain clusters of ideas about origin and about the place of the groups in the world, i.e. about their symbolic capital.

But we can also look at the social organization of the groups, and how specific networks or certain centers may play key roles in such reproduction. In addition, we need information on how members of the groups see themselves and their history. Thus we can see how various forms of validation are used to establish acceptance for a certain version of history, or of certain genealogical facts. I say "facts" but the analytical point is that they are not facts, but rather "claims" about how the world is organized. Hence, we are looking at different world views.

Following the basic argument in this book, I argue that on a general level we can link historical epochs with types of identities, discourses, and world views, and that in periods of general change the basis for all these can be problematized and made the focus of new types of debates among people.

Such debates relate to the field of religion in that the stratification system may be both defended and attacked through arguments based on an understanding of Islamic history. But they also show that different groups among Hadramis have different ways of perceiving themselves as groups, thus making it necessary to broaden the discussion to one about different types of Hadrami historicity. It is my argument, then, that such broad discussions are necessary in order to understand the dynamics of the stratificational system found in Hadramaut, a system which is also found in Southern Arabian communities in general. The way the system operates, and the ways people relate to it show a lot of variation, in Southern Arabia as well as in Hadramaut, and even more so in the diasporic communities.

Social stratification in the homeland

In the most comprehensive analysis of the social stratification system in Hadramaut, Abdalla Bujra (1971) identified the important building block in Hadrami society as descent and descent status (*nasab*). Hadramis recognize two lines of descent, that of the Prophet Mohammed's line, which is the northern Arabian lines of Adnan, and Qahtan. These two ultimate ancestors are ranked, with those of the Prophet being ranked higher than that of Qahtan. Those Hadramis who do not descend from these lines are in the lowest status groups. This system allows for an easy categorization of people into three categories within which marriage is possible. The preference is always for marriage with a person of equal social status. However, other factors may intervene in this.

According to Bujra, the Hadrami theory of descent implies that any group of people that traces its descent to a common ancestor shares not only agnatic ties but also other characteristics which stem from that ancestor. Thus the Sada (in Bujra's case, al Attas, from Hureida, relatives of al Attas whom we met in Singapore) insist that their descent from the Prophet is *mutsalsil* (linked like a chain).This means that the descent is a true one and is meticulously documented. The powers of the Prophet have been passed down to the contemporary members, both noble blood and powers to intercede with God.

The Sada are superior in status to other lineages that may be religious but descend from local holy men (in Hureida, this would be Basahl). Thus the *silsilah* of such a group (Basahl) is not chain-like, given that there are gaps in the links back to Qahtan. Such ancestries go back to a known ancestor some time back, but after that the specific ancestors are not known. Other groups also descended from Qahtan can follow their links back to specific persons known as warriors. The Mesakin (the poor ones) are also believed to inherit specific qualities, but from ancestors only three to five generations back.

For Hureida then, Bujra presents a picture with al Attas as the Sada family at the top of the stratificational system, a system that also includes Mashaikh and Qabail. The Masakin, or Duafa (the weak ones), are also included with specific groups called Hirthan (whose ancestors were farmers), Akhdam (servants), and Subyan (laborers, servants, and artisans). Sylvain Camelin (1997) has challenged the generality of this system of stratification and claims that Bujra has presented an ideal system based on the Hureida situation, a system that has become central to our understanding of social stratification in Hadramaut in general. Camelin shows how other authors, having undertaken studies in other areas, find regional variation in the way groups are classified. The empirical cases presented by authors such as Hartley (1961) on the Beduin Nahdi group, Camelin herself from the fishing town of Shihir and Mathisen from Ghail Bawasir, founded by a *mahaiyykh* and where there are few Sada, is proof enough that Camelin's point is well taken and certainly merits attention.

However, even if Bujra's case is only valid for the situation in Hureidha, the discussion continues to be valid. One important factor maintaining the system observed by Bujra was the equality of marriage partners—*kafa'a*. Thus the Attas argued that a man should marry someone who is equal in descent to himself, but that if there is no such person, a man may marry a woman from lower descent. This is because the children of such a union will be considered to descend from the father. However, spouses from the same agnatic line are preferred, or at least from a family of comparable status in wealth and religious prestige. A woman, however, should never be allowed to marry a man of lower descent since the children in such a case would be of the lower descent of the father.

In addition to marriage and genealogical links, al Attas also base their position on the institution of *hawtah*, through which they can exploit their religious status to mediate between the tribes in the region, a mediation that creates links that provide protection of the town. A *hawtah* is an area controlled by a "holy man" in which people can seek refuge in times of trouble, protected by the general authority and prestige of such a person.

When the Qaity and Kathiri sultanates were established in the nineteenth century, many Sada were brought in as administrators. They were able to further exploit their position through education, wealth, and relations with sultans. Economically, their elite status depended on their ownership of land. The agricultural system under the Kathiri and Qu'ayti sultanates, as already indicated in the case from Hureidha, consisted of a few small landholdings cultivated by the owners, but in some cases there were large subtribe/clan holdings cultivated exclusively by sharecroppers, on contracts of ten to twenty years (*mukhabara*). The sharecroppers were almost always from different subtribes or families. In the rare cases when they were from the landowning group, they would work the land on the same basis as other sharecroppers. The land-owners were mostly from the Sada group.

The contracts showed a basic relationships between what inputs (pumps, seeds, fertilizers, means of mechanization) the parties involved brought to the cultivation process and the share of the harvest they would receive. Which of course meant that contracts varied a lot. But certain general patterns were found. For instance, sharecroppers who provided all the inputs got 90 percent of their harvest for themselves, paying their landlords 10 percent for the use of their land. In irrigated areas, 2.5 percent of the harvest went to the party who had invested in irrigation technology (wells, pumps, canals). There were other factors as well, but as most of the inputs in reality came from the side of the landlords, this meant also that the landlord was left with the lion's share of the harvest, and the sharecropper only received the part assigned to "labor," roughly 25 percent.

A dynamic system

The system was dynamic in that it was affected by different types of change. Colonial rule was one such factor. In the late 1930s, Harold Ingrams was the British government's resident advisor to Qaity and Kathiri. The Qaity Sultan-ate was then a protectorate of the British government, with a resident advisor to the government based in Mukalla. He kept close contact with the *Wazir* (prime minister) and the members of the Council of State, was responsible for external relations and internal security, and had control over the Hadrami Bedouin Legion. Militarily, he was backed by the Royal Air Force (RAF) and British troops based in Aden. Below this top level were the governors of the five provinces, each having two or three districts looked after by a *ga'im* (district administrative officer). Courts dealt with civil cases according to Islamic Law while a chief justice or *Qadi* sat in the Supreme Court in Mukalla. Local councils represented the lowest level in the system.

Despite the changes brought by the colonial administration, however, the Sada families in Hadramaut managed to maintain their dominant position also under the new circumstances. To use al Attas, the Sada family of Hureida as example, this particular family managed to dominate the local council in the town. They also controlled the local courts and exploited new opportunities through education. They also issued certificates of good conduct as a basis for passports for labor migrants. Al Attas is thus a typical case of the Sada adapting to new situations and contexts, maintaining their elite position in the process.

The British strengthened their rule through their relationships with prominent Sada families, involving them in the making of policy and giving them preferential treatment. Not surprisingly, a second "wind of change" produced social forces in strong opposition to the position of the Sada. This development related to the emergence of new ideological trends in the region, including Arab nationalism and a growing call for independence for Arab states. In Hureida, non-Attas people organized around the "language of nationalism" and the Basahl group became the leaders of opposition to the Attas. Clubs were formed, expressing these lines of difference. Lower strata also could claim new positions of equality through involvement in trade unions, receiving ideological support from a new generation of radicalized Arab leaders. In the late 1960s, the Qaity and Kathiri sultanates, together with other Southern Arabian sultanates, remerged as the People's Democratic Republic of Yemen, with a communist regime, proclaiming farmers, fishermen, and workers as heroes, and condemning the Sada as "feudalists."

There were also profound changes in the Wadi Hadramaut agricultural system and the position of the Sada within it. Independence in 1967 was the beginning of a turbulent period. The Land Reform Law of 1968 established the legal grounds for the expropriation of all lands belonging to sultans, emirs, and sheikhs. It also established maximum holdings per family for those who would receive portions of the confiscated land. But the law was largely unimplemented. Two years later, in 1970, a second Land Reform Law (no. 27 of 1970) was passed and implemented, in some cases by force.

All holdings exceeding 2.5 feddans of well-irrigated, and five feddans of spate-irrigated (from a river or a stream) land were expropriated and redistributed among sharecroppers and laborers who were given usufruct rights. Farmers were also encouraged to join cooperatives, and in the case of those who had received land through the new agrarian reform legislation such cooperative membership was even made compulsory. To ensure implementation of the law and to encourage peasants to continue their opposition of the former regime, the National Liberation Front (NLF), which took power at independence, organized a series of *intifadhat* or sponsored uprisings, during which groups of peasants accompanied by NLF cadres took the land by force for redistribution. The land was now owned by the state and only usufruct rights were granted. Throughout the 1970s the regime continued its socialization of all productive industries. Cooperatives were seen as a step towards the collectivization of agriculture. After an initial rise in production in the mid-1970s, production fell, and problems of organization became apparent.

This led to a reconsideration of policy which also affected the running of cooperatives. In particular, farmers wanted tenure documents showing their rights to the land received through the earlier agrarian reform. The issuing of such documents for individual plots had been seen as incompatible with the ultimate aim of collective agriculture and hence, none were issued. Although formal ownership to land and water was impossible due to state ownership, in the 1980s the government started issuing tenure documents giving farmers long-term usufruct rights to their land, including security of tenure and the right to pass on land to inheritors. The state continued, however, to assert its right to repossess land that was left uncultivated. The changes had only started at the time of unification. Collective cultivation had not been widely adopted and in most cases peasants insisted on working their own land. However, group farming had taken place in certain places, particularly where new irrigation techniques were introduced, including the Wadi Hadramaut Development Project (see Lackner 1985, for a history of the PDRY).

After the unification of North and South Yemen in 1990, Prime Ministerial Decree No. 65 of 1991 laid out the principles and procedures to be followed for the return of land to former owners and the payment of compensation to the dispossessed former land reform beneficiaries in the PDRY. A number of committees were formed to carry out the decree: The higher committee was headed up by the minister of agriculture and included the ministers of local administration, justice, legal affairs, and *awqaf*—deputy ministers of agriculture and governors of the relevant governorates.

In each governorate, subcommittees were established under the presidency of the governor; in each district a subcommittee was made up of a leader, then the director of agriculture, a representative of the legal department and also a number of selected individuals. A report (International Development Association 1992), summarizing the situation in Wadi Hadramaut, stated that compensation for the loss of land following the return of confiscated land had been largely completed within five years of passage of the new decree. The remaining cases were those that required further legal attention.

Sada – non-Sada dynamics

The above stories reflect longstanding problems in Hadramaut, and involve Sada and non-Sada groups. During the period of early nationalist awakening the Sada were targeted by the Arabic language radio stations. Bujra provides an example of this type of ideologically charged rhetoric:

> The hour of Arab nationalism in South Arabia has arrived. Let the Hashemite reactionaries fold their network of intrigues and conspiracy, for the free Yemenis have placed the last nail in the coffin of the Hashemites, who shall never return. (Bujra 1971: 173, fn. 1)

The contemporary situation shows elements of the same Sada/non-Sada tension as depicted above. The social and political climate in Hadramaut is in recent years dominated by the fallout of former landowners returning to reclaim their land, the lower groups having relinquished the land they were given under communist rule. One dramatic example of what occurred is presented by Eng Seng Ho (1997b). The case involved a mosque in Hadramaut in which local farmers were thrown out after prayer by armed men representing the former Sada owners. The mosque was part of *waqf* land that had been given to the farmers under the communists. The mosque was on the burial place of a famous Sada saint and was a center of *howlias* and pilgrimages. The farmers went on to build a mosque nearby and were assisted by a rich Hadrami migrant living in Saudi Arabia. But as this new mosque was on land belonging to another *waqf*, also controlled by Sada, the dispute continued. Due to the conflict, the Sada declared the prayers in this mosque to be religiously invalid. But at a later date, when the Sada mosque needed repairs, the local Sada could find no one to carry out the work and had to import laborers from North Yemen. The laborers' mosque became a center for the Islamic reform movement and a platform of anti-Sada agitation, including criticism of the grave visits and pilgrimages related to Sada traditions (Ho 1997b: 10).

The case shows several things of interest to our analysis. First, the old conflicts continue under new circumstances. The non-Sada groups are attracted to the Wahhabi ideology of Islamic fundamentalism, and one might argue that one reason why this is so is that it provides a new platform for a politicized criticism of Sada hegemony. The Sada—criticised as "Hashemites" under nationalism, as "feudalists" under the Communists—are now blamed for being un-Islamic promoters of *shirk* (polytheism) and *tawassul* (mediation) (Ho ibid.).

This also explains why Hadramaut was the only region in which the Islah Party received more votes that the government's Congress Party in the last elections in 1997. The Islah Party (Yemeni Congregation for Reform) has an ideology that is dramatically different from that of the communists, but as a mass organization it can mobilize many of the same groups who supported communism, providing new rhetoric, but talking about old divisions in Hadrami society. It is also interesting to observe how the non-Sada can punish the Sada by refusing to offer their labor power.

It clearly shows that local production systems in Hadramaut, although stratified along strict lines, were also integrated in the sense that landowners depended on the labor of the landless. Workers were needed in agriculture, doing work such as tilling before and after flood; clearing weeds, sand, and stones; overseeing water flows; and keeping watch during harvesting. Other labor was required from people in craft occupations such as smiths, carpenters, potters, and masons, and for leading ceremonial services connected to marriages, births, and funerals. Under the new policies of privatization, some of these economic relations are being reestablished, particularly in areas where the conflicts have been few and less intense. In areas where conflict has continued, the new situation allows for class-based struggles that have religious overtones.

Hadramis in the diaspora

Moving from the local situation in Hadramuat, we can now follow Hadramis into the diaspora and see how members of the various groups of Hadramis have adapted and related to each other there. First we need to establish the basic historical perimeters of this early migration history. Hadramis participated in early developments through which the Indian Ocean became an important arena for travel, trade, and learning. Historically, Muslim merchants and ship owners operating along the Arabian coastal towns dominated the western part of the Indian Ocean. Throughout, Hadramis met with people from other parts of the world. To illustrate this, the following comes from Tome Pires' list of visitors and residents in early sixteenth-century Melaka:

> Moors from Cairo, Mecca, Aden, Abessynians, men of Kilwa, Malindi, Ormuz, Parsees, Rumes, Turks, Turkomans, Christian Armenians, Gujaratees, men of Chaulk, Dabhol, Goa, the Kingdom of Deccan, Malabars and Klings, merchants from Orissa, Ceylon, Bengal, Arakan, Pgu, Siamese, men of Kedah, Malays, men of Pahang, Paani, Cambodia, Champa, Cochin China, Chinese, Legueos, men of Brunai, Lucoes, men of Tamjompura, Laue, Banka, Linga (they have a thousand other islands), Moluccas, Banda, Bima, Timor, Madura, Java, Sunda, Pamembang, Jambi, Tongkal, Indragiri, Jappatta, Menangkabau, Siak, Argua, Aru, Bata, country of the Tomjano, Pase, Pedir, Maldives (Pires, *Suma Oriental*, qtd. in Curtin 1984: 130).

In spite of all intermingling in such towns, Muslims remained a distinct group, their lives organized around the *mosque*. Membership in the group of Muslims was through faith. Basic symbols to define group membership were food habits, articles of clothing, and housing, which all signaled social and religious identities, and helped to keep groups apart. Rules about avoidance of pork for Muslims, beef for Brahman Indians, and milk and dairy products for the Chinese were thus basic markers for members of the various communities. Clothes also helped to differentiate, based on whether people were wearing trousers or robes as dress, and whether the clothing was tailored or not. Public buildings expressed the spiritual force of Islam, but also displayed the connection between imperial power and architecture. But, leaving the question about a Muslim identity aside, the question is about how, in this type of historical context, could an identity as Sada be maintained?

The Sada in the diaspora – the importance of the Tariqa al-Alewiyya

We have seen in the beginning of this chapter that a Sada identity among Hadramis depended on an explanation of their origin as direct descendants from the Prophet (*ahl al-bayt*). Through the *kafa'a* marriage practice, the Sada have also been able to link this notion of origin with the reproduction of their own group. A major organization only mentioned briefly in chapter five came to be of great importance in the diaspora—the Tariqa al-Alewiyya. This sufi-oriented organization provided the Sada with a vehicle that enabled the reproduction of their notions as Sada, both as they traveled to new areas in the Indian Ocean, and as new generations were born in the diaspora, without direct access to the home areas in which their own history was embedded. The establishment of this organization came several hundred years after the arrival to Hadramaut from Basra of the first Sada, Ahmad al Muhajir, in the mid tenth century. Although open to discussion on historical grounds (Knysh 1993, 1997, 1999), the Sada understanding of their identity is closely tied up with the coming of al-Muhajir, and that everything is related to his *hijra*, in terms of his migration from Basra, but also in terms of his links to local Beduin tribes who offered protection where the *sayyid* settled.

It is likely that in the early years of Sada presence in Hadramaut, they did not stand out in the same way as we see today. Rather, indications are that Sada were attached to different tribal groups, that they carried weapons, and were involved in many violent activities that would not be conducive to the contemporary understanding of proper Sada behavior. A question to be asked is therefore in what ways the Sada managed to establish their particular version of their own history?

The Tariqa al-Alewi is an important part of the answer to this question. The importance is in keeping together the various patronymic sections, or houses (sing. *bayt*; pl. *buyut*), of Sada descent categories around the spread of religious knowledge and education. There are large houses and small ones, all ranked by wealth, education, and profession, and all stressing the importance of their genealogical position. Thus they combine what Bourdieu (1986) calls "economic capital" and "symbolic capital." Some big families maintain relationships with power holders; smaller ones share in the poverty of rural people. What grew out of this history may be called a Sada tradition of knowledge. Knowledge about themselves as a group, and about their historical role in society, has evolved over time and established a specific tradition in which we can define a corpus of knowledge, a social organization of knowledge, and specific technologies for transmitting knowledge (e.g., Barth 1990).

Kazuhiro Arai (2004) has elaborated on the history of al-Attas family from Hureidha. Although al-Attas is not among the eldest Hadrami Sada families (they were established in the seventeenth century by the founding ancestor, Umar b. Abdel al-Rahman al-Attas) they represent a family which includes members related to the local Kathiri sultans, but who also traveled widely in the Indian Ocean. Through various chronicles, the family's history is told through the life stories of its most prominent personalities. The primary area of settlement for such individuals was Southeast Asia, but there are also family members in India and east Africa. Some traveled to the Hijaz, particularly for education. Most of these migrants were involved in trade alongside their religious activities.

Although most attention has been given to saints and religious scholars among the Sada families, over time Hadrami Sada took up other occupations, not only in trade but also in administration and higher learning. While many enjoyed substantial success, there is no doubt that the charismatic saints are the legendary figures of the Hadrami migration saga. They are respected for their religious knowledge and the deeds they carried out during their lifetime, and their tombs are important meeting points both for their descendants and other Hadramis. The yearly visits to the tombs (*hawl*) are important meeting points for diasporic Hadramis.

I mention this to underline my point that it is important not to confuse the ideological level with the level of concrete groupness. Most contemporary Sada do not devote their lives to the pursuit of religious knowledge and are now found in various professional occupations. Irrespective of social position, however, many Sada believe they are the carriers of an important part of Hadrami history, and that the history of Hadramaut is, somehow, their own history. They continue to honor the tradition of the *kafa'a* marrage in order to keep the *bayt* together. There is thus no direct relationship between an identity as Sada and the type of activity pursued. This is so because it is not enough to be born a *sayyid*.

Children are not expected to take up the vocation of preaching unless particular circumstances lead them in that direction. The *sulb* (support that gives strength) of the Prophet is a dormant quality, which has to be activated through the acquisition of knowledge and action. The specific knowledge is *ilm*, which includes knowledge of God, but less divine knowledge is also revered. As the ultimate knowledge lies with the Prophet, the Sada through their genealogical links to him carry a special responsibility to manage this type of knowledge. But education is also important, as it can improve a person's character, and make him care more for others (Bang 2003; Freitag 2001, 2003).

Building a moral economy—the role of *al waqf*

In Hadramaut the Sada played an important role in making alliances with political leaders, supporting specific rulers by writing their histories and legitimizing their positions. They could also undermine the position of leaders by leaving the area controlled by a certain leader, performing *hijra*, which in the Islamic tradition means to leave the "territory of sin" and establish their "sacred area," *hawta,* somewhere else, under a different leader. Combining religion and politics was thus common. The Sada also combined religion and economics. Unlike the northern Yemeni *zaydis,* Hadrami Sada have always combined religious duties with trading activities (see e.g., von Bruck 2005). Teaching is a duty and no payment is expected. But trade is another matter. In trade the aim is to make a profit. As missionaries and traders, the Sada have combined two processes: establishing themselves as pious persons, and at the same time conducting trade in a profitable manner. The way trade was carried out, and particularly how one spent one's wealth were important for an individual's status. Hadrami involvement in publishing serves as an example of an activity in which they could combine commercial interests with the production of religious texts. Similarly, putting trade profits into libraries would also indicate the person's learning and raise his status.

This expands our discussion on Hadramis from one of religious and genealogical status to a broader discussion on how Hadramis have maintained themselves as "moral community." On this level, status appears as a complex notion among Hadramis. Basic factors for the maintenance of honorable status among Hadrami men include economic position, occupation, education, descent line, degree of cultural refinement, etiquette, social skills, and generosity. Command of Arabic is also part of this cultural capital.

It is interesting to note that a preoccupation with money in itself is viewed negatively. Economic wealth does not automatically create status. It has to be mediated through accepted channels that are both material and spiritual at the same time. Much of this is symbolic work. Money can lead to many unwanted things and has to be transformed into something inalienable (e.g., Weiner 1976). Material wealth must be combined with inner strength. This resonates with Simmel's view that value is not an intrinsic quality of objects but "a judgment upon them which remains inherent in the subject" (Simmel 1990). Thus, a continuous challenge for the successful trader is to show an ability to restrain "desire" in spite of efforts to accumulate money. Islam offers ways through which to achieve this balance.

One specific institution that Hadramis have made use of to solve the above problem is the *waqf* (pl. *awqaf*). All Islamic schools of law allow Muslims to endow part of their property as *waqf,* an institution that provides a means for Muslims to support various charitable activities, thus transforming capital that would normally go to the market sector, in which notions of profit and selfishness dominate, to an arena in which capital can be transformed into "moral capital" that can sustain the trader as a moral person. By facilitating such processes the institution of the *waqf* became an important mechanism for the maintenance of the Sada hegemonic position in the diaspora. It allowed them to combine their involvement in trade with their missionary activities, and all activities together helped strengthen the position of the Tariqa al-Alewia.

The *waqf* works in the following way (Freitag 2002): The donor (*waqif*) must have full right over the property and that which is endowed must be of a tangible and permanent nature and yield a revenue. This would include rural and urban real estate, but also moveables like animals, books, and furniture. The endowed object is endowed for perpetuity (i.e., withdrawn from circulation) and cannot be given away as a gift, inherited, sold, or mortgaged. And it should be *fi sabil Allah*, for the sake of God, meaning that the revenues must revert to a charitable purpose, such as to a mosque, a hospital, or for the relief of the poor. If revenues go directly to charity it is called *waqf khayri* (charitable). The person can also direct the revenues to relatives and other private people. But after these named people die, the revenues revert to charitable purposes. This is called *waqf dhurri*, or *waqf ahli* (family). Such a *waqf* is administered by a *mutawalli*.

The *waqf* is an institution that has played an important role in the development of the Hadrami economy. But its importance is not so much as a direct economic institution but rather as a mechanism that facilitates links between the market sphere and the moral sphere, which raises the issue of Hadrami notions of morality in the economic sphere. Education is a case in point. Schools could be funded by such *waqfs* and thus facilitate the drive towards education which was so important to the Ba Alewi. The education of others was for them a drive towards the "inner mission," both at home where they educated nomads so that they could educate their children, and in the diaspora. This is then coupled with the modernist vision of education, which also contains social aims. This was so in the past, and is still the case today.

The issue can be linked to the development of the Hadrami economic success in Southeast Asia. Hadramis, who were at the forefront during various periods of modernization in that region, saw their commercial success slow down in the twentieth century, and they lost out compared to members of other groups, particularly when compared to the success of the Chinese. The Hadramis kept their family firms and continued investing in *waqfs*, investing in cultural capital. If we use Maurice Bloch and Jonathan Perry's (1989) terms of "short term and long term cycles of accumulation," it is clear that whereas the short term was focused on capital accumulation, the long term was directed towards a moral economy in which many factors were relevant. This practice resulted in the continuation of earlier business practices, rather than the introduction of new practices or risk-taking that the contemporary economic situation demanded. But this is a matter of scale. If we look at the case of Hadramis in Africa the family firm has been sufficient to make Hadramis compete with other types of economic enterprises, but in southeast Asia, where the globalized economy is most pronounced, we see the differences most clearly.

Opportunities for the non-Sada

One factor that characterizes the modern history of Hadramis is that a new type of migrant emerged at the end of the nineteenth century. Members of non-Sada groups began to travel and benefit from new opportunities around the Indian Ocean. But their migration and their conceptualization of it represent a different pattern from that of the Sada within the Tariqa al-Alewiyya. Members of these groups do not recognize deep genealogical lines but most usually stop after the third generation. Names of more distant ancestors are not known. Affinal relationships tie these groups together, also along the lines of the home areas. Rather than building their social organization on deep genealogies and networks of religious scholars, these groups build their immediate community along the lines of a business enterprise: more specifically, the family firm. Family members had to learn the trade and then work their way up, eventually taking on greater responsibility for decision making and longer term planning.

The biographies of these people look somewhat alike. Their ancestors came from Hadramaut, often driven into the diaspora by drought, famine, and tribal wars, and they established themselves in some type of trade. They all seem to share a narrative that underlines the hardships of the early travelers, how they started out in a small and modest way, but also emphasizes that they were pious and careful and built wealth through time. The accounts tell of men who began as wandering petty traders, then made wise investments that allowed a more settled life. Children were socialized into the family's business and the whole enterprise was clearly linked to the conditions of where they lived and based on local values. In these accounts, those who failed did so because they had not had the proper training, or because historical forces affected them in unfair ways. The homeland is always characterized by images of deprivation, powerlessness, and violence. Consistent with this depiction of the hardships life at home, the migrants are shown as committed to assisting those who have not migrated. The most wealthy of Hadrami migrants, such as bin Talib in Singapore, are considered to have worked to fulfil this aim.

Prevailing conditions today are the legacy of earlier economic successes, and failures. We have seen how Hadramis in Hyderabad struggled to maintain their economic position after the Police Action of 1948. Petty traders in Borana and Sudan struggle to turn a profit in small, local economies. We also see larger traders developing new commercial interests in the homeland as a place of emerging economic opportunity, not as a place of ancestral purity.

The Arab Association in Singapore and the Yemeni Community Association in Addis Ababa are both involved in building trade relationships with Yemen. These networks are also promoted by the Yemeni government. Yemeni President Ali Abdalla Saleh routinely travels to diasporic communities seeking investment capital from Yemenis living outside the country. The investors may make small talk with the president about their origins in Hadramaut, but their meetings are about business, with questions about the existing investment climate in Yemen, the security of their investments, and what measures the president is taking to combat the proverbial Yemeni corruption.

The situation in the diaspora—discourses about identities

This type of perspective not only looks at the changes in a religious and theological context but also draws on broader historical circumstances. This model can be used to examine developments among Hadramis in the diaspora as well, developments that show the continuing tension between the Sada and the non-Sada groups there. A famous case is the Alewi-Irshadi debate which took place in Southeast Asia after 1905 (Bujra 1967; Kostiner1984; Ho 1997b). This case illustrates my argument that the Sada struggled to maintain their hegemonic position in the diaspora during the early decades of the twentieth century and that new types of historical consciousness emerge in the process.

The starting point of the debate was whether a *sharifa* (a female member of the Sada) can marry a non-*sayyid*. The debates about this particular issue were formed as debates about hierarchy and equality: They were debates about the stratification system. And as Muslim scholars were involved, such debates took the form of *fatwas*, issued by scholars who try to provide religious legitimacy for different positions. Several scholars have summarized the debates (see Bujra 1967; Kostiner 1984), and here I draw on Eng Seng Ho (1997b).

On a question in the Cairo based journal *Al Manar* about marriage between a *sharifa* and a Muslim of non-*sharif* descent, Rashid Rida argued that such a marriage should be possible as the important thing was whether or not the groom is to be a Muslim. A Hadrami Sada from Sumatra reacted in the following way:

> Know you that equality (*al-kafa'a*) in matrimony is a necessity/duty. And it is by way of pedigree in 4 degrees, thusly: First: to be Arab. Those of non-Arabs are not equal to them. Second: to be of Quraysh. Other Arabs are not equal to them. Third: to be of the Banu Hashim. Others among the Quraysh are not their equals. Fourth: the descendants of Fatima al-Zahra', through her sons Hasan and Husayn; others of the Hasimites ae not their equals. ... Know you

that nobility (*al-sharaf*) is of two divisions, essential (*dhati*) and attributional (*si-fati*). The *ulama* have deemed correct that the essential nobility of the prophet is linked to his descendants. So, as the Prophetic essence has been set aside for him from all of existence, God has made it a repository for every praiseworthy quality. And it still runs in his folk, the purity within the repository. God has gone to great lengths in the perfection of its purity. Not by work do they manufacture it, nor by pious deeds, but by God's preexisting effort upon them. As such, the effects of the Prophetic emanation is not known by the greatest of saints who is not of them, even if he expends the greatest effort till eternity. Of this secret, God says: "Say: No reward do I ask of you except the love of those near of kin." (*surat al-Shura*) ... So, it is not permitted that a non-*sayyid* marry a *sharifa* even if she waives the *kafa'a* and consents and her guardian does too, for the right to do so is not theirs. Nobility of essence is not something they gained which they can give away, but belongs to the Prophet and all the sons of Hasan and Husayn, and their consent is inconceivable. And it has been established that they are masters over all the other human beings, according to the text of the *hadith*: Whomever I was master of, Ali is his master." And it is permissible that a slave marry his lady/mistress? (Ho 1997b: 7)

Ho argues that the *fatwa* is a sign of a more active policy among the Sada to define the boundaries of their identity, and that people of the Sada carry a religious essence that is beyond the will of any individual member of the group. The debate responds to a globalized situation in which local authorities are being challenged by established authorities elsewhere. A second characteristic is that the earlier social world of the Indian Ocean, characterized by mixing and syncretism, is being replaced by a racialized imperialist world view. The increased travel, possible with the introduction of steamships, brought new groups of people with "pure" identities, both among the European and the Arab parts of the population, a fact that gave the discourse a different direction.

It was in this context that the Sada developed a new type of genealogy, collected in a work entitled *Shams al-Zahira al-Dahiyya al-Munira* (*The Luminescent, Encompassing Mid-day Sun*), written in 1890 by 'Abd al-Rahman bin Muhamad al-Masshur. The "mid-day sun" is a metaphor for the bright light of the Sada religious heritage, a metaphor that occurs also in other books written by Hadrami Sada about their own tradition (see Ho 2006). According to Ho (1997b, 2006), this important book combined four different things: It set out a comprehensive scheme of descent from the Prophet Mohammed; within the scheme it located major family groups and explained the origin of the family names; it provided information about prominent ancestors within each family; and it mentioned the pattern of migration for the different families.

A central registry was set up in Jakarta and the information is kept up to date to this day, making this conscious effort on the part of the Sada to define and limit their identity as a central element in the maintenance of the Sada consciousness. The reason why this movement took off in Indonesia, rather than in other parts of the diaspora, can be related to Dutch colonial policies. Generally, Hadramis living in parts of the British-ruled Malay world were better off than those who lived under Dutch rule in Indonesia. The British created mechanisms to administer religious practice. After generations as advisors to Malay sultans, Hadramis were well positioned to become members of the bureaucracy. By 1914 the *Minhaj al-Talibin,* the standard Shafi'e *fiqh* manual, had been translated into English, and the Hadramis were favored by the British when filling positions.

This was very different from the situation in Indonesia where the Dutch marginalized the Arabs (Ho 1997b; de Jonge 1997). The strategic position of the Sada group in Indonesia to claim a superior status was thus weaker, and members of the non-Sada groups could challenge this superiority. This challenge could also be expressed in the form of counter-*fatwas* to the ones produced by the Sada. An example of this is a *fatwa* written by the Sudanese scholar and teacher Ahmad al-Surketti, who in the early years of the twentieth century wrote:

> Verily, most of the people of religions are agreed, without dissent, that the origin of all people is one. And that no one is superior to another by the essence (*dhat*) of his blood and flesh. Rather, they are superior by virtue of (personal) qualities/attributes and deeds and good upbringing. Just like different fruits taken from one tree, they are preferred (one over the other) for sweetness of taste, largeness of size and lack of rot. So too are people preferred/superior by virtue of knowledge and works and moral character.
>
> The seed which is taken from a small tree will produce a large tree possessing great fruit as a result of good cultivation and effort, surpassing its original in sweetness and grace. In like wise, the seed taken from a great big tree of the same type, its fruit will be small, not sweet, and rotten if it is cultivated badly and effort is not expended upon it.
>
> So too is the situation of the sons of Adam, of the son of every great man. For the son of the generous, learned, excellent/superior, morally upright man could be doltish, cowardly, vile and corrupt is his upbringing is bad. And the son of one who is idiotic, foolish, vile and cowardly, could be generous, brave, excellent, learned and upright if his upbringing is excellent. So, there is no place of conceit on account of descent from one who is generous, learned or one of the prophets. (Ho 1997b: 7)

Clearly, the *fatwa* can be read as a reply to the Sada point of view that we quoted above. But the issue of identity was only part of the debate, and soon different organizations were created around the positions expressed in the debates. In 1914, the Jamiyyat al-Islah al-Islamiyya was formed in opposition to the Sada, establishing non-Sada schools and newspapers. The Sada organized themselves in al-Rabita al-Alawiyya. To illustrate that the organizations now were engaged in battles that went beyond the issue of internal identities among Hadramis, it is interesting to note that both organizations competed for support both in the Ottoman court in Istanbul and with the Sharif of Mecca, the Imam of Yemen and the Quaity and Kathiri sultans at home in Hadramaut.

Hadrami historicity

Hadramis discussed in this chapter differ in the way they see their own identities. Clearly, the Sada group maintains a specific identity due to their claimed genealogical relations to the Prophet Mohammed, as do certain Mashaikh groups to an ancestor who began the specific link of religious learning. For other groups it is not their genealogical descent, but rather their activities in the diaspora that are underlined. A new term, *mashaikh bi-l ilm* emerged, denoting people who obtained religious status not through genealogies but "*bi-l ilm*," through religious knowledge obtained by studies. Masakin and others accumulated wealth and, through their improved financial status, were better able to challenge the hegemony of the traditionally rich Sada, for instance through education. Opposition was also based on religious criteria (see von Bruck 1998, 2005 for such an argument for groups in North Yemen).

The basic process here is how the different actors see themselves as "becoming persons." In doing this we need to take into consideration how the different actors embrace certain identities, and how they themselves relate to the history of their group, their family and their own individual careers. Under this line of argument, certain patterns stand out, certain "discursive possibilities" for the different Hadramis we have met in this book, discursive possibilities that also affect identity making (e.g., Bloch 1998).

The religiously oriented Sada, as represented by Tariqa al-Alewia, conceptualize history as being embodied in the actions of their ancestors and thus are the product of kinship relationships. History is a kind of kinship reckoning, and the individual's "becoming a person" is related to the memory of ancestors who belong to the house of the Prophet. This type of religiously oriented Sada recirculate the past as a form of knowledge, and they invest in keeping this image of the past alive, in genealogies (e.g. *Shams al Zahira*) and on the walls of the homes as well as in pilgrimages to the graves of the important ancestors. A quote from Nietzsche may further illustrate what I mean by this:

> [H]istory belongs to the preserving and revering soul—to him who with loyalty and love looks back on his origins; through this reverence, he, as it were, gives

thanks for his existence. By tending with loving hands what has long survived he intends to preserve the conditions in which he grew up for those who will come after him—and so he serves life. The possession of ancestral furniture changes its meaning in such a soul: for the soul is rather possessed by the furniture. The small and limited, the decayed and obsolete receives its dignity and inviolability in that the preserving and revering soul of the antiquarian moves into these things and makes itself at home in the nest it builds there. The history of his city becomes for him the history of his self ... And so ... he looks beyond the ephemeral, curious, individual life and feels like the spirit of the house, the generation, and the city. (Nietzsche 1874/1980).

The successful traders of non-Sada descent have no such sense of history and their "houses" are not metaphorically embedded in history, but are new and large and luxurious. Their history is that of traders who became visible through their commodities. Those people who started the activities on which people now depend exist in living memory and are important for the present. While the notion of the past may relate to memories of the homeland, these memories often have negative characteristics, focused on those events that led their forebears to leave. And the homeland is still barren, and has not contributed to present successes. Today's traders are self-made men, their success made through their own deeds.

In this way of understanding history the knowledge that counts is the knowledge needed to create wealth. And those who return to Yemen spend this wealth not on traditional items of consumption but on Western goods such as four-wheel-drive cars, TVs and satellite antennas, and modern houses. They make their history felt through capital investments. Whereas the Sada brought religious texts these people bring commodities. While the religious, literate Sada construct a present through the past, these people create the present in terms of an imagined future. They erase the past, and try to establish a counter-hegemonic history of civil society liberties and free trade. Memory is not part of a symbolic heritage. Identity is in the making, not modeled on the past. Migration has allowed them not only to dream about this world but actually to create it.

It is of course risky to pursue this debate as one in which two groups, the Sada and the non-Sada, are pitched against each other. The ideological currents we are referring to did not divide Hadramis strictly along a group basis. There were spokespersons for most viewpoints in all groups, in the diaspora as well as at home in Hadramaut. Members of the Sada group have developed their careers as traders and belong to this group. One example is the al-Kaf family whom we met in the chapter on Singapore. This family, at least as represented through the history presented here, were major traders, maintaining links to the homeland and acting as key reformers there (see Freitag 2002).

But several families with a history from the more recent migration to the Gulf and to Saudi Arabia also operate in this manner, and are also reformers at home.

We can talk about these processes using a notion of different Hadrami traditions of knowledge. Rather than looking for groups, we can look for discourses available among Hadramis, and then see to what extent various Hadramis become part of and embrace such discourses. People identify with the past in different ways, and the extent to which they project their identities into the past varies. Many Hadramis are not what they are through ancestral substance, but through knowledge in the present, in contexts of kinship and their knowledge of the "the world at large." To such people, their forebears indeed represent an important past, but the past is also characterized by the groups of exploiters, such as the Sada, who made it impossible for their forbears to make a living at home.

History is here not understood as continuity but rather as a transformation that led to their present type of existence. Such differences also influence the claims different people make to a position in the social and political order. The transformations of such orders in the homeland, as well as in the diaspora, have forced Hadramis to reconsider such orders. New opportunities are also taken up by members of the groups, and new legitimizations arise to explain where the different groups "belong" in such a changing world. The following section examines the various ways these processes have occurred in Hadramaut and in the diaspora.

Conclusion

The cases in this chapter show two particular situations in which identities are being formed. Rather than seeing a person's identity as something given at birth, identity is a continuous process of "becoming." Identity is based both on performative action and on ancestry. Through migration and the building of a new life in the diaspora, a person's self-definition is re-evaluated. As well, due to processes both in the diaspora and in the homeland, formerly underprivileged or marginalized strata are encouraged to claim their share of power. In the case of Hadramis, several elements in their identity formation fit this logic well. Through their practices, as explored above, we can say that the Sada have "negotiated the duration of time" in a way that presents their social positions and identities as being timeless.

At the same time, members of the non-Sada groups have engaged in modern activities that challenge the Sada representation of history. With a growing number of non-Sada migrating outside Yemen, a battle over group identities has emerged. Over and above such struggles, however, are rituals that provide what all rituals do—repetition, formalization and fixing experience in time. As Muslims, Hadramis engage in Muslim rituals, and we have seen how the Sada, and members of Tariqa al-Alewia, play important roles here, both in terms of ongoing activities, but also as apical ancestors around whom rituals such as *hawlia* are organized. There is thus a constant tension between Hadramis in everyday affairs and Hadramis as participants in cultural traditions. The Sada seem to stand at the center of this tension, a tension that revolves around a transformation of their position from one of power to one of rank. This means that their position is ritualized, taken out of history and given a rigid, essentialized meaning that cannot be questioned.

Looking at the history of the Hadrami people, it must be said that this strategy of Sada identity formation has been very successful. But if our focus is on specific moments of history we also see that the success is being challenged. And in such moments of challenge we see how the earlier successes of the Sada, and the way they have built up an ideological justification of their position within the social hierarchy can limit the flexibility of discourse about the various identities available to the Sada. This was apparent when the Sada were challenged by the new groups who came up through nationalism and market relationships as "self-made men" in the diaspora, or as new landowners, as was the case in contemporary Hadramaut. The challenge is not so much to the Sada as a general identity, but rather to the way the identities are ranked.

CHAPTER SEVEN

Resisting the West

Muslim Universalism Versus Western Globalization in the Indian Ocean

People with history

The representation of Hadrami diasporic communities in chapters one to four, and the more specific discussions in chapters five and six, make several general conclusions. The earlier chapters show that there are "world system" dynamics at play, that the Indian Ocean region is a meeting place of "civilizations," and, indeed, that from a very early period there have been elements we now associate with "globalization." These elements include the movement of large numbers of people across the ocean and the early formation of diasporic communities, primarily in trading towns, now perhaps better described as "world cities" of their time.

In this chapter we draw on the earlier discussion to further understand some broader regional and global dynamics in the Indian Ocean, and to further explain how Hadramis have participated in these dynamics. The discussion is not particularly focused on any of the four places that this book has addressed thus far. Rather, here I want to generalize and look at the spread of "the West" in the Indian Ocean, represented by global capitalism, colonialism and imperialism, as well as Western modernity. I see these processes as a part of the ongoing cycles of globalization, through which local communities are drawn into large-scale processes of global reach. Hence the discussion also will touch on issues that are of relevance to our understanding of globalization in general. An important point is that globalization cannot be taken to mean processes of homogenization.

Hadramis and other Muslims certainly react to these historical processes, but not in any one, homogeneous way. Some people embrace change, while others resist it. The Hadramis and other Muslims were active participants in these developments, with some gaining and some losing in the process. It is important to take a closer look at regional dynamics in the Indian Ocean, to see how processes observed in the specific Hadrami communities relate to wider regional dynamics. As Muslims, Hadramis were players in a regional game that was characterized by economic, political, and cultural continuities, as well as by the emergence of new dominant groups, and the constant definition and redefinition of place.

The Muslim identity

Our earlier discussions have shown that in spite of all the variations in Hadrami identities and processes of ethnic assimilation, Hadramis always consider themselves to be Muslims. As seen elsewhere, over time the migrant individual's ethnic identity seemed to be pushed into the background and became subordinate to religious identity. Such a religious identity is expressed through specific actions, and is also shaped through participation in religious organizations. But it also has a global element, in that Muslims, as part of the *umma,* are considered members of "an imagined community" with a global reach. At the same time, religion's global dimensions must be balanced against its local expression. This is also the case with Hadramis.

Hadramis were at the forefront of developments which led the Indian Ocean to become an important arena for travel, trade, and learning. Historically, Muslim merchants and ship owners operating from the Arabian coastal towns dominated the western part of the Indian Ocean. The Turkish conquest of Gujarat (1303–1304) gave Muslim traders from Siraf, Oman, and Hadramaut access to Gujarati coastal towns. These Gujarat-based traders established communities all along the coast, as far as Malacca. A middle region connected the Indian coast with the "Hinduized" southeast Asian regions of Sumatra and Malaya; an eastern circuit linked Java with China, thus bringing Muslims into the realm of Buddhism and Confucianism.

By the end of the thirteenth century, city states appeared throughout the coastlines of Southeast Asia, with Muslim trading groups spreading Islam and at the same time providing Europe with spices. Two centuries later, Islam had begun to penetrate the interior of Java. There the Muslims did not encounter European traders, as they did in the coastal towns, but a Hindu-Buddhist civilization. Similar processes brought Islam to Africa: via the trans-Saharan trade routes between north and west Africa; across the Red Sea to Sudan; across the Indian Ocean to the Swahili coast; and up the Nile Valley, from Cairo, which after the fall of Baghdad became the region's most important Muslim city and the seat of the Mameluk dynasty.

From the tenth century, trade links flourished. Oral traditions, as well as archaeological excavations and Arab geographers, refer to the kingdom of Zanj on the East African coast, and Ibn Battuta's journeys to Mogadishu and Kilwa in 1328 are part of the remarkable story of trade links between East

Africa, Daybul, and Cambay in India, Aden, Suhar, and Shiraf. Again, we see the familiar configuration of Indian Ocean trading cities. Trade, administration of political kingdoms, religious instruction, and the manufacture of industrial products—all these functions were closely woven into the fabric of Asian cities (Chaudhuri 1985: 98). Yemen and Oman were important points in the western reaches of the Arab-Asian trade, and Aden, Zabid, Suhar, and later Muscat were important trade cities, offering a wide choice of commodities, currencies, and banking services, as well as shipping berths and docking facilities.

The traces of this history are most vividly present in the ancient trading towns. There you will find a vibrant mix of cultures, identities, and ideas, all linked through cultural forms, kinship relations, business networks, and travel routes, as well as through loyalty to the religious center of the diaspora. This medieval world of the Indian Ocean and the Red Sea has been termed "the Geniza World." The name is taken from the *geniza,* or storeroom, of an Old Cairo (Fustat) synagogue in which the papers, written from about 870 to as late as 1880, were found. The historian S.D. Goitein has made an outstanding contribution to our understanding of ancient transnational cultures through his study of the everyday documents found in the *geniza* (see Ghosh 1992 for a wonderful description of the finds; also Clifford 1994: 305).

The Indian Ocean was greatly affected by the arrival of European imperial powers beginning in the 1500s. Being a major commercial area, the Indian Ocean caught the attention of the Portuguese in the sixteenth century. They were looking for trade routes and access to the most profitable of commodities, gold. Ottoman Turkey later emerged as a competitor for influence in the region, as did the French, the British, and the Dutch. Each of these powers were important for developments in Hadramaut: the Ottomans and British as occupying colonial rulers in South Yemen; the French and British in constant competition for control of India, with the British East India Company providing the means for Hadrami settlements there; and the Dutch as the colonial power in Southeast Asia, which was of importance to the significant Hadrami community on Java.

In Africa, Germany also entered into the picture as a colonial power on the Tanzanian coast and in Zanzibar, where they were in competition with the Omani Sultanate on Zanzibar. Despite political and economic competition, the early centuries of European presence were not characterized by their dominant position, but rather by the ways they were absorbed by the Indian Ocean world. For two centuries the Europeans carried out their trade, and adapted to realities in the region alongside all other groups. They were not dominating. But this was to change from the second half of the eighteenth century, and it is this period that will be the focus of the next section.

Exploring dynamics

In order to capture the complexity of the situation hinted at above, I find the writings of Michael Busawoy et al. (2000) useful. In *Global Ethnography*, Busawoy focuses on what he calls "forces," "connections," and "imaginations." But whereas Busawoy and his group dealt with the postmodern world, I am more concerned with using this perspective on longer periods through which we can see different historical periods come and go. With a long perspective, we can see the continuity and variation in the forces of globalization—economic, political, and cultural. We can also better recognize how these forces exist through connections in the world, and identify people's reactions to globalizing processes. Looking at such factors through a long historical perspective facilitates a historically grounded, theoretically driven macro-ethnography, combining comparative history and ethnography.

Furthermore, it is important to be specific about the historical periods we are dealing with, as well as the groups and types of reactions. In order to provide a base for such a historical presentation, I use the concept of epoch, not as a history of detail but as a heuristic device to focus on transformations and the factors at play in such epochs. I draw here on Stuart Hall's (1991) terminology, in which he talks about "global imperialism" to refer to the time of the British Empire, and "global postmodernism" to refer to the period of U.S. global dominance. The selection of these two epochs is obviously based on the chronology of our Hadrami diasporic communities. The aim is to further problematize the three elements hinted at above, i.e., to describe the forces operating within larger systems and look at how these forces are manifested in specific places, and then to address people's perceptions and discourses about the workings of the world.

The epochs are also particular phases in the ongoing processes of globalization. Globalization represents tendencies of a worldwide reach and impact; connectedness of social phenomena; and a world-encompassing, or global, awareness among social actors (Therborn 2000: 154). With such a general view on what globalization means, we are free to look at many processes that relate to a spatialization of the social. This requires a focus on the extension and connectivity of the social as such processes move towards a globally encompassing system. Such processes are clearly multidimensional, and must not be reduced to economics only (Wallerstein 1974), cultural dynamics (Appadurai 1990) or to the dynamics of systems in themselves (Luhman 1995). We should look at broad "moments of reconfiguration" and see what perceptions and discourses develop during such periods. Hadrami cases contain examples of cooperation with imperial and nationalist forces, as well as examples of resistance against such forces. Both strategies may result in increased problems and the closure or opening of opportunity. The effects of this depend on who you are and where you are.

A final, but basic point to make is that despite the processes of differentiation among Hadrami Muslims and the emergence of different identities and responses to historical processes, we are still looking at Muslims who treasure their religion and participate in these discussions without questioning their identities as Muslims. This is consistent with arguments I have presented earlier (Manger 1999) that we should build our understanding of Muslim communities less on the notion that Islam is static and more on the notion that these are dynamic communities engaging in "world systems interrelationships." To capture the dynamism, a static, Orientalist image of Islam and Muslims will not do. Rather, we need to look in the direction of Talal Asad's (1986) suggestion that we look at Islam as a discursive tradition, in which our task is to understand the production of knowledge and the institutional conditions for the production of that knowledge.

We should not assume that religion and culture make up any *a priori* system of meaning, and we should not look for what is essential in Islam. Rather, we should look for historical formations through which that which is taken to be essential is being produced. In this perspective, Islam is not an agent but an arena of many processes that become Islamic because they belong to the discursive tradition of Islam. The tradition consists essentially of discourses that seek to instruct practitioners on the correct form and purpose of a given practice that, precisely because it is established, has a history. The discursive tradition also has its social organization, including experts on different levels, with knowledge, specific technologies for transferring knowledge, and internal hierarchies, but also having relations with rulers. The question here is not what is the essence of Islam, but what are the historical conditions necessary for the existence of particular religious practice and discourse.

From this starting point, specific histories can more clearly come to the surface. The lives of Muslims can be portrayed against that history, i.e., lives not only affected by integrated localities organized according to Islamic principles, but as lives lived in arenas in which complex historical processes have taken place and will continue to do so. Trade relationships in the Indian Ocean activated not only capital but organizational patterns that dealt with credit, legal patterns that gave security to contractual agreements and so on. In such situations, Islam was not only a religion. *Shari'a* provided a legal code for the handling of business and for dealing with conflicts. People well versed in *shari'a* therefore also acted as judges, arbitrators, and so on. They drew on their knowledge about earlier cases from elsewhere, as well as their interpretation of the text itself. But the same processes also provided arenas in which Muslims met, and in which Muslims met with non-Muslims, thereby experiencing themselves as Muslims in their particular world.

So much for my conceptual preferences. Let us now turn to the historical analyses themselves.

Global imperialism

The Hadrami communities referred to in this book were established in the late eighteenth and nineteenth centuries. I have described the specific historical circumstances in which the development of these communities took place. In this section, a broader canvas of events will show the wider "global" dynamics in the Indian Ocean, with Muslims becoming important actors in the region. This is particularly important since it was during the late eighteenth century that we see the beginning of the imperial period, in which European colonial powers moved from the control of trade to the control of territory.

C.A. Bayly (1989) argues that the rise of British power in the eighteenth century is connected to the decline of regional political powers, including the Ottomans, Safavids, and Mughals, as well as the small Java state of Mataram. For the British, an important colonial milestone was when they took control of Bengal through the East India Company. Following the battle of Plassey in 1757, the company collected land rents on the authority of the *nawab* of Bengal, making the company the chief revenue officer (*diwan*); this continued until 1858, when the company was dissolved. For Holland, its hold over Java through the Dutch East India Company, dating from 1752, was challenged by the British. Holland regained control of Java in 1816, when the Dutch government took power and renamed the colony the Netherland Indies.

The glorious past of the Muslim empires was at an end. This was not because of Ibn Khaldounian processes of corruption in the leadership, city life, and wealth, but rather as a result of the emergence of new regional economies and new classes. The unifying effects of trade had produced processes of local differentiation. But trade was not the only factor. Population growth began to stagnate in the sixteenth century and the same period saw an increasingly uneven economic development, with urban areas becoming privileged at the expense of the rural areas. The introduction of a monetary system as part of a general process of commercialization led peasants into bondage by larger landowners who held large estates. State land was broken up and sold, ownership becoming less dependent on having some form of political office and more on the principle of "freehold property." General expenditures were to an increasing degree shifted from the central to regional leaders, who shifted the burden onto the peasants. Commercialization, urbanization, and the growth of landed classes brought profound change, a change which was also influenced by external forces, including trade links with Europe. The export of raw materials and the import of precious metals also played a role, leading to the establishment of a financier class.

But the export link also increased the region's vulnerability to price fluctuations elsewhere, thus increasing systemic interdependencies. The new regional power centers that developed within this context weakened the old, established imperial centers. Egypt under Mohamed Ali is a case in point, weakening the Ottoman Empire, and so is Hyderabad under the Asaf Jahs, weakening the Mughal Empire. At the same time, "tribal warlords" rebelled. Afghan and Turkik tribes from Central Asia (the Rohillas, "men of the hills") challenged both the Safavids and the Mughals. The Wahhabis in what was to become Saudi Arabia also belong to this pattern of eighteenth-century rebellion, as did the Maratha Hindu soldiers in India. Tribal societies were also transformed into military dynasties, often creating internal unity through their attacks on others.

But trade links remained important, and many of the places where the new tensions developed were those areas where the field of trade had been contested for a long time. Puritanical movements like the Wahhabis represented an ideological response to these developments. In India, the leaders of Awadh promoted Shi'ism over the dominant Sunni Mughal. One consequence of these processes of revolt was the emergence of new political units that were more effectively organized than the loose imperial confederacies they replaced. In fact, they might be said to have taken the first steps towards forming nation states. The rulers sought to monopolize and protect trade and settle their people in order to tax them (Bayly 1989: 47). Professional armies were employed, often recruited from minority groups such as Circassians, Georgians, Afghans, and Arabs, including Hadramis. New areas of land were cultivated, new sources of labor power were sought, and nomads were settled. Thus control of primary producers was important. But so was trade, and wars soon broke out over the control of trade routes. Because the export of primary agricultural products was flourishing at this time, the control of producers and the control trade routes was linked. The race for ever expanding profits was on (e.g. ,Bose 2006).

This was thus the period in which we started to see the processes so common under colonialism and imperialism. The colonial state began to aggressively discipline and control marginal groups, land ownership was privatized, and a market economy was introduced. Rather than the spread of free trade, the colonial powers—both Britain and Holland—sought territorial revenues. It was during this era that the notion of Britain as a "Christian Roman Empire" was born (Bayly 1989: 11; see also Cooper and Stoller 1997). A more rigidly defined racial hierarchy was also developing, alongside other forms of British prejudice, such as their dislike of urban elites and their romanticization and "protection" of nomads and "tribal" people. A number of "consuls" were dispatched to represent the interests of European powers and to act as key agents of Western commercialization. They represented the new European arrogance.

Muslim and Hadrami reactions

Conventional Western historiography on Muslims in the eighteenth century has portrayed the period described above as a "dark age," with a focus on the disintegration of the gunpowder empires and a general defeat at the hands of Western powers. This Western view of Islam, portraying Muslim societies as stagnant and barbaric, came to dominate. Not surprisingly, the situation is more complex. For counter examples of Muslim gains in the fields of agriculture, scientific knowledge and technology, seafaring, and navigation see Watson (1983), Al-Hassan and Hill (1986) and Tibbetts (1981). Muslims were not merely passive observers of the new age. We have already mentioned John Voll's (1984) description of four different styles of Islamic reaction to developments in the eighteenth century: adaptionist, conservative, fundamentalist, and, finally, one inspired by sufi beliefs. We see examples of each of these reactions during this period.

For instance, new theological interpretations signaled a new fundamentalism based on the writings of Ibn Taymiyyah, who argued that Muslims should let their actions be directed by God through the Koran. Such ideas were transformed into political action, as represented by the Wahhabis in Saudi Arabia. We saw in chapter six how these different positions were underpinned by the Sada/non-Sada identities among Hadramis, and how they evolved into conflicts that divided Hadrami society along new lines. Other people, in other places made other choices.

Shah Wali Allah al-Dihlawi (1702–1762) and his establishment of schools is a local Indian example of an attempt to deal with the disunity of Muslim society (Hardy 1971, 1972). Al-Dihlawi reformulated Islam on a basis that was broader than any one tradition, making Indian Islam more receptive to outside influences than, for instance, the Arabian version of Wahabism. Southeast Asian Islam was also affected by these trends. The region's many trading states had embraced Islam, but the religion was by no means dominant. Also, Muslims had adapted to the local traditions of Hinduism and Buddhism, bringing the pantheistic elements of Islam to the fore. Over time the Dutch presence in Indonesia led Muslim leaders to depend on their Dutch colonial masters for support, in the process accepting many Western ways. This is just one backdrop for the growth of religious fundamentalism as a form of resistance against such developments.

In the same period, or epoch, the social organization of the basic unit in sufism, the *tariqah*, expanded. Better organized and more activist *tariqahs* appeared and became vehicles for revival rather than passive adaptation. The general economic and political situation developed in ways that allowed these groups to mobilize outside the religious platform, and increased travel brought these groups in closer contact with each other. Malay Muslims regularly trav- eled to Mecca, and it is an interesting fact that some of the leaders behind the Padri movements in Sumatra were present in Mecca during the times the Wahhabi revolt emerged. It is likely that there was cross-fertilization between the different Muslim resistance groups on the question of how to respond to their marginalization. Scholars traveled widely, participating in transnational networks often centered on Mecca and Medina because of the *hajj*. But other Middle Eastern cities were also important, including Cairo and Damascus (Eickelman and Piscatori 1990). Religion became the basis for the emergence of new local identities, and religious scholars increasingly formed alliances with nationalistic activists and political figures.

Hadramis were, of course, participants in these developments, particularly through the building of regional networks. For centuries, they had been trav- eling to India's Gujarati and Malabar coasts, and during this period they also decisively established themselves in Southeast Asia. Hadrami families inter- married with the families of Sultans in many of the eighteenth-century Malay States (Jamal al-Layl in Kedah, Abu Bakr in Perak, Al Aydarus in Trengganu, al-Bahrayn in Kelantan, al-Attas in Johore, al-Qadri in Negeri Sembilan, Bin Shihab in Selangor, and al-Attas in Pahang [Othman 1997]). They were traders but also religious and political leaders. In Indonesia, Hadramis played a central role in Acheh, and there were Hadrami imams in mosques on the islands of Bangka and Madura, in Pontianak at Borneo, at Ternate in the Mo- luccas, as well as central towns on Java and Sumatra (Riddell 1997). And the Hadramis were no longer so dependent on the patronage of the local sultans. Their appearance in these far-flung regions was connected to the growing influence of southern Arabia and Aden during this period, both in trade and as a natural stopover for pilgrims traveling to Mecca from the east and south. In such contexts we see the Hadramis developing a power base of their own, based both on their economic roles and on their religious reputation.

Nineteenth-century globalization

The nineteenth century represents an intensified period of globalization. New maritime technology played a crucial role, for instance the team ship technology that developed through the nineteenth century (Hugill 1993: 30) reducing transport times as well as costs. The innovations appeared in the commercial sphere first, and later in the military sector allowing *Pax Bri- tannica* to develop after 1815. Wood and coal were the main fuel sources, necessitating the establishment of coaling stations along the major shipping lines. The opening of the Suez Canal, shortening shipping times, dramatically reduced the number of stops required, and hence the required number of secure coaling stations. Oil fuel freed ships from many of the problems of coal, the diesel engine further making shipping more efficient in the twentieth century.

The Industrial Revolution restructured the international economy. The search for raw materials such as raw cotton and timber was a part of this, preceding a shift in the global division of labor because of industrialization. Changes to banking, finance, transport, and communication, as well as the move from steam to diesel-powered transoceanic shipping, brought new Western influences to the region. In the 1830s, a letter sent from Europe to India took five to eight months to round the Cape on a sailing ship. To receive an answer might take up to two years. By the 1850s, the letter sent from London to Calcutta would take thirty to forty days. Only two decades later, in the 1870s, a message sent in the form of a telegram from Britain to India could be sent and replied to in one day.

New technologies made many "diasporic" ways of conducting business and trade obsolete, and traditional links between various points in the diaspora were replaced by direct links to the center. British shipping, with coal stations around the world and communication by telegraph to increase efficiency, for sailing orders and commercial contracts, was run from England. Greater use of river transport saw shippers extend their reach inland to the world's major grain producers. These developments were surpassed in the twentieth century when oil and petroleum took over as the main energy sources, producing diesel engines for ships, cars and tractors, and later airplanes, which not only changed the nature of trade but also the technological basis for warfare (Hugill 1993). On the social side, the massive migration out of Europe (O'Rourke and Williamson 1999) also helped change the world order, first towards Germany, and later the United States.

Industrial production now revolved around wheat and cotton: wheat to feed the people, and cotton to provide raw material for the factories. As populations grew and Irish wheat production fell following the Potato Famine, Britain's importation of wheat increased. The United States, Argentina, Australia, and Russia all became important wheat producers. Because cotton could not be grown in Britain, the textile industry had to be supplied by the colonies. Among the colonies, India remained the most important for British economic interests. The construction of railroads, the use of steamships and the opening of the Suez Canal transformed India into a major source of both cheap food and raw materials for Europe. Tea, wheat, oil seeds, cotton, and jute all came from there. At the same time, India was becoming an important market for British finished products. Large surpluses originating from trade with India were central to Britain's capital accumulation and London's important position in international finance (Arrighi 1999: 263).

The integration of the world's economy into a single, interdependent whole further developed in the period 1870–1914. Three factors were central: further advances in the means of communication; the spread of rail transport outside Europe and North America; and the expansion of world shipping, both in tonnage, and through the shift from sail to steam which reduced travel time and improved punctuality. Canal constructions, including the Suez Canal in 1869 and the Panama Canal in 1914, helped cut distances and travel times (by 41 percent on a trip from Liverpool to Bombay; and by 60 percent from New York to San Francisco). Finally, cables laid beneath the oceans linked the continents, for instance enabling the telephone (international lines from 1887).

All of this paralleled a boom in commerce, with the tripling of foreign trade volumes between 1870 and 1914. This is the period of "finance capital" in the imperial age, an expansion related to increased pressure on the profitability of capital within Britain itself. This led investors and financial houses to channel capital through the City (London's financial district) to distant places, directly linking up with the imperial project (see Hobson 1938). However, most of all this was a finance relationship among powerful countries indicating an increasing global inequality. Only 11 percent of world trade took place among the primary producers themselves, and investments from the West into these countries supported not their development but further colonization. These investments relate to the introduction of the gold standard for European currencies in 1863–1874. At the same time that capital was flowing into the colonies, surplus labor was dispatched from Europe, leading to the Europeanization of many territories.

But other, non-European areas also tried to modernize. Some were colonies, like India and Indonesia, while others were quasi-independent, like Egypt. The old urban artisan communities in the Islamic world were replaced by new forms of indigenous capitalism, partly, but only partly, linked to the Industrial Revolution in Europe. In the wake of the French Revolution, peasant rebellions flourished. Rural sufi groups followed suit. Millenarian movements signaled this breakdown of the old order and the onset of colonialism. People sought new legitimizations, and local issues were replaced by universal ones like Islam versus Christianity. The Sanusiyya in North Africa, Naqsbandiyya in China, Salawiyya in the Nile Valley, and Padri in Indonesia were all movements that heralded such reformulations.

The Mappilas of southwestern India provide an example of this change. The traditional pepper trade was controlled by the Muslim Mappilas, who competed with Hindu Nayyar chieftains, as well as the Christian Portuguese. Tipu Sultan's successful Muslim rule in Mysore helped the Mappilas, but the

British defeat of Mysore in 1793 turned the tables against the Muslims and allowed the Nayar to regain control. This is just one example of a type of development which shows that not only trade and religion was at stake. Trade and religion certainly belong to the picture, but so do factors such as ethnic identities, indigenous state formations, and the intervention by colonial powers, all working together to shape ongoing conflicts.

Several other examples could also be mentioned. The Wahhabis in Saudi Arabia challenged the traditional Muslim leadership, and also European colonialists. And their activities had far-reaching consequences. The printing press helped "textualize" issues in new ways. People within the regions and Europe were more in touch with each other than before. Indonesian Muslims, for instance, present in Mecca during the emergence of the new and radical Wahhabi religious discourse, brought back to the Padri the Wahhabi message about the need to purify Islam. In India, the Parsis of Bombay and the Hindu gentry of Calcutta, among other groups, adapted to the new situation by founding schools, newspapers, and reform societies.

Two Muslim attempts to modernize stand out in the nineteenth century, the most outstanding of which was led by Muhamed Ali (1805–1849) in Egypt, but the Ottoman Tanzimat, started by Mahmoud II in Istanbul in 1839 and lasting until 1876, is also important. These initiatives, and others like them, looked to the West to find solutions to their societies' problems. This in turn brought Islamic fundamentalist reactions. In Istanbul, opposition from the "Young Turks" was liberal in nature, while more conservative, Islamic responses took various forms. One was to emphasize the role of the Sultan as a pan-Islamic ruler (Abdel Hamid II from 1876). The other was to enter a debate with the West and develop a Muslim understanding of modernism. The famous Muslim modernist thinker, Al Afghani, was a key figure here (1839–1897). The third theme was the growing absolutism of the Ottoman ruler, as exemplified by Abdel Hamid II (ruling from 1867 until 1909), who used Muslim clerics to shore up his rule and claim legitimacy. This ended when the Young Turks movement revolted and took power in 1909. Nationalistic sentiment, both Arab and Turkish, also grew, thus making the Ottoman empire an example of the dilemmas and tensions Muslims experienced at the end of the nineteenth century. The two last Sultans of the Empire, Mehmed V (1909–1918) and Mehmed VI (1918–1922), who ruled until the end of the Ottoman era in 1922, could do nothing much to influence the flow of history, neither the first by declaring jihad against the Allies in 1914, nor the latter who lived to see the emergence of the Turkish Republic in 1924.

In Egypt, Muhamed Ali's successors (Abbas 1849–1854, Said 1854–1863, and Ismail 1863–1879) modernized and rebuilt cities and transportation systems. The end result of this policy was that Egypt, rather than developing as a regional Red Sea and Gulf of Aden power, became financially dependent on the West, ending up as a British colony in the 1880s. Also here Al-Af-ghani played an important role in formulating critiques of the Muslim way of meeting the challenges of the West, and his follower Mohamed Abduh (1849–1905) even more so. Abduh's aim was to integrate modern Western and Islamic ideas and innovations. His public position (as mufti of Egypt from 1899) enabled him to spread his message to a wider public, inspiring both fundamentalism and revivalism.

In other areas local states were not strong enough to act as reformers by themselves, and European colonial powers led the modernization, which inevitably created an Islamic backlash. In India, several groups and movements formed to oppose the modernist drive. After the Indian Mutiny in 1857, the British controlled the Muslim areas of India, and Indian Muslims had to balance between accepting the modernizing drive of the British presence and a Muslim orientation leading their political loyalties towards the Ottoman Empire. Sayyid Ahmad Khan (1817–1898) was a key figure in this, trying to combine Western learning with Islamic teachings, and establishing schools that used an integrated approach, drawing from both Western and Islamic thought. The Deobandis favored a more traditionalist, Islamic line. In 1906 The Muslim League was formed, to act as an umbrella organization representing all Indian Muslims, but came under increasing criticism for being too pro-British. This criticism led to the establishment of the Khilafat Committee in 1919, which advocated a more pro-Ottoman position (Manger, Ane 2007).

Similar developments can bee seen on a more local level. In Kerala, the famous Hadrami *sayyid*, Sayyid Fadl b. 'Alawi b. Sahl played a central role in a Muslim-inspired rebellion, or jihad, against the British. His family held the title of *tannals* of the Mappilas. In the middle of the nineteenth century, Sayyid Fadl inspired several attacks by Kerala Muslims on Hindu groups. The attacks were more in the tradition of earlier skirmishes with Hindu groups over the spice trade than a real resistance against the British. Nevertheless, Sayid Fadl was expelled by the British in 1852 and traveled to Istanbul, Mecca, and Dhofar (see Dale 1997; Bang 2003).

In Southeast Asia, the tension between a localized, syncretist faith and a rigorous, cosmopolitan faith existed alongside the tension over how to respond to Dutch colonialism. Opposition movements were active throughout the nineteenth century. The earliest was the Padri movement in Sumatra, followed by the Java War from 1825 to 1830. In 1873, there was an uprising in Acheh after the Dutch invaded. All of the anti-colonial actions included an element of holy war, as they were led by *ulema* and were influenced by the pan-Islamic movement.

All of these movements benefited from modern transport. Political leaders could now go on pilgrimage to Mecca, thereby keeping in touch with the center of the Islamic world. New communication technologies also helped organizations stay up to date with emerging intellectual currents throughout the region. For instance, Shaykh Muhammad Tahir ibn Jalal al-Din (1867–1957) spread the ideas of Muhamed Abduh's Salafiyyah through his Singapore-based newspaper, *Al-Imam*, trying to place events occurring during his time in a Muslim intellectual context. In London, several Indian activists ran newspapers (*Muslim Outlook, Islamic News, Muslim Standard*) propagating the cause of the Khilafat movement (Manger, Ane 2007).

Mecca and Madina were also affected, although their religious leadership was conservative and cooperated with the Egyptian and Ottoman rulers against neo-Sufism. It was the Sharif of Mecca who kept in touch with the wider Islamic world. In Oman, the maritime empire declined, and Oman became increasingly dependent on the British. The same can be said about the British takeover of Aden in 1839 which created a new situation in southern Arabia that blocked the development of any particular Muslim reaction.

The global postmodern

Muslim responses to twentieth-century globalization tendencies are not very different from those of earlier historical periods. But many contextual factors are different. One basic factor that changed in the past century was the emergence of nation states and nationalism. In the early part of the century this process was seen by many Muslims as a threat to Muslim global unity. The issue of the Caliphate is one example. This was an attempt to restore the Ottoman Sultan as the leader of the Muslims, which led to a call for holy war during World War I. Of course, the Sultan was not returned to power and no effective holy war emerged. From 1919 to 1924, the Indian Caliphate Movement was rather strong, seeking the restoration of the Caliphate, but the Ottoman era was over. They lost the war to the Western, allied nation states, and they lost the sultanate to the new, Turkish nation state (Manger, Ane 2007).

Instead of revitalizing the Caliphate then, the struggle for independence encouraged nationalism. New organizations were formed to voice those nationalistic sentiments, often using poetry and literature to express the growing confidence of newly independent peoples. In the post-independence period, political reforms and policies aimed at modernization were undertaken. In many cases, the changes were made under the banner of Arab socialism, signifying a regionally specific form of nationalism that differed from that of the West. Among the leaders who promoted nationalistic aspirations were Egypt's Gamal Abdel Nasser, Algeria's Ben Bella, and Indonesia's Sukarno. Muslim leaders usually went along with this development, although political movements like the Muslim Brotherhood sprang up after World War I in reaction to a growing secularism. A key voice in this reaction was the Egyptian Muhamad Rashid Rida (1865–1935). His Salafiyya inspired views, arguing for a return to a "true Islam" were presented in the journal, *Al-Manar*, which was distributed throughout the Muslim world. Rida argued against secularization and called for a re-establishment of a Muslim state based on the model of the early Muslim empires. Consequently, he ended up a supporter of the Saudi state. The radical stance of the Muslim Brothers was just one further continuation of this line of thinking. Other, more moderate trends were also present in the debates. Journals and other publications during this period engaged in heated discussion and promotion of the new ideas spreading throughout the region, often representing Islam as an alternative to the model of the capitalist West, but also to communism and socialism.

Also in the years before and after World War I, in India, Muhamed Iqbal and the Muslim League (formed in 1906) formulated an Islamic response on behalf of Indian Muslims facing a Hindu majority, which eventually led to the formation of Pakistan, engineered by Muhamed Ali Jinnah. In the meantime, the Khilafat movement (1918–23) had put different priorities (Manger, Ane 2007). More conservative forces among the *ulema* in Jamiyat al-ulema-i-Hind wanted more pragmatic policies, whereas al-Mawdudi's Jama'at i-Islami advocated radical ideas that placed Islam above nationalism. The platform of Tablighi Jama'at was somewhere in between (Metcalf 1999). In Malaya, the British had preserved the old sultanates which meant that conservative, traditionalist forces retained power. But new thinking emerged with a new generation, for instance the Young Group in Singapore (Kaum Muda), which looked at the Muslim experience in the context of living as a minority group within the Chinese and Indian majority.

Singapore was a center for the publication of religious literature. Students from all over the archipelago who wanted to further their studies in Islamic doctrine or law went either to Mecca or to the Straits Settlement, where they "sat at the feet" of itinerant scholars from Hadramaut, Patani, Acheh, Palembang, and Java. Most of these scholars had themselves studied in Mecca. The city thus stood at the heart of a communication network which fed a constant stream of revived "orthodox" Muslim thought from the Hejaz into the Malay peninsula and Indonesian archipelago.

The efforts to spread the many various viewpoints among Muslims were greatly helped by the publishing facilities which had sprung up in Singapore. Material originally published in Arabic, particularly from Egypt, spread into Southeast Asia. Although the readership of Arabs, Malay, and *Jawi Pernakan* (locally born Muslims, the offspring of South Indian Muslim and Malay unions) was rather small, they represented an elite. Contacts between this educated group and the wider local population helped spread the emerging ideas into nonliterate quarters (Roff 1964: 83). Jutta E. Bluhm (1983), for instance, discusses the particular impact of the Cairo-based *Al-Manar,* during its period of publication from 1898 to 1936. Articles also appeared in *Al Imam,* published in Singapore, and *Al Munir,* published in Padang.

Malayan Muslims joined forces with the conservative traditional leadership of the Chinese and Indian communities, in opposition to radical Chinese elements who were influenced by Communism. In Indonesia, Muhammadiyya and Sarekat Islam were established in 1912, the former having *Salafiyya* overtones of a need to purify Islam; the latter being an organization for traders and businessmen, later developing into a nationalistic, anti-Dutch organization. The Nahdatul Ulema, formed in 1926, was an organization representing conservative *ulema.* Regardless of their particular interpretation of Islam, and their political leanings, all of the organizations were Muslim in character and arose in response to the historical circumstances in the first part of the twentieth century.

Hadramis were politically active in the diaspora during these years, but the general trend saw them join national movements that emphasized their Muslim identity rather than their identity as Arabs. Many actually left the areas they had migrated to because of anti-Arab, anti-foreign sentiments. Those who stayed behind became increasingly assimilated, and identified with nationalistic sentiment in their new home countries. The mid twentieth century is thus the starting point for a new distancing between diasporic Hadramis and the homeland. The lack of economic development in Hadramaut, due to the rule of conservative sultans, was a factor. For a short period, the growth of Aden as a global city allowed many Hadramis to continue to carry out trade in their homeland, regardless of conditions in Hadramaut itself. But this was short-lived. The British left in 1967, and the Quaity and Kathiri sultanates quickly became part of the People's Democratic Republic of Yemen. When the new state opted to ally itself with the communist East Bloc, diaspora-homeland relationships were further weakened.

Between nation state and empire

The will for political nationalism was soon counteracted by yet another turn in the process of economic globalization. In the second half of the twentieth century the greater geographical mobility of capital, combined with a crisis of Fordist (Keynesian) mass production led to flexible specialization. Legal constraints on production were being bypassed by the proliferation of personal and family entrepreneurial economic activity. According to Arrighi (1999), we are again seeing a new systemic cycle of accumulation. Some speak of the end of organized capitalism (Lash and Urry 1987) and the emergence of disorganized capitalism, i.e., precisely the functional de-concentration and decentralization of corporate powers earlier referred to. David Harvey (1989) calls this a period of flexible accumulation.

The main elements of this development can be sketched as follows. In terms of hegemonic power, the twentieth century is of course characterized by the rise of the United States as a new hegemonic power after the United Kingdom. Two world wars and economic recession periods which helped destroy the gold standard on which British financial dominance was built helped bring the United States to its dominant position. The regime of accumulation shifted to one in which multinational companies dominated world markets. In Britain, spinning, weaving, finishing, and marketing were handled by different companies. The U.S. model brought these different components of production together in vertically integrated units, whereas the British used "flexible specialization." The United States, as did West Germany, learned this lesson during the Great Depression of 1873–1896.

The world had moved from colonial rule to independent nation states, with organizations such as the United Nations acting as fora in which such nation states could supposedly work out their differences, rather than reverting to armed conflict. But the nation state also became the main vehicle for development of a world economy, although the United States dominated here as well. The Bretton Woods institutions, the International Monetary Fund, and the World Bank are as much instruments of U.S. hegemony as they are mediators between independent nation states. World money was now a part of state-building.

The development of a U.S. market after the American Civil War helped secure a strong national economy, partly through protectionist policies, but it did not develop a global, U.S.-driven world economy. This is where the multilateral financial institutions became important agents for U.S. interests. It was corporate capital that conquered the world, not finance capital. But once success was assured, foreign markets proved to be limited. The rebuilding of western Europe (through the Marshall Plan) and Japan, in response to Soviet power, became the answer to this problem. As well, there was increased and sustained U.S. military expenditure abroad, after the Korean War until the end of the Vietnam War in 1973. This all created a long period of sustained growth in the world economy.

Technological developments have continued, with oil bringing Arab countries back into the global picture as oil producers, but also as victims of that position within the current *Pax Americana*. The use of oil has led to further developments in transportation, with air traffic as the most significant example. The more recent revolution in information technology, enabling the decentralization of production processes, with access to finance capital as a key resource is also part of this.

The cycle ended, however, when an international recession was brought on by rising oil prices set in the 1970s. Surplus capital was in private hands, and national governments manipulated currency rates to attract it. At the same time, fluctuating national currencies invited financial speculation. The result might seem like a global financial revolution, but it was not entirely new. Rather, it represented a return to the historical phase of finance capitalism that has occurred after each period of capitalist expansion. Regardless of its larger scale, scope and technical sophistication, it was a continuation of a *longue durée* tendency dating back to the time when Italian city states dominated the world economy. The trend saw ever stronger blocks of governmental and business organizations acting as the lead agencies for international capital accumulation.

What the crisis of the early 1970s marked was thus the decline of the US hegemony. It also signaled the contradiction of the global capitalist system. The dominance of US capital in international markets dating from the 1950s led to the establishment of the Euro-currency market into which US money also started to flow. This accumulated effects of this created a financial market beyond the control of any nation state or any of the Bretton Woods institutions. It also created European competition for the American multinational corporations.

At the same time, in the early 1970s, the world price of oil exploded. This increased available capital, but much of it was spent on financial speculation rather than productive investments. The focus on increased purchasing power in the world economy, rather than investment in trade and production, created a crisis. But the crisis was not without its precedents. A preoccupation with finance capital and high tolerance for rising debt loads, the deregulation of the economy, "flexible specialization," and "informalization" had all occurred in Edwardian Britain, Periwig Holland, and Genoese Spain as well (Arrighi 1999: 314).

Attempts by national governments to control their economies led to capital flight. Those with investment dollars sought new, more profitable places for their capital, which again increased the possibility of second and third world states pursuing their own economic strategies. But the U.S. policies also changed, further marginalizing the position of the Third World countries. Easily borrowed money in the 1970s became heavy debt burdens in the 1980s and 1990s. But some regional economies did recover, and new economic giants emerged in Asia, including Japan, Hong Kong, Taiwan, Korea, Singapore, Malaysia, and Indonesia. This happened through both industrialization as well as these countries' positions in the ongoing financial expansion.

The growing status of East Asian nations as the center of international business implied that the nation that controls military power no longer controls surplus capital. These tendencies are not conducive to the maintenance of a single dominant world power and produce increased instability.

The role of the diaspora

It is at this point that we return to the Hadrami diaspora. In chapter three we saw how Osama bin Laden can be seen as a reaction to the global developments outlined above, and as such he assumes a role that earlier Hadramis have also had. Similarly, al-Qaida as an organization may be considered a new phenomenon but, again, individual Hadramis headed up resistance movements in earlier times as well. *Madrasas*, mosques, and sufi brotherhoods have all acted as focal points in such developments. In such a context, Osama is only a recent example of a long history of resistance that originated in the diaspora and of which several Hadramis have played important roles.

The list can be made longer. Historically, Abdel Rahman b. Muhammad al-Zahir was involved in anti-colonial resistance in Acheh against the Dutch (Reid 1967, Ho 2004), and Zein al-Din al-Malibari opposed the Portuguese along the Malabar coast of India (Ho ibid.). Earlier in this chapter we saw that centuries later, Sayyid Fadl (1836–1921) did the same against the British also on the Malabar coast (Dale 1997). For contemporary examples, the Indonesian Islamist leader convicted in connection with the Bali bombings, Abu Bakar Ba'asyir, is of Hadrami descent. And, given the way networks have been organized throughout the Southeast Asian region (see Abuza 2003)—including the Jamaah Islamiya and Mujahidin Council of Indonesia—it would be surprising if more Hadramis were not involved.

In Hyderabad as well, there are indications of Hadrami involvement in anti-state activities. *The Times of India* reported on 13 July 2004 that a certain Abdul Rahman Aidrus, father of Habeeb Hasan, had demanded a probe into the killing of his son in Mumbai (Bombay). Habeeb was accused of being involved in two bombings carried out on 25 August of that year. In a press conference in Barkas, the father demanded that the authorities reveal what evidence they had to call his son a terrorist. And he had another explanation for his son's presence in Mumbai on the day of the bombing: Habeeb had gone to Mumbai to get a Yemeni visa for his sister so she could join her husband there. In the same newspaper it was also reported that the alleged mastermind of the Mumbai operations, Adul Aydeet (alias Naseer), was known to have frequented Hyderabad. He was born in Mumbai of a Yemeni father and a mother who came from Hyderabad. He therefore often visited his relatives in Barkas, the paper said. But what some saw as family visits, others claimed were meetings at which the bombings were planned.

Diaspora and Empire in the long durée

What we see from the above section is that the relationship between Hadramis and various colonial, imperial, and nation-state authorities goes back a long way, and that there are earlier precedents for contemporary political events. We have seen that the Hadrami diaspora developed in specific ways, with associations and organizations that were partly Hadrami, Yemeni, and Arab, as well as Muslim, in character. As such, Hadramis among their own community and in the wider population have played important roles throughout the diaspora.

The religious dimensions of this diaspora are crucial, in that the early Hadramis were central in the very processes of Islamization that have come to characterize many of these regions. The universalizing mission encouraged people to spread into ever new areas, both for reasons of trade and to spread the faith. When people adopted Islam, they became part of a tradition that was not only religious but which also contained political, social, and economic institutions that forged links between Hadramis and local populations. Drawing on Ellen Meiksins Woods (2003) Hadramis were part of an "Empire of Commerce" established by the Arabs. Islam was the main organizational vehicle of an empire that competed for trade with Venice and Florence, and was later superseded by other Muslim forces like the Mughals and the Ottomans, and still later, by the European powers. While new political centers and state formations emerged, the original networks of traders continues until today.

The focus in this chapter is on resistance, and how some of these discourses of resistance have led to concrete political action, some of which have been violent. In contrast to the drama represented above, which could easily lead to references to a "clash of civilizations," it should be noted that the vast majority of Hadramis live uneventful, "normal" lives. The Hadramis encountered in Singapore are a good example of this. We saw in chapter one how their lives were shaped by the establishment of Singapore as a global city, a financial center for world capital and with ambitions of creating the most technologically advanced of economies. As Hadramis are part of this, they are also close to the globalizing forces of the contemporary southeast Asian world. Hadramis in Singapore have entered the globalization debate through the specific, southeast Asian experience.

After three decades as an "economic miracle," insular southeast Asia (Malaysia, Indonesia, Singapore) was hit by a deep recession in 1997. Three years later there were signs of economic recovery, and parts of the region are going through restructuring and transformations in both economic and sociopolitical fields—transformations that seem to have produced economic recovery, at least in Malaysia and Singapore. Keeping in mind the continued problems

in the Indonesian economy, this period of southeast Asian history is a success story in terms of overall economic development, although the adverse
effects of increased inequity, labor exploitation, environmental degradation,
and violations against minority groups have also been significant.

The political reactions to these adverse effects of the economic boom were
profound. Suharto's thirty-two-year rule of Indonesia finally came to an end
in May 1998, and the country carried out its first free election in forty-four
years in June 1999. In Malaysia we have seen a dramatic political struggle
among the political elite, culminating with the dismissal and prosecution of
the deputy prime minister, Anwar Ibrahim. The implications of this move
are still unclear, but the situation following this political showdown has high-
lighted discussions on the role of Islam and political reform in the country. In
both Indonesia and Malaysia we see tension between a political center trying
to balance a complex ethnic and religious situation in the two countries, and
regional powers advocating Islamic rule and the introduction of sharia. Finally, Singapore was also hit by the economic crisis but to a lesser extent than
its neighbors, and the political situation there seems less turbulent.

Osama Bin Laden and al-Qaida aside, Hadrami entrepreneurs, as a historical case, are especially interesting. They did not promote a Western-style, capitalist development but couched their commercial activities in the language
of Islam. Because of this, there were different social consequences compared
to the experience of other entrepreneurial groups. The early importance of
Hadramis in the regional economy is connected to their involvement in the
establishment of early trading states in the coastal areas of the Malay world.
This involvement developed into commercial interests in shipping between
the islands of Indonesia, to and from Singapore and also in the pilgrimage
traffic to Jeddah and Mecca. Early involvement in the East Indonesian spice
trade was later transformed into Hadrami involvement in money lending, the
supply of plantation labor, urban estate developments in Singapore and Batavia (Jakarta), and in the establishment of newspapers and printing houses.
Arabs also entered the important batik sector, in competition with the Chinese, thus also engaging themselves in the manufacturing sector.

Hadramis were central agents in global exchanges that facilitated commercialization and organizational change in local economies. At the same time,
they also affected the "moral economies" in their areas of operation. Families
of entrepreneurs have supplied important Islamic scholars and teachers, influencing the region far beyond a purely economic impact. Hadramis became
important agents for the Islamization of the region. They appeared on the
scene as teachers, judges, and advisors, not only among commoners, but were
also close to the founders and rulers of various sultanates. In the early twentieth century they were involved in the pan-Islamic movement, calling upon
the Ottoman Empire to protect their rights, sending youth to Istanbul for ed-

ucation and establishing contacts with Islamic presses in Istanbul, Cairo, and Beirut. These developments helped make Hadramis forerunners of the Islamic reformist movement in Southeast Asia at the turn of the twentieth century, a process that also, interestingly, facilitated the development of incipient na-tionalist movements, especially Sarekat Islam. Through the establishment of schools, involvement in printing houses, dissemination of literature both in Arabic and in Malay, and as imams in mosques, Hadramis play a major role in social and political movements at the turn of the century.

Similar processes are at work in contemporary southeast Asia. Hadrami Arabs engage with other Muslim groups, particularly among the large Malay population. Hadrami mosques are still central fora where people come for ad-vice and help. The mosques are sites for the negotiation of such varied issues as marriage, relations between in-laws, food regulations, religious conversions, and anxieties about the perceived secularization of society. But the mosques are also sites that reveal contemporary relationships between Hadramis and various power holders in the region. The influence of Hadrami religious fig-ures is evident in a report about the Masjid Ba'alewi, the Hadrami mosque in Lewis Street, carried in the Singaporean magazine *Al-Mahjar* in 2001:

> Heads of State of the ASEAN Nations and their Foreign Ministers visited Sin-gapore for the Four-Day ASEAN Informal Meeting which ended on the 26 th November 2000. A truly informal kind of summit took place during the ASEAN Informal Summit on Friday 24 November 2000. The congregation at Singapore's Ba'alewi Mosque has the honour of joining a number of ASEAN dignitaries for Friday prayers. Dignitaries present included Dr. Mahathir Mo-hammad, Prime Minister of Malaysia and Syed Hamid Albar, his foreign min-ister together with Prince Mohamed Bolkiah of Brunei Darussalam, Dr. Alwi Shahab of Indonesia and Dr. Surin Pitsuwan of Thailand. Syed Hassan bin Mu-hamad Alattas led the Friday Prayer. In addition to his normal Friday invoca-tions, in his closing *do'a*, Syed Hassan asked for Allah's blessing for Muslims in the region and their leaders. Datuk Hamid Albar and Dr. Alwi Shahab stayed for lunch at the invitation of Syed Hassan Alatas, the Imam of Ba'alwi Mosque and met local Arabs who regularly attended the Friday prayers and see it as an opportunity to fulfil their *silatulrahim*. (*Al-Mahjar*, 2001: 9)

Clearly, what such an example shows is that we need to overcome the sim-plistic dichotomies that project fundamental distinctions between "modern" and "traditional," "rational" and "pre-rational," and "monetary" and "pre-monetary" worlds. In southeast Asia, as well as in other regions, the presence of entrepreneurial groups and extensive labor and commodity markets long predates the coming of so-called modernity. The present developments should therefore be seen in the context of a historical continuity. The present-day globalization is in fact only a recent, though intensified, phase in longstand-ing relations of global interchange. The question is thus not so much whether or not southeast Asia has "become modern," but how present-day forms of global interchange differ from former means and modes of interregional engagements. The Bin Laden case shows that such global interchanges can lead to violent reactions and to processes not characterized by accommodation but by a "clash of civilizations."

Whatever can be said about these stories, one conclusion is that the simple stance taken by various modernization theorists, more or less assuming Western-like transformations leading to a universal spread of *homo economicus*, will not take us far. To stay with the case of southeast Asia, we need a higher level of empirical precision, in which we can document how the economic field is embedded in various regional and local socio-cultural contexts. Rather than assuming a continuous "dis-embedding" of the economy from the social field, we see a "re-embedding" of social life within new politico-economic regimes. The forms of capitalism that have emerged are deeply dependent on regional and local organizational forms, cultural meanings, and moralities, and the forging of new links between the economic and sociopolitical fields should be studied, taking such factors into consideration. Islam is an important basis for these conditions in southeast Asia, and Hadramis, although not alone, are important providers of premises that help define the ways local people interpret their new realities.

The image of a monolithic capitalism thus has to be deconstructed in favor of models that recognize the variable articulation of capitalist institutions with, among others, cultural meaning, religious ideologies, kinship, gender systems, and the state. Rather than passively submitting to the macro forces at work, individuals and communities engage in order to evade, resist, or transform the contexts in which they are placed. It is important to acknowledge that such engagements within the overall globalizing context are integral to the shaping of the region's political economy.

❋ Bibliography

Abaza, Mona. 1997. "A Mosque of Arab Origin in Singapore: History, Functions and Networks." *Archipel* 53.

Abdi Sheikh-Abdi. 1993. *Divine Madness: Mohammed Abdulle Hassan (1856–1920)*. London: Zed Books.

Abir, Mordechai. 1965. "The Emergence and Consolidation of the Monarchies of Enarea and Jimma in the First Half of the Nineteenth Century." *Journal of African History* VI (2).

———. 1965. "Brokerage and Brokers in Ethiopia in the First Half of the 19th Century." *Journal for Ethiopian Studies* III (1).

———. 1968. "Caravan Trade and History in the Northern Parts of East Africa." *Paideuma* XIV.

———. 1970. "Southern Ethiopia," in *Pre-colonial African Trade: Essays on Trade in Central and Eastern Africa before 1900*. Eds. R. Gray and D. Birmingham. London: Oxford University Press.

Abrahams, Philip. 1982. *Historical Sociology*. Ithaca: Cornell University Press.

Abu Lughod, Janet. *Before European Hegemony: The World System AD 1250–1350*. New York: Oxford University Press.

Abuza, Zachary. 2003. *Militant Islam in Southeast Asia: Crucible of Terror*. Boulder, Col.: Rienner

Al Hassan, Ahmad Y. and Donald R. Hill, 1986. *Islamic Technology: An Illustrated History*. Cambridge: Cambridge University Press.

Alatas, Syed Farid. 1997. "Hadhramaut and the Hadhramaut Diaspora: Problems in Theoretical History." in *Hadhrami Traders, Scholars and Statesmen in the Indian Ocean, 1750s–1960s*. Eds. U. Freitag and W.G. Clarence-Smith. Leiden: Brill.

Algadri, Hamid. 1994. *Dutch Policy Against Islam and Indonesians of Arab Decent in Indonesia*. Jakarta: Pustaka LP3ES

Alikhan, Raza. 1990. *Hyderabad 400 Years (1591–1991)*. Hyderabad: Zenith Services.

Aljuneid, 1996. *The Spice of Life That is Aljuneid*. Singapore: Dominie Press.

Alkaff, Alwee. 1982. *Pioneers of Singapore*, A 000124/24/04–reel 01. National Library of Singapore.

Al-Mahjar, 1997. *Al-Mahjar* 2, no. 1.

Al-Mahjar, 1998. *Al-Mahjar* 3, no. 2.

Al-Mahjar, 2001. *Al-Mahjar* 6, no. 1.

Al-Qaddal, Muhamed Saeed. 1997. *Al-Shaykh al-Qaddal Pasha*. Aden: Aden University Press.

Alpers, Edward. 1983. "Futa Benaadir: Continuity and Change in the Traditional Cotton Textile Industry of Southern Somalia, c. 1840–1980." In: Laboratoire Connaissance du Tiers-Monde (ed), *Enterprises et Entrepreneurs en Afrique XIX et XX*. Paris:L'Harmattan, 77–98.

Alsagoff, Syed Mohsen. 1963. *The Alsagoff Family in Malaysia AH 1240 (AD 1824) to AH 1382 (AD 1962)*. Singapore: Mun Seong Press.

Anderson, Benedict. 1991. *Imagined Communities: Reflections on the Origin and Spread of Nationalism*. London: Verso.

———. 1998. *The Spectre of Comparison: Nationalism, Southeast Asia and the World*. New York: Verso.

Anthias, Floya. 1998. "Evaluating 'Diaspora': Beyond Ethnicity?" *Sociology* 32, no. 3: 557–80.

Antoun, Richard. 1989. *Muslim Preachers in the Modern World: A Jordanian Case Study in Comparative Perspective*. Princeton: Princeton University Press.

Anwar Ibrahim, 1996. *An Asian Renaissance*. Kuala Lumpur: Times International.

Appadurai, Arjun. 1990. "Disjuncture and Difference in the Global Cultural Economy." in *Global Culture: Nationalism, Globalisation and Modernity*. Ed. M. Featherstone. London: Sage.

———. 1996. *Modernity At Large: Cultural Dimensions of Globalisation*. Minneapolis: University of Minnesota Press.

———, ed. 2001. *Globalization*. Durham, NC: Duke University Press.

Arai, Kazuhiro. 2004. "Arabs Who Traversed the Indian Ocean: The History of the Al-'Attas Family in Hadramawt and Southeast Asia, c. 1600–c. 1960." PhD diss., University of Michigan.

Arrighi, Giovanni. 1999. *The Long Twentieth Century: Money, Power, and the Origin of Our Times*. London: Verso.

———, 2005. "Hegemony Unravelling I & II." *New Left Review* 32 and 33.

Asad, Talal. 1986. "The Idea of an Anthropology of Islam." *Centre for Contemporary Arab Studies*, Occasional papers series. Washington: Georgetown University.

———. 1993. *Genealogies of Religion: Discipline and Reasons of Power in Christianity and Islam*. Baltimore: John Hopkins University Press.

———. 2003. *Formations of the Secular: Chrisitianity, Islam, Modernity*. Stanford: Stanford University Press.

Ashenden, Sangatha, and David Owen, eds. 1999. *Foucault Contra Habermas*. London: Sage.

———. 1999. "Questions of Criticism: Habermas and Foucault on Civil Society and Resistance." in *Foucault Contra Habermas*. Eds. S. Ashenden and D. Owen. London: Sage.

Asiaweek. 1992. July 31, 1992. A Question of Identity. (section on "controversies")

Astuti, Rita. 1995. *People of the Sea: Identity and Descent among the Vezo of Madagascar*. Cambridge: Cambridge University Press.

Austin, Ian. 1992. *City of Legends: The Story of Hyderabad*. Delhi: Viking Penguin, India.

Axel, Brian Keith. 2002. *From the Margins: Historical Anthropology and Its Futures*. Durham, NC: Duke University Press.

Ayubi, N.N., 1995. "Rethinking the Public/Private Dichotomy: Radical Islamism and Civil Society in the Middle East."*Contention* 4, no. 3: 79–105.

Azra, Azyumardi. 2000. "Hadramis as Educators: Al-Habib Sayyid Idrus ibn Salim al-Jufri (1889–1969) and al-Khairat." *KULTUR* 1, no.1: 91–104.

Baali, Fuad. 1988. *Society, State and Urbanism: Ibn Khaldun's Sociological Thought*. Albany: State University of New York Press.

Bafana, Harasha. 1997. "The Singapore Arabs of Today: Living in the Past." *Al-Mahjar* 2, no. 1.

Bahru, Zewde. 2002. *A History of Modern Ethiopia, 1855 – 1991*. Oxford/Athens, Ohio: James Currey/Ohio University Press

Bajunied, Omar Farouk. 1997, 1998, 1999. "Arabs and the Nation State in Southeast Asia." *Al-Mahjar* 2 (nos. 1 and 2); 3 (nos. 1 and 2); 4 (nos. 1 and 2).

Bamyeh, Mohammed A. 1999. *The Social Origin of Islam: Mind, Economy, Discourse*. Minneapolis: University of Minnesota Press.

Bang, Anne Kathrine. 2003. *Sufis and Scholars of the Sea: Family Networks in East Africa, 1860–1925*. London: Routledge Curzon.

Bangstad, Sindre. 2006. Diasporic Consciousness as a Strategic Resource: A Case-Study from a Cape Muslim Community. in *Diasporas Within and Without Africa: Dynamism, Hetereogeneity, Variation*. Eds. L. Manger and M. A. Assal. Uppsala: The Nordic Africa Institute.

Baosman, Osman. n.d. *Hindustan me Arabon ki aamad*. Hyderabad: Aajaz Press.

Barendse, Rene J. 2000. "Trade and State in the Arabian Seas: A Survey from the Fifteenth to the Eighteenth Century." *Journal of World History* 11, no. 2: 173–225.

Barth, Fredrik. 1969. *Ethnic Groups and Boundaries*. Oslo: Norwegian University Press.

———. 1983. *Sohar: Culture and Society in an Omani Town*. Baltimore: John Hopkins University Press.

———. 1984. "Problems of Conceptualizing Cultural Pluralism, With Illustrations from Sohar, Oman." in *The Prospects for Plural Societies*. Eds. S. Plattner and D. Maybury-Lewis. Washington: 1982 Proceedings of the American Ethnological Society.

———. 1987. *Cosmologies in the Making. A Generative Approach to Cultural Variation in Inner New Guinea*. Cambridge: Cambridge University Press.

———. 1989. "The Analysis of Culture in Complex Societies." *Ethnos* 54, nos. I–II.

———. 1990. "The Guru and the Conjurer: Transactions in Knowledge and the Shaping of Culture in Southeast Asia and Melanesia." *Man* 25.

———. 1992. "Towards a Greater Naturalism in Conceptualising Societies." in *Conceptualizing Society*. Ed. A. Kuper. London: Routledge.

———. 1993. *Balinese Worlds*. Chicago: University of Chicago Press.

———. 1994a. "A Personal View of Present Tasks and Priorities in Cultural and Social Anthropology." in *Assessing Cultural Anthropology*. Ed. R. Borofsky. New York: McGraw.

———. 1994b. "Nye og evige temaer i studiet av etnisitet." in *Manifestasjon og prosess*. Oslo: Universitetsforlaget.

———. 1999. "Comparative Methodologies in the Analysis of Anthropological Data." in *Critical Comparisons in Politics and Culture*. Ed. J. Bowen and R. Petersen. Cambridge: Cambridge University Press.

———. 2000. "Boundaries and Connections." in *Signifying Identities: Anthropological Perspectives on Boundaries and Contested Values*. Ed. A.P. Cohen. London: Routledge.

———. 2002. "An Anthropology of Knowledge." *Current Anthropology* 2, no. 1.

Bawa, Vasant Kumar. 1992. *The Last Nizam: The Life and Times of Mir Osman Ali Khan*. Delhi: Viking Penguin, India.

Baxter, Peter T.W. 1969. "Acceptance and Rejection of Islam among the Boran of the Northern Frontier District of Kenya." in *Islam in Tropical Africa*. Ed. I.M. Lewis. London: IAI.

Bayly, Christhopher A. 1983. *Townsmen and Bazaars: North Indian Society in the Age of British Expansion, 1770–1870*. Cambridge: Cambridge University Press.

———. 1989. *Imperial Meridian: The British Empire and the World, 1780–1830*. London: Longman.

Bayly, Susan. 1989. *Saints, Goddesses and Kings: Muslims and Christian in South Indian Society, 1700–1900*. Cambridge: Cambridge University Press.

Beals, Alan R. 1955. "Interplay Among Factors of Change in a Mysore Village." in *Village India*. Ed. M. Marriot. Chicago: University of Chicago Press.

Beeston, Alfred Felix Langdon. 1937. *Sabaean Inscriptions*. Oxford: Oxford University Press.

———. 1972. "Kingship in Ancient South Arabia." *Journal of Economic and Social History of the Orient* xv: 1–3.

———. 1984. *Sabean Grammar*. Manchester: *Manchester Journal of Semitic Studies*, monograph no. 6.

Bender, John, and David E. Wellbery. eds. 1991. *Chronotypes: The Construction of Time*. Stanford: Stanford University Press.

Bentley, Jerry H. 1993. *Old World Encounters: Cross-Cultural Contacts and Exchanges in Pre-Modern Times*. New York: Oxford University Press.

Bezabeh, Samson A. 2004. *Yemenis in Dire Dawa, Eastern Ethiopia: A Study in Migration and Identity*. MA-thesis, Department of Sociology and Social Anthropology, Addis Ababa University.

———. 2008. *Among People With History. Yemni Diaspora and Ethiopian State Interaction in Historical Perspective*. M.Phil-thesis, Department of Social Anthropology, University of Bergen.

Birch, David. 1999. "Reading State: Communication as Public Culture." in *Reading Culture: Textual Practices in Singapore*. Ed. P.G.G. Chew and A. Kramer-Dahl. Singapore:Times Academic Press.

Bloch, Maurice. 1992. "What Goes Without Saying: The Conceptualization of Zafimaniry Society." in *Conceptualizing Society*. Ed. A. Kuper. London: Routledge.

———. 1998. *How We Think They Think: Anthropological Approaches to Cognition, Memory, and Literacy*. Boulder, CO: Westview Press.

———. and Perry. Jonathan. 1989. *Money and the Morality of Exchange*. Cambridge: Cambridge University Press.

Blom Hansen, Thomas. 1997. "The Saffron Wave." PhD diss., Roskilde University.

———. 1998. *The Saffron Wave: Democracy and Hindu Nationalism in Modern India*. Princeton: Princeton University Press.

Bluhm, Jutta E. 1983. "A Preliminary Statement on the Dialogue Established Between the Reform Magazine *Al-Manar* and the Malyo-Indonesian World." *Indonesian Circle*, 32: 35–42.

Bodansky, Yossef. 1999. *Bin Laden: The Man who Declared War on America*. Roseville, CA: Forum.

Boddy, Janice. 1989. *Wombs and Alien Spirits: Women, Men and the Zar Cult in Northern Sudan*. Madison: University of Wisconsin Press.

Bose, Sugata. 2006. *A Hundred Horizons: The Indian Ocean in the Age of the Global Empire*. Cambridge, Mass.: Harvard University Press.

Bourdieu, Pierre. 1977. *Outline of a Theory of Practice*. Cambridge: Cambridge University Press.

———. 1982. "The Economics of Linguistic Exchanges." *Social Science Information* 16, no. 6: 645–68.

———. 1986. "The Forms of Capital". in *Handbook of Theory and Research for the Sociology of Education*. Ed. John G. Richards. Santa Barbara: Greenwood Press.

Boustead, Hugh. 1971. *The Wind of Morning: The Autobiography of Hugh Boustead*. London: Chatto and Windus.

Bowen, John. 2002. "Islam in/of France: Dilemmas of Translocality." Accessed at http://www.cari–sciences–po.org.

———. and Richard Petersen eds. 1999. *Critical Comparisons in Politics and Culture*. Cambridge: Cambridge University Press.

Brah, Avtar. 1996. *Cartographies of Diaspora: Contesting Identities*. London: Routledge.

Braukamper, Ulrich. 2002. *Islamic History and Culture in Southern Ethiopia*. Hamburg: LIT Verlag.

Brenner, Suzanne. 1998: *The Domestication of Desire. Women, Wealth, and Modernity in Java*. Princeton: Princeton University Press.

Brubaker, Roger. 2004. *Ethnicity Without Groups*. Cambridge, MA: Harvard University Press.

Bruner, Jerome. 1990. *Acts of Meaning*. Cambrdige. MA: Harvard University Press.

Bujra, Abdalla. 1967. "Political Conflict and Stratification in Hadramaut, I and II." *Middle Eastern Studies*. 3, no. 4 and 4, no.1.

———. 1970. "Urban Elites and Colonialsm: The Nationalist Elite of Aden and South Arabia." *Middle Eastern Studies* 6:189–211.

———. 1971. *The Politics of Stratification: A Study of political Change in a South Arabian Town*. Oxford: Clarendon Press.

———. 1987. *Conceptualizing the Indian Ocean Programme: The Historical and Contemporary Socio-Economic Role of the Hadramis (from South Yemen) in the Indian Ocean, Preliminary Reflections*. Bergen: Centre for Development Studies/The Chr. Michelsens Institute.

Burckhardt, Johann Ludwig. 1822/1978. *Travels in Nubia*. London: Murray.

Burke, Peter. 1992. *History and Social Theory*. Cambridge: Polity Press.

Burton, Richard Francis. 1894. *First Footsteps in East Africa or, An Exploration of Harar*. London: Tylston and Edwards.

Busawoy, Michael. et.al. 2000. *Global Ethnography: Forces, Connections and Imaginations of a Post-Modern World*. Berkeley: University of California Press.

Butt, Helen B. 1990. *The Composite Nature of Hyderabadi Culture*. Hyderabad: Inter-cultural Cooperation, Hyderabad Chapter and Osmania University.

Calhoun, Craig. 2002. "Imagining Solidarity: Cosmopolitanism, Constitutional Pa-triotism, and the Public Sphere." in *Toward New Imaginaries* (*Public Culture* 14, no.1). Eds. D.P.. Gaonkar and B. Lee. Durham, NC: Duke University Press.

Camelin, Sylvain. 1997. "Reflections on the System of Social Stratification in Hadh-ramaut." in *Hadhrami Traders, Scholars and Statesmen in the Indian Ocean, 1750s–1960s*. Ed. U. Freitag and W.G. Clarence-Smith. Leiden: Brill.

Cantwell Smith, Wilfred. 1950. "Hyderabad: Muslim Tragedy." *Middle East Journal*, no. 4.

Carapico, Sheila. 1998. *Civil Society in Yemen: The Political Economy of Activism in Modern Arabia*. Cambridge: Cambridge University Press.

Carr, David. 1974. *Phenomenology and the Problem of History: A Study of Husserl's Transcendental Philosophy*. Evanston: Northwestern University Press.

Carrithers, Michael. 1992. *Why Humans Have Cultures: Explaining Anthropology and Social Diversity*. Oxford: Oxford University Press.

Cassanelli, Lee. 1982. *The Shaping of Somali Society: Reconstructing the History of a Pastoral People, 1600–1900*. Philadelphia: University of Pennsylvania Press.

Castells, Manuel. 1996. *The Rise of the Network Society, Vol. I–The Information Age: Economy, Society and Culture*. Oxford: Blackwell.

———. 1997. *The Power of Identity, Vol. II–The Information Age: Economy, Society and Culture*. Oxford: Blackwell.

———. 1997. *The End of the Millennium, Vol. III–The Information Age: Economy, Society and Culture*. Oxford: Blackwell.

Castoriadis, Cornelius. 1987. *The Imaginary Institution of Society*. Cambridge: MIT Press.

Census of India. 1981. *Special Report on Hyderabad City*. Part XE, Series 2. Hyderabad: Directorate of Census Operations.

Chatterjee, Partha. 1999. "On Religious and Linguistic Nationalisms: The Second Partition of Bengal." in *Nation and Religion: Perspectives on Europe and Asia*. Eds. P. van der Veer, and H. Lehmann. Princeton: Princeton University Press.

Chartier, Roger. 1988. *Cultural History: Between History and Representations*. Cam-bridge: Polity Press.

Chaudhuri, Kirti Narayan. 1985. *Trade and Civilization in the Indian Ocean: An Economic History From the Rise of Islam to 1750*. Cambridge: Cambridge University Press.

———. 1991. *Asia Before Europe: Economy and Civilization of the Indian Ocean from the Rise of Islam to 1750*. Cambridge: Cambridge University Press.

Che Man, W.K. 1991. "The Administration of Islamic Institutions in Non-Muslim States: The Case of Singapore and Thailand." *Teaching and Research Exchange Fel-lowships Report No. 10*.

Chiew Sen Kong. 1985. "The Socio-Cultural Framework of Politics." in *Understand-ing Singapore Society*. Ed. Ong Jun Hui, Tong Chee Kiong and Tan Ern Ser. Singa-pore: Times Academic Press.

Clarence-Smith, William G. 1997. "Hadhrami Entrepreneurs in the Malay World, c. 1750 to c. 1940." in *Hadhrami Traders, Scholars and Statesmen in the Indian Ocean, 1750s–1960s*. Eds. U. Freitag and W.G. Clarence-Smith. Leiden: Brill.

Clark, Hugh R. 1995. "Muslims and Hindus in the Culture and Morphology of Quanzhou from the Tenth to the Thirteenth Century." *Journal of World History* 6, no. 1.

Clifford, James. 1988. *The Predicament of Culture: Twentieth-Century Ethnography, Literature, and Art*. Cambridge, MA: Harvard University Press.

———. 1994. "Diaspora." *Cultural Anthropology*. 9, no. 3.

———. 1998. *Routes: Travels and Translation in the Late 20th Century*. Cambridge, MA: Harvard University Press.

Cohen, Anthony. 1994. *Self Consciousness: An Alternative Anthropology of Identity*. London: Routledge.

———, ed. 2000. *Signifying Identities: Anthropological Perspectives on Boundaries and Contested Values*. London: Routledge.

———. 2000. "Introduction: Discriminating Relations—Identity, Boundary and Authenticity. in *Signifying Identities: Anthropological Perspectives on Boundaries and Contested Values*. Ed. A. Cohen. London: Routledge.

Cohen, Robin. 1997. *Global Diasporas, An Introduction*. London: University College London Press.

Cole, Jennifer and Deborah Durham. 2007. "Introduction: Age, Regeneration, and the Intimate Politics of Globalization". in *Generations and Globalization. Youth, Age, and Family in the New World Economy*. Eds. J. Cole and D. Durham. Bloomington: Indiana University Press

Collins, Randall. 1999. *Macrohistory: Essays in the Sociology on the Long Run*. Stanford: Stanford University Press.

Collins, Randall. 2000. *The Sociology of Philosophies: A Global Theory of Intellectual Change*. Cambridge MA: Harvard University Press.

Comaroff, Jean. 1985. *Body of Power, Spirit of Resistance: The Culture and History of a South African People*. Chicago: University of Chicago Press.

Comaroff, John and Jean Comaroff. 1992. *Ethnography and the Historical Imagination*. Boulder, CO: Westview.

———. 1991 and 1997. *Of Revelation and Revolution*; vol. I, *Christianity, Colonialism and Consciousness in South Africa* and vol. II, *The Dialectics of Modernity on a South African Frontier*. Chicago: University of Chicago Press.

Connerton, Paul. 1989. *How Societies Remember*. Cambridge: Cambridge University Press.

Cooper, Fredrick and Anne L. Stoller, eds. 1997. *Tensions of Empire: Colonial Cultures in a Bourgeoise World*. Berkeley: University of California Press.

Crone, Patricia. 1987. *Meccan Trade and the Rise of Islam*. Princeton: Princeton University Press.

Curtin, Philip. 1984. *Cross-Cultural Trade in World History*. Cambridge: Cambridge University Press.

———. 2000. *The World and the West: The European Challange and the Overseas Response in the Age of Empire*. Cambridge: Cambridge University Press.

Dale, Stephen F. 1980. *Islamic Society on the South Asian Frontier: The Mappilas of Malabar 1498–1922*. Oxford: Clarendon Press.

———. 1997. "The Hadrami Diaspora in South-Western India. The role of the sayyids of the Malabar coast." in *Hadrami Traders, Scholars and Statesmen in the Indian Ocean, 1750s–1960s*. Eds. U. Freitag and W.G. Clarence-Smith. Leiden: Brill.

Dalleo, Peter T. 1975. "Trade and Pastoralism: Economic Factors in the History of the Somali of Northeastern Kenya, 1892–1948." PhD diss., Syracuse University.

Darnton, Robert. 1984. *The Great Cat Masssacre and Other Episodes in French Cultural History*. New York: Vintage.

Das, Veena. 1995. *Critical Events: An Anthropological Perspective on Contemporary India*. Oxford: Oxford University Press.

de Jonge, Huub. 1997. "Dutch Colonial Policy Pertaining to Hadrami Immigrants." in *Hadhrami Traders, Scholars and Statesmen in the Indian Ocean, 1750s–1960s*. Eds. U. Freitag and W.G. Clarence-Smith. Leiden: Brill.

———— and Nico Kaptein, eds. 2002. *Transcending Borders. Arabs, Politics, Trade and Islam in Southeast Asia*. Leiden: KITLV Press.

de Waal, Alex, ed. 2004. *Islamism and Its Enemies in the Horn of Africa*. London: Hurst.

Dean, Mitchell. 1999. "Normalising Democracy: Foucault and Habermas on Democracy, Liberalism and Law." in *Foucault Contra Habermas*. Eds. S. Ashenden and D. Owen. London: Sage.

Deo, S.B. 1991. "Roman Trade: Recent Archaeological Discoveries in Western India." in *Rome in India: The Ancient Sea Trade*. Eds. V. Begley and R. D. de Puma (eds.), Madison: University of Wisconsin Press.

Derlugian, Georgi M. and Scott L. Greer, eds. 2000. *Questioning Geopolitics: Political Projects in a Changing World-System*. Westport: Praeger.

Devji, Feisal. 2005. *Landscapes of the Jihad: Militancy, Morality, Modernity*. London: Hurst.

————. 2008. *The Terrorist in Search of Humanity: Militant Islam and Global Politics*. New York: Columbia University Press.

Dirks, Nicholas B., Geoff Eley, and Sherry B. Ortner. 1994. "Introduction". in *Culture/Power/History. A Reader in Contemporary Social Theory*. Eds. N.B. Dirks, G. Eley and S. Ortner. Princeton: Princeton University Press.

Dirlik, Arif. 1997. *The Postcolonial Aura: Third World Criticism in the Age of Global Capitalism*. Boulder, CO: Westview Press.

————. 2000. *Postmodernity's Histories: The Past as Legacy and Project*. Lanham: Rowman & Littlefield.

Donaldson Smith, Arthur. 1897. *Through Unknown African Countries*.

Donham, Donald. 1999. *Marxist Modern: An Ethnographic History of the Ethiopian Revolution*. Berkeley: University of California Press.

————. 2000. "Thinking Temporally or Modernizing Anthropology." Unpublished paper presented at Department of Anthropology, Emory University.

Dresch, Paul. 1989. *Tribes, Government, and History in Yemen*. Oxford: Clarendon Press.

————. 2000. *A History of Modern Yemen*. Cambridge: Cambridge University Press.

Dumont, Louis. 1972. *Homo Hierarchicus: The Caste System and its Implications*. London: Paladin.

————. 1977. *From Mandeville to Marx: The Genesis and Triumph of Economic Ideology*. Chicago: University of Chicago Press.

Eaton, Richard M. 1978. *Sufis of Bijapur, 1300–1700*. Princeton: Princeton University Press.

————. 1990. *Islamic History as Global History: Essays on Global and Comparative History.* American Historical Association.

————. 2000. *Essays on Islam and Indian History.* Oxford: Oxford University Press.

Edens, Christopher. 1992. "Dynamics of Trade in the Ancient Mesopotamian 'World System'." *American Anthropologist* 94, no. 1: 118–39.

Ehret, Christopher. 1998. *An African Classical Age: Eastern and Southern Africa in World History, 1000 BC to AD 400.* Charlottesville: University of Virginia Press; Oxford: James Curry.

Eickelman, Dale and James Piscatori. 1990. *Muslim Travellers: Pilgrimage, Migration, and the Religious Imagination.* London: Routledge.

————, and Jon W. Anderson, eds. 1999. *New Media in the Muslim World: The Emerging Public Sphere.* Bloomington: Indiana University Press.

El Edroos, Syed Ahmed (with L.R. Naik), 1994. *Hyderabad of the "Seven Loaves": A Historical Account of the Asaf Jahi Dynasty with an Autobiographical Sketch of the Author, Covering the Events of Hyderabad's Merger with the Indian Union.* Hyderabad: Laser Print.

Elias, Norbert. 1994. *The Civilizing Process.* London: Blackwell.

Ellingson, Loyd. 1978. "The Origin and Development of the Eritrean Liberation Front. In *Proceeding of the Fifth international Concerence of Ethipian Studies.*

Engineer, Asgharali A. 1984. *Hyderabad Riots: An Analytical Report.* In *Communal Riots in Post-Independence India.* Ed. A.A. Engineer. London: Sangam Books.

Ensminger, Jane. 1996. *Making a Market: The Institutional Transformation of an African Society.* Cambridge: Cambridge University Press.

Eriksson, Erik H. 1968. *Identity: Youth and Crisis.* London: Faber.

Erlich, Haggai. 1994. *Ethiopia and the Middle East.* Boulder, CO: Lynne Rienner Publishers.

Evans-Pritchard, Edward Evan. 1961. *Anthropology and History.* Manchester: University of Manchester Press.

Evers, Hans-Dieter and Heike Schrader, eds. 1994. *The Moral Economy of Trade: Ethnicity and Developing Markets.* London: Routledge.

Ewald, Janet and W.G. Clarence-Smith. 1997. "The Economic Role of the Hadrami Diaspora in the Red Sea and Gulf of Aden, 1820s to 1930s." in *Hadrami Traders, Scholars and Statesmen in the Indian Ocean, 1750s–1960s.* Eds. U. Freitag and W.G. Clarence-Smith. Leiden: Brill.

Ewing, Kantherine, ed. 1988. *Shari'at and Ambiguity in South Asian Islam.* Berkeley: University of California Press.

Fabian, Johannes. 1983. *Time and the Other: How Anthropology Makes its Object.* New York: Columbia University Press.

Fakhry, Majid. 1970. *A History of Islamic Philosophy.* NY: Colombia University Press.

Featherstone, Mike, Scott Lash, and Roland Robertson, eds. 1995. *Global Modernities.* London: Sage.

Forbes, Andrew D.W. 1981. "Southern Arabia and the Islamicisation of the Central Indian Ocean Archipelagoes." *Archipel* 21.

Foucault, Michel. 1991. "Governmentality." in *The Foucault Effect: Studies in Governmentality.* Eds. G. Burchell et.al. London: Harvester.

Fowler, Bridget. 1997. *Pierre Bourdieu and Cultural Theory: Critical investigations*. London: Sage.

Fredriksen, Margrete. 2005. "Perspectives on the Public Sphere and Some Scientific Implications." Unpublished paper presented at Department of Social Anthropology, University of Bergen.

Freitag, Ulrike. 1997. "Hadhramis in International Politics c. 1750–1967." in *Hadrami Traders, Scholars, and Statesmen in the Indian Ocean, 1750s–1960s*. Eds. U. Freitag and W.G. Clarence-Smith. Leiden: Brill.

——— and William G. Clarence-Smith, eds. 1997. *Hadrami Traders, Scholars, and Statesmen in the Indian Ocean, 1750s–1960s*. Leiden: Brill.

———. 2001. "Hadrami Migrants and Reform in their Homeland (c. 1800–1967)." Habitilation diss. University of Munchen.

———. 2002. "Arab Merchants in Singapore: An Attempt at a Collective Biography." In Huub de Jonge and Nico Kaptein (eds.), *Transcending Borders. Arabs, Politics, Trade and Islam in Southeast Asia*. Leiden: KITLV Press.

———. 2003. *Indian Ocean Migrants and State Formation in Hadramaut. Reforming the Homeland*. Leiden: Brill.

Friedman, Jonathan. 1994. *Cultural Identity and Global Process*. London: Sage.

Galaty, John. 1982. "Being 'Masai': Being 'People of Cattle': Ethnic Shifters in East Africa." *American Ethnologist* 1, no. 9: 1–20.

Gallagher, John and Ronald Robinson. 1953. "The Imperialism of Free Trade." *The Economic History Review*, second series VI, no. 1.

Gallie, Walter B. 1964. *Philosophy and the Historical Understanding*. London: Chatto & Windus.

Gaonkar, Dilip P. and Benjamin Lee. 2002. *New Imaginaries* (*Public Culture* 14, no. 1). Durham, NC: Duke University Press.

Gaonkar, Dilip P. 2002. "Towards New Imaginaries: An Introduction." In *New Imaginaries* (*Public Culture* 14, no. 1). Eds. D.P. Gaonkar and B. Lee. Durham, NC: Duke University Press.

Gavin, R.J. 1975. *Aden Under British Rule, 1839–1967*. London: C. Hurst.

Geertz, Clifford. 1968. *Islam Observes: Religious Development in Morocco and Indonesia*. New Haven: Yale University Press.

———. 1972. *The Interpretations of Cultures*. New York: Basic Books.

———. 1980. *Negara: The Theatre State in Nineteenth-Century Bali*. Princeton: Princeton University Press.

———. 1983. *Local Knowledge: Further Essays in Interpretive Anthropology*. New York: Basic Books.

———. *Available Light: Anthropological Reflections on Philosophical Topics*. Princeton: Princeton University Press.

Gellner, Ernest. 1981. *Muslim Society*. Cambridge: Cambridge University Press.

———. 1992. "Anthropology and Europe." *Social Anthropology* 1, part 1: 1–7.

Ghosh, Amitav. 1992. *In An Antique Land*. New York: Vintage.

Giddens, Anthony. 1981. "A Contemporary Critique of Historical Materialism." In A. Giddens, *Power, Property and the State*. Berkeley: University of California Press.

————. 1982. *Profiles and Critiques in Social Theory*. Berkeley: University of California Press.

————. 1984. *The Constitution of Society:Outline of the Theory of Structuration*. Cambridge: Polity Press.

————. 1990. *The Consequences of Modernity*. Cambridge: Polity Press.

Gilroy, Paul. 1993. *The Black Atlantic: Modernity and Double Consciousness*. London: Verso.

Gledhill, John. 1988. "Introduction: The Comparative Analysis of Social and Political Transitions." In *State and Society: The Emergence and Development of Social Hierarchy and Political Centralization*. Eds. J. Gledhill, B. Bender and M.T. Larsen. London: Routledge.

Goldzhiher, Ignaz. 1981. *Introduction to Islamic Theology and Law*. Princeton: Princeton University Press.

Göle, Nilüfer. 2002. "Islam in Public: New Visibilities and New Imaginaries." in *New Imaginaries (Public Culture* 14, no. 1). Eds. D.P. Gaonkar and B. Lee, Durham, NC: Duke University Press.

Goody, Jack. 1996. *The East in the West*. Cambridge: Cambridge University Press.

Gosh, Devleena and Stephen Muecke, eds. 2007. *Cultures of Trade: Indian Ocean Exchanges*. Newcastle: Cambridge Scholars Publishing

Gottschalk, Peter. 2000. *Beyond Hindu and Muslim: Multiple Identity in Narratives from Village India*. Oxford: Oxford University Press.

Gramsci, Antonio. 1971. *Selections from the Prison Notebooks*. London: Lawrence and Wishart Granovetter.

Griffith, V.L. 1938. A.C.E.C. 28/38–India Office Library and Records, Ref: IOR R/20 File Jos/38.–14 July 1938, 28/38. (C.A. Grossmith, Official Secretary).

Grønhaug, Reidar. 1971. "Etablering av tegn i sosial forløp." Mimeo, University of Bergen.

————. 1978. "Scale as a Variable in Analysis: Fields in Social Organization in Herat, Northwest Afghanistan." in *Scale and Social Organization*. Ed. F. Barth. Oslo: Norwegian University Press.

Gudeman, Stephen. 2001. *The Anthropology of Economy: Community, Market and Culture*. Oxford: Blackwell.

Gupta, Akhil and James Ferguson. 1997. *Culture, Power, Place. Explorations in Critical Anthropology*. Durham: Duke University Press.

————, and James Ferguson, eds. 1997. *Anthropological Locations: Boundaries and Grounds of a Field Science*. Berkeley: University of California Press.

Hobson, John M. 2004. *The Eastern Origins of Western Civilization*. Cambridge: Cambridge University Press

Håland, Gunnar. 1985. *The Global Context of Economic and Political Development in South Yemen (Vol. I & II)*. DERAP Publications, no. 191. Bergen: The Chr. Michelsens Institute.

————. 1986. "Evolution of Socio-Economic Dualism in the Maldives." Paper presented to ILO.

————. 2005. "From Nepali Hill Farmers to Business Managers in Thailand: Explaining Causes in Evolving Contexts." Mimeo.

Halbwachs, Maurice. 1992. *On Collective Memory*. Chicago: University of Chicago Press.

Hall, John R. 1999. *Cultures of Inquiry. From Epistemology to Discourse in Sociohistorical Research*. Cambridge: Cambridge University Press.

Hall, Stuart. 1991. "The Global and the Local: Globalisation and Ethnicity." in *Culture, Globalisation and World-System*. Ed. A. King. Binghamton: Department of Art History, State University of New York at Binghamton.

Handelman, Don. 1977. "The Reorganization of Ethnicity." *Ethnic Groups* 1.

Hanks, William F. 1996. "Exorcism and the Description of Participant Roles." in *Natural Histories of Discourse*. Eds. M. Silverstein and G. Urban. Chicago: Chicago University Press.

———. 2000. *Intertexts: Writings on Language, Utterance and Context*. Lanham, Maryland: Rowman & Littlefield.

Hannerz, Ulf. 1992. *Cultural Complexity: Studies in the Social Organization of Meaning*. New York: Columbia University Press.

Hardt, Michael and Antonio Negri. 2000. *Empire*. Cambridge, MA: Harvard University Press.

———. 2004. *Multitude: War and Democracy in the Age of Empire*. New York: The Penguin Press.

Hardy, Peter. 1971. *Partners in Freedom and True Muslims: The Political Thought of Some Muslim Scholars in British India, 1912–1947*. Lund: Scandinavian Institute of Asian Studies Monograph Series.

———. 1972. *The Muslims of British India*. Cambridge: Cambridge University Press.

Harn, L.C. n.d. *The Arab Population of Singapore. 1819–1959*. BA diss. National University of Singapore.

Hartley, John G. 1961. "The Political Organization of an Arab Tribe of the Hadramaut." PhD diss. University of London.

Hartwig, Friedhelm. 2000. *Hadramaut und das insische Furstentum von Hyderabad. Hadramitische Sultanatsgrundungen und Migration im 19. Jahrhundert*. Wutzburg: Ergon Verlag.

Harvey, David. 1989. *The Conditions of Postmodernity. An Inquiry into the Origin of Cultural Change*. Oxford: Blackwell.

———. 1989. *The Conditions of Postmodernity. An Inquiry into the Origin of Cultural Change*. Oxford: Blackwell.

———. 2003. *The New Imperialism*. Oxford: Oxford University Press.

Hasan, Mushirul. 1997. *Legacy of a Divided Nation: India's Muslims Since Independence*. London: C. Hurst.

Hefner, Robert, ed. 1998. *Market Cultures: Society and Morality in the New Asian Capitalisms*. Boulder, CO: Westview Press.

Hertzfelt, Michael. 1997. *Cultural Intimacy: Social Poetics in the Nation State*. NY: Routledge.

Hess, Robert L. 1966. *Italian Colonialism in Somalia*. Chicago: University of Chicago Press.

Hickinbotham, Tom. 1958. *Aden*. London: Constable Co.

Hill, Richard. 1959. *Egypt in the Sudan, 1820–1881*. London: Oxford University Press.

Ho, Eng Seng. 1997a. "Hadhramis Abroad in Hadhramaut: The *Muwalladin.*" in *Hadrami Traders, Scholars and Statesmen in the Indian Ocean, 1750s–1960s.* Eds. U. Freitag and W.G. Clarence-Smith. Leiden: Brill.

———. 1997b. "Group Identity and Religious Conflict in Modern Hadrami History." Paper presented at Leiden University.

———. 2002. "Before Parochialization. Diasporic Arabs Cast in Creole Waters." in *Transcending Borders: Arabs, Politics, Trade and Islam in Southeast Asia.* Ed. Huub de Jonge and Nico Kaptein. Leiden: KITLV Press

———. 2004. "Empire Through Diasporic Eyes: A View From the Other Boat." *Society for Comparative Study of Society and History,* 46: 210–46.

———. 2006. *The Graves of Tarim: Geneaology and Mobility across the Indian Ocean.* Berkeley: University of California Press.

Hobsbawm, Eric. 1979. *The Age of Capital 1848–1875.* New York: New American Library.

Hobson, John A. 1938. *Imperialism: A Study.* London: George Allen & Unwin.

Hofheinz, Albrecht. 1996. "Internalizing Islam: Shaykh Muhammad Majdhub, Scriptural Islam and Local Context in the Early Nineteenth-Century Sudan." PhD diss. University of Bergen.

Holden, Philip. 1999. "The Free Market's Second Coming: Monumentalising Raffles." in *Reading Culture: Textual Practices in Singapore.* Eds. P.G.G. Chew and A. Kramer-Dahl. Singapore: Times Academic Press.

Hopkins, Anthony G, ed. 2002. *Globalization in World History.* London: Pimlico.

Hugill, Peter J. 1993. *World Trade Since 1431: Geography, Technology and Capitalism.* Baltimore: John Hopkins University Press.

Hui, Ong Jin, Tong Chee Kiong, and Tan Ern Ser, eds. 1997. *Understanding Singapore Society.* Singapore: Times Academic Press.

Hunt, Lynn, ed. 1989. *The New Cultural History.* Berkeley: California University Press.

———. 1989. "Introduction: History, Culture and Text." in *The New Cultural History.* Ed. L. Hunt. Berkeley: California University Press.

Huntington, Samuel. 1993. "The Clash of Civilizations." *Foreign Affairs,* 72, no. 3: 22–49.

———. 1996. *The Clash of Civilzations and the Remaking of the World Order.* New York: Simon & Schuster.

Hunwick, John. 1999. "Islamic Financial Institutions: Theoretical Structures and Aspects of their Application in Sub-Saharan Africa." in *Credits, Currencies and Culture: African Financial Institutions in Historical Perspective.* Eds. E. Stiansen and J. Guyer. Uppsala: NAI.

Iggers, Georg G. 1997. *Historiography in the Twentieth Century: From Scientific Objectivity to the Postmodern Challenge.* Hanover, NH: Wesleyan University Press.

Ilias, M.H. 2007. Mappila Muslims and the Cultural Content of Trading Arab Diaspora on the Malabar Coast. *Asian Journal of Social Science,* 35: 434–456.

Inde, Jonathan X. and Renato Rosaldo, eds. 2002. *The Anthropology of Globalization. A Reader.* Oxford: Blackwell.

Ingrams, Harold. 1937. *A Report on the Social, Economic and Political Condition of the Hadhramaut.* London: His Majesty's Stationary Office.

————. 1966. *Arabia and the Isles*. London: Murray.

International Development Association. 1992. *Report On The Committee for the Selection of Beneficiaries of Project Land development*. Sanaa: Ministry of Agriculture and Water Resources.

Issawi, Charles P. 1998. *Cross-Cultural Encounters and Conflicts*. Oxford: Oxford University Press.

Jacobsen, Frode F. 2000. "Trade and Ethnic Complexity among Hadhrami Arabs on the Indonesian Islands of Bali, Lombok and Sumbawa." Unpublished paper presented at University of Bergen.

————. 2009. *Hadrami Arabs in Present-day Indonesia. An Indonesia-oriented group with an Arab signature*. London: Routledge.

Jamieson, Ian. 1980. *Capitalism and Culture: A Comparative Analysis of British and American Manufacturing Organisations*. Farnborough: Gower.

———— and M. Miyoshi, eds. 1998. *The Culture of Globalization*. Durham: Duke University Press.

Jay, Martin. 1996. For Theory. *Theory & Society* 25, no. 2: 167–83.

Jenkins, Richard. 1996. *Social Identity*. London: Routledge.

Jumabhoy, Rajabali. 1981. Pioneers of Singapore. (A 000074/37–reel 26).

Kahn, Joel S., ed. 1998. *Southeast Asian Identities: Culture and the Politics of Representation in Indonesia, Malaysia, Singapore and Thailand*. Singapore: Institute of Southeast Asian Studies.

Kakar, Sudhir. 1996. *The Colors of Violence: Cultural Identities, Religion, and Conflict*. Chicago: University of Chicago Press.

Kalb, Don and Herman Tak, eds. 2005. *Critical Junctions: Anthropology and History Beyond the Cultural Turn*. New York: Berhahn.

Kapferer, Bruce. 1988. *Legends of People, Myths of State: Violence, Intolerance, and Political Culture in Sri Lanka and Australia*. Washington: Smithsonian Institution Press.

————. 2000. "Star Wars: About Anthropology, Culture and Globalisation." *The Australian Journal of Anthropology* 11, no. 2: 174–98.

Kapteijns, Lidwin and J. Spaulding. 1989. "Class Formation and Gender in Precolonial Somali Society: A Research Agenda." *Northeast African Studies* 11, no. 1: 19–38.

Katznelson, Ira. 1997. "Structure and Configuration in Comparative Politics." in *Comparative Politics, Rationality, Culture, and Structure*. Eds. Mark I. Lichbach and Alan S. Zuckerman. Cambridge: Cambridge University Press.

Kearney, Michael. 1995. "The Local and the Global: The Anthropology of Globalization and Transnationalism." *Annual Review of Anthropology* 24: 547–65.

Keesing, Robert. 1987. Anthropology as Interpretive Quest. *Current Anthropology* 28: 161–76.

Kelly, John. 1998. "Time and the Global: Against the Homogeneous, Empty Communities in Contemporary Social Theory." *Development and Change*, 27, no. 4: 839–71.

Khalidi, Omar. 1987. "The Arabs of Hadramawt, South Yemen in Hyderabad." *Islam and the Modern Age* 18, no. 4: 203–29.

————. 1988. "The 1948 Military Operations and Its Aftermath: A Bibliographical Essay." in *Hyderabad: After the Fall*. Ed. O. Khalidi. Wichita: Hyderabad Historical Society.

————, ed. 1988. *Hyderabad: After the Fall*. Wichita: Hyderabad Historical Society.

————. 1995a. *Indian Muslims Since Independence*. Delhi: Vikas Press.

————. 1995b. "The Role of the Hyderabad Hadhramis in the Politics of Hadramawt in the 19th Century." Paper presented at SOAS, London.

————. 1997. "The Hadhrami Role in the Politics and Society of Colonial India, 1750s–1950s." in *Hadhrami Traders, Scholars and Statesmen in the Indian Ocean, 1750s–1960s*. Eds. U. Freitag and W.G. Clarence-Smith. Leiden: Brill.

Khalidi, Tarif. 1994. *Arabic Historical Thought in the Classical Period*. Cambridge: Cambridge University Press.

Khalidi, Usama. 1988. "From Osmania to Birla Mandir: An Uneasy Journey." in *Hyderabad: After the Fall*. Ed. O. Khalidi. Wichita: Hyderabad Historical Society.

Khan, Rashiduddin. 1988. "Major Aspect of Muslim Problem in Hyderabad." in *Hyderabad: After the Fall*. Ed. O. Khalidi. Wichita: Hyderabad Historical Society.

Kluckhohn, Clyde. 1962. "The Konso Economy of Southern Ethiopia." in *Markets in Africa*. Eds. P. Bohannan and G. Dalton. Evanston: African Studies, no. 9, Northwestern University.

Knodt Eva M. 1995. "Foreword." in *Social Systems*, by N. Luhman. Stanford: Stanford University Press.

Knysh, Alexander. 1993. "The Cult of Saints in Hadramawt: An Overview." in *New Arabian Studies* 1. Eds. R.B. Serjeant, R.L. Bidwell and G.R. Smith, Exeter: Exeter University Press.

————. 1997. "The Cult of Saints and Islamic Reformism in Early Twentieth Century Hadramawt." in *New Arabian Studies 4*. Eds. C.R. Smith, J.R. Smart and B.R. Pridham, Exeter: Exeter University Press.

————. 1999. "The Sada in History: A Critical Essay on Hadrami Historiography." in *Cultural Anthropology of Southern Arabia: Haramawt Revisited*. Eds. M.N. Souvorov and M. Rodinov. St. Petersburg: Museum of Anthropology and Ethnography/Russian Academy of Sciences.

Korotayev, Andrey. 1994. "Some Trends of Evolution of the Sabaean Cultural-Political Area: From Clan Titles to Clan Names." in *New Arabian Studies* 2. Eds. R.L. Bidwell, C.R. Smith and J.R. Smart (eds.), Exeter: University of Exeter Press.

————. n.d. "Some General Trends and Factors of Evolution of North-East Yemen Socio-Political Systems in the Last Three Millennia." Unpublished paper.

————. 1997. "The Chiefdom: Precursor of the Tribe." Unpublished paper.

————. 1997. "Religion and Society in Southern Arabia and Among the Arabs." Unpublished paper.

————. et al. 1999. "Origins of Islam: Political-Anthropological and Environmental Context." *Acta Oerientaia Academiae Scientiarum Hun* 52.

Koselleck, Reinhardt. 1979. *Futures Past: On the Semantics of Historical Time*. Boston: MIT Press.

Kostiner, Joseph. 1984. "The Impact of Hadrami Emigrants in the East Indies on Islamic Modernism and Social Change in Hadramaut During the 20th century." in *Islam in Asia (Vol. III): Southeast and East Asia*. Eds. R. Israeli and A.H. Jones. Boulder, CO: Westview.

Krech III, Shepard. 1991. "The State of Ethnohistory." *Annual Review of Anthropology* 20: 345–75.

Krogstad, Anne. 2000. "Antropologisk sammenligning i 'tykt' og 'tynt': ti kjetterske teser." *Norsk Antropologisk Tidsskrift* 11, no. 2: 88–107.

Kuper, Adam, ed. 1992. *Conceptualizing Society*. London: Routledge.

———. 1999. *Culture: The Anthropological Account*. Cambridge, MA: Harvard University Press.

Kymlicka, Will. 1995. *Multicultural Citizenship: A Liberal Theory of Minority Rights*. Oxford: Clarendon.

LaCapra, Dominick. 1983. *Rethinking Intellectual History: Text, Context, Language*. Ithaca: Cornell University Press.

Lackner, Helen. 1985. *P.D.R. Yemen: Outpost of Socialist Development in Arabia*. London: Ithaca Press.

Lacoste, Yves. 1989. *Ibn Khaldun: The Birth of History and the Past of the Third World*. London: Verso.

Lakoff, George. 1987. *Women, Fire, and Dangerous Things*. Chicago: Chicago University Press.

Lambek, Michael. 1992. *Knowledge and Practice in Mayotte: Local Discourses of Islam, Sorcery and Spirit Possession*. Toronto: University of Toronto Press.

———. 1995. "Choking on the Quran and Other Consuming Parables from the Western Indian Ocean Front." in *The Pursuit of Certainty: Religious and Cultural Formulations*. Ed. W. James. London: Routledge.

Larson, Pier M. 2009. *Oceans of Letters. Language and Creolization in an Indian Ocean Diaspora*. Cambridge: Cambridge University Press

Lash, Scott. 1999. *Another Modernity: A Different Rationality*. Oxford: Blackwell.

——— and John Urry. 1987. *The End of Organized Capitalism*. Madison: University of Wisconsin Press.

Launey, Robert. 1992. *Beyond the Stream: Islam and Society in a West African Town*. Berkeley: University of California Press.

Le Guennec-Coppens, Francoise. 1997. "Changing Patterns of Hadhrami Migration and Social Integration in East Africa." in *Hadrami Traders, Scholars, and Statesmen in the Indian Ocean, 1750s–1960s*. Eds. U. Freitag and W.G. Clarence-Smith. Leiden: Brill.

Lekon, Christian. 1997. "The Impact of Remittances on the Economy of Hadraut, 1914–1967. in *Hadrami Traders, Scholars and Statesmen in the Indian Ocean, 1750s–1960s*. Eds. U. Freitag and W.G. Clarence-Smith. Leiden: Brill.

Leonard, Karen. 1971. "The Hyderabad Political System and Its Participants." *Journal of Asian Studies* 30, 2: 569–82.

———. 1981. "Banking Firms in Nineteenth Century Hyderabad Politics." *Modern Asian Studies* 15, no. 2.

———. 1994. *Social History of an Indian Caste*. Hyderabad: Orient Longman.

Lewis, Ioan M., ed. 1968. *History and Social Anthropology*. ASA Monograph 7.

Lewis, Oscar. 1951. *Life in a Mexican Village: Tepotzlan Restudied*. Urbana: University of Illinois Press.

Li, Tanya. 1989. *Malays in Singapore: Culture, Economy and Ideology*. Singapore: Oxford UO.

Lim, Lu Sia. 1986/7. The Arabs of Singapore:A Sociographic Study of Their Place in the Muslim and Malay World of Singapore. B. Sc.-diss. National University of Sinagapore

Little, Tom. 1968. *South Arabia, Arena of Conflict*. London: Pall Mall Press.

Luhman, Niklas. 1995. *Social Systems*. Stanford: Stanford University Press.

Lyons, T. 1986. "The United States and Ethiopia. The Politics of Patron Client Relationship." *Northeast African Studies*. 8, nos. 2–3.

Maclagan, Ianthe. 1994. "Food and Gender in a Yemeni Community." in *Culinary Cultures of the Middle East*, 159–72. Eds. S. Zubaida.and R. Tapper. London: I.B. Tauris Publishers.

Mahmood, Saba. 2005. *Politics of Piety: The Islamic Revival and the Feminist Subject*. Princeton: Princeton University Press.

Mandal, Sumit K. 1997. "Natural Leaders of Native Muslims: Arab Ethnicity and Politics in Java under Dutch Rule." in *Hadhrami Traders, Scholars and Statesmen in the Indian Ocean, 1750s–1960s*. Eds. U. Freitag and W.G. Clarence-Smith. Leiden: Brill.

Mandalios, John. *Civilization and the Human Subject*. Lanham, MD: Rowman & Littlefield.

Mandaville, Peter. 2001. "Reimagining Islam in Diaspora: The Politics of Mediated Community." *Gazette* 63, nos. 2–3: 169–86.

Manger, Ane. 2007. "The Indian Muslim Factor." A study of the Indian Muslim groups in London and their involvement in questions related to Pan-Islam, Indian and turkey during the period 1918–24. MA diss. University of Oslo (in Norwegian).

Manger, Leif, ed. 1984. *Trade and Traders in the Sudan*. Bergen: Bergen Studies in Social Anthropology.

———. 1991. "Yemeni Themes: Exploration of Some Important Building Blocks Within Yemeni State and Society." Unpublished paper presented at University of Bergen.

———.1992. "On the Study of Islam in Local Contexts." *Norwegian Journal of Development Studies* 1.

———, et al., eds. 1996. *Survival on Meagre Resources: Hadendowa Pastoralism in the Red Sea Hills*. Uppsala: The Nordic Africa Institute.

———, ed. 1999. *Muslim Diversity: Local Islam in a Global Context*. London: Curzon Press.

———. 1999a. "Introduction." In *Muslim Diversity: Local Islam in a Global Context*. Ed. L. Manger. London: Curzon Press.

———. 1999b. "The Hadrami Diaspora in the Indian Ocean." in *Cultural Anthropology of South Arabia—Hadramaut Revisited*. Eds. M.N. Souvorov and M. Rodionov. St. Petersburg: Museum of Anthropology and Ethnography/Russian Academy of Sciences.

———. 2001a. "Hadramis in Singapore: Making Muslim Space in a Global City." *Bulletin of the Royal Institute for Inter-faith Studies* 3, no. 2).

———. 2001b. On the Indian Ocean World in a "Long Durée": Empires, World Systems and the Historicising of Globalisation. Unpublished manuscript.

———. 2001c. "On the Concept of Diaspora and the Theorising of Identity." Unpublished paper.

————. 2002. "September 11 and October 7: From Human Tragedy to Power Politics." *Social Analysis* 46, no. 1.

————. 2005. "Understanding Globalization: The Need for a Historicized Anthropology." in *Social Anthropology in the Era of Globalization: Issues and Concerns*. Ed. K. Misra. Hyderabad: Hyderabad University Press.

————. 2006a. "Connectivity in the Long Durée: Hadramis from South Yemen in an Indian Ocean World." in *Connectivity in Antiquity: Globalisation as Long Term Historical Process*. Eds. Øystein LaBianca and Sandra Scham. London: Equinox.

————. 2006b. "Empires, World-Systems and Globalization." Online at www.global moments.org.

————. 2006c. "Globalization on the African Horn: Yemenis in Southern Somalia and Ethiopia." in *The Global Worlds of the Swahili: Interfaces of Islam, Identity and Space in 19th and 20th Century East Africa*. Eds. Roman Loimeier and Rüdiger Sesemann. Bayreuth: LIT (Beiträge zur Afrikaforschung, Band 26).

———— and Munzoul A.M. Assal, eds. 2006. *Diasporas Within and Without Africa: Dynamism, Hetereogeneity, Variation*. Uppsala: The Nordic Africa Institute.

———— and Munzoul A.M. Assal. 2006. "Diaspora Within and Without Africa: An Introduction." in *Diasporas Within and Without Africa*. Eds. L. Manger and M.A.M. Assal (eds.). Uppsala: The Nordic Africa Institute.

————. 2006. "A Hadrami Diaspora in the Sudan: Individual Life-Courses in Regional and Global Contexts." in *Diasporas Within and Without Africa*. Eds. L. Manger and M.A.M. Assal. Uppsala: The Nordic Africa Institute.

————. 2007a. Hadramis in Hyderabad: From Winners to Losers. *Asian Journal of Social Science* 35: 405–433.

————. 2007b. "Building a Moral Economy: The Historical Success of Hadrami Sada in Singapore (c. 1820–1920)." in *Embedded Rationalities: Southeast Asian Cases of Entrepreneurship*. Ed. E. Bråten. (in preparation, Routledge)

Mann, Michael. 1986. *The Sources of Social Power (Vol. I): A History of Power from the Beginning to AD 1760*. Cambridge: Cambridge University Press.

————. 1993. *The Sources of Social Power (Vol. II): The Rise of Classes and Nation States, 1760–1914*. Cambridge: Cambridge University Press.

————. 2005. *The Dark Side of Democracy: Explaining Ethnic Cleansing*. Cambridge: Cambridge University Press.

Mannheim, Karl. 1936. *Ideology and Utopia*. London: Routledge and Kegan Paul.

————. 1986. *Conservatism: A Contribution to the Sociology of Knowledge*. London and New York: Routledge and Kegan Paul.

Marcus, George E. 1995. "Ethnography in/of the World System: The Emergence of Multi-Sited Ethnography." *Annual Review of Anthropology* 24: 95–117.

————. 1999. *Ethnography Through Thick and Thin*. Princeton: Princeton University Press.

———— and Michael M.J. Fisher. 1986. *Anthropology as Cultural Critique: An Experimental Moment in the Human Sciences*. Chicago: University of Chicago Press.

McDonald, Terrence J., ed. 1996. *The Historic Turn in the Human Sciences*. Ann Arbor: University of Michigan Press.

Meissner, Jeffrey R. 1987. "Tribes at the Core: Legitimacy, Structure and Power in Zaydi Yemen." PhD diss. Columbia University.

Messick, Brinkley. 1978. "Transactions in Ibb: Economy and Society in a Yemeni Highland Town." PhD diss. Princeton University.

———. 1993. *The Caliographic State: Textual Domination and History in a Muslim Society*. Berkeley: University of California Press.

Metcalf, Barbara D., ed. 1984. *Moral Conduct and Authority: The Place of Ada in South Asian Islam*. Berkeley: University of California Press.

———. 1996. "Introduction: Sacred Words, Sanctioned Practice, New Communities." in *Making Muslim Space in North America and Europe*. Ed. B.D. Metcalf. Berkeley: University of California Press.

———. 1999. "Nationalism, Modernity, and Muslim Identity in India before 1947." in *Nation and Religion: Perspectives on Europe and Asia*. Ed. P. van der Veer and H. Lehmann. Princeton: Princeton University Press.

Meyer, Birgit and Peter Gesciere, eds. 1999. *Globalization and Identity: Dialectics of Flow and Closure*. Oxford: Blackwell.

Miller, Roland E. 1976. *Mappilla Muslims of Kerala*. Madras: Orient Longman.

Mink, Louis O. 1969. *Mind, History, and Dialectic: The Philosophy of R.G. Collingwood*. Middletown, CT: Wesleyan University Press.

Mink, Louis O., Brian Fay, Eugene O. Golob, and Richard T. Vann. 1987. *Historical Understanding*. Ithaca: Cornell University Press.

Mintz, Sidney. 1998. "The Localisation of Anthropological Practice." *Critique of Anthropology* 18, no. 2: 117–33.

Mittelman, James H. 1994. "The Globalization Challenge: Surviving at the Margins." *Third World Quarterly* 15, no. 3: 427–44.

———. 2000. *The Globalization Syndrome: Transformation and Resistance*. Princeton: Princeton University Press.

Mobini-Kesheh, Natalie. 1999. *The Hadrami Awakening: Community and Identity in the Netherlands East Indies, 1900–1942*. Ithaca: Cornell Southeast Asia Program Publications 28.

Moore, Henrietta. 1996. "The Changing Nature of Anthropological Knowledge: An Introduction." in *The Future of Anthropological Knowledge*. Ed. H. Moore. London: Routledge.

———, ed. 1999. *AnthropologicalTheory Today*. Cambridge: Polity Press.

Mukund, Kanakalatha. 1990. *Andhra Pradesh Economy in Transition*. Hyderabad: Centre for Economic and Social Studies and Booklinks.

Munslow, Alun.1997. *Deconstructing History*. London: Routledge.

Nash, Junr. 1991. "Ethnographic Aspects of the World Capitalist System." *Annual Review of Anthropology* 10: 393–423.

Nader, Laura. 1994. "Comparative Consciousness." in *Assessing Cultural Anthropology*. Ed. R. Borofsky. New York: McGraw-Hill.

Naidu, Ratna. 1990. *Old Cities, New Predicaments: A Study of Hyderabad*. Delhi: Sage.

Niethammer, Lutz. 2000. "Maurice Halbwachs: Memory and the Feeling of Identity." in *Myth and Memory in the Construction of Community: Historical Patterns in Europe and Beyond*. Ed. Bo Stråth. Brussels: PIE Lang.

Nietzche, Friedrich. 1874/1980. *On the Advantage and Disadvantage of History for Life*. Indianapolis: Hacket Publishing.

Noer, Deliar. 1973. *The Modernist Muslim Movement in Indonesia, 1900–1942*. Singapore: Oxford University Press.

O'Brien, Patricia. 1989. "Michel Foucault's History of Culture." in *The New Cultural History*. Ed. Lynn Hunt. Berkeley: California University Press.

Ohnuki-Tierney, E. 2001. "Historization of the Culture Concept." *History and Anthropology* 12, no. 3: 213–54.

———, ed. 1990. *Culture Through Time: Anthropological Approaches*. Stanford: Stanford University Press.

Ong, Aiwa. 1999. *Flexible Citizenship, The Cultural Logic of Transnationality*. Durham: Duke University Press.

O'Rourke, Kevin O. and Jeffrey G. Williamson. 1999. *Globalization and History: The Evolution of a Nineteenth-Century Atlantic Economy*. Cambridge, MA: MIT Press.

Ortner, Sheryy. 1973. "On Key Symbols." *American Anthropologist* 75, no. 5: 1338–1346.

———. 1984. "Theory in Anthropology Since the Sixties." *Comparative Studies in Society and History* 26, no. 1.

———. 1990. "Patterns of History: Cultural Schemas in the Founding of Sherpa Religious Institutions." in *Culture Through Time: Anthropological Approaches*. Ed. E. Ohnuki-Tierney. Stanford: Stanford University Press.

———. 1997. "Fieldwork in the Postcommunity." *Anthropology and Humanism* 22, no. 1: 61–80.

———, ed. 1999. *The Fate of Culture: Geertz and Beyond*. Berkeley: University of California Press.

———. 1999. "Introduction." in *The Fate of Culture: Geertz and Beyond*. Ed. S. Ortner. Berkeley: University of California Press.

———. 2005. "Subjectivity and Cultural Critique." *Anthropological Theory* 5, no. 1: 31–52.

Othman, Mohammad R. 1997. "Hadhramis in the Politics and Administration of the Malay States in the Late Eighteenth and Nineteenth Centuries." in *Hadhrami Traders, Scholars and Statesmen in the Indian Ocean, 1750s–1960s*. Eds. U. Freitag and W.G. Clarence-Smith. Leiden: Brill.

Özkirimli, Umut. 2005. *Contemporary Debates on Nationalism: A Critical Engagement*. New York: Palgrave MacMillan.

Pan, Lynn, ed. 1998. *The Encyclopedia of the Chinese Overseas*. Singapore: Landmark Books.

Pankhurst, Richard. 1965. "Trade of Southern and Western Ethiopia and the Indian Ocean Ports in the 19th and early 20th Centuries." *Journal of Ethiopian Studies* 3, no. 2.

———. 1968. *Economic History of Ethiopia, 1800–1935*. Addis Ababa: Haile Sellassie I University Press.

Parkin, David. 1974. "Congregational and Interpersonal Ideologies in Political Ethnicity." in *Urban Ethnicity*. Ed. A. Cohen. London: Tavistock.

Pearson, Harold F. 1955. *People of Early Singapore*. London: University of London Press.

Peel, John D.Y. 1987. "History, Culture and the Comparative Method." in *Comparative Anthropology*. Ed. L. Holy. Oxford: Blackwell.

Peirce, Charles. 1982. *Writings of Charles S. Peirce*. Bloomington: University of Indiana Press.

Perkin, Kenneth J. 1993. *Port Sudan: The Evolution of a Colonial City*. Boulder, CO: Westview Press.

Perlin, Frank. 1994. *Unbroken Landscape. Commodity, Category, Sign and Identity: Their Production as Myth and Knowledge from 1500*. Aldershot: Variorum.

Pinault, David. 1992. *The Shiites*. New York: St.Martin's Press.

Pliny. n.d. *Natural History*, Book 12, Ch. 32, Sec. 63.

Pratt, Mary Louise. 1992. *Imperial Eyes: Travel Writing and Transculturation*. London: Routledge.

Prestholdt, Jeremy. 2003. "East African Consumerism and the Genealogies of Globalization." PhD diss. Northwestern University.

Putnam, Hilary. 1987. *The Many Faces of Realism*. La Salle: Open Court.

Rafael, Vincente C. and Itty Abraham, eds. 1992. "Southeast Asian Diaporas." *Sojourn* 12, no. 2.

Raj, Sheela. 1987. *Mediaevalism to Modernism: Socio-Economic and Cultural History of Hyderabad, 1869–1911*. Bombay: Popular Prakashan Pvt.

Rao, P. Raghunadha. 1993. *History of Modern Andhra Pradesh*. Selhi: Sterlinger Publishers.

Rao, Sudhakar. 1996. *Hadramis in Hyderabad*. CDS Report Series. Bergen: Center for Development Studies, University of Bergen.

Ray, Himanshu P. and Edward A. Alpers, eds. 2007. *Cross Currents and Community Networks. The History of the Indian Ocean World*. New Delhi: Oxford University Press.

Reade, Julian, ed. 1996. *The Indian Ocean in Antiquity*. London: Kegan Paul.

Reese, Scott S. 1996. *Patricians of the Benadir: Islamic Learning, Commerce and Somali Urban Identity in the Nineteenth Century*. PhD diss. University of Pennsylvania.

Reid, Andrew. 1967. "Nineteenth Century Pan-Islam in Indonesia and Malaysia." *Journal of Asian Studies* 26, no. 2: 267–83.

Rhoden, David. 1970. "The Twentieth Century Decline in Suakin." *Sudan Notes and Records* LI: 7–22.

Ricoeur, Paul. 1984. *Time and Narrative (Vol. 1)*. Chicago: University of Chicago Press.

Riddell, Peter G. 1997. "Religious Links Between Hadhramaut and the Malay-Indonesian World, c. 1850–c. 1950." in *Hadhrami Traders, Scholars and Statesmen in the Indian Ocean, 1750s–1960s*. Eds. U. Freitag and W.G. Clarence-Smith. Leiden: Brill.

Robertson, Roland. 1995. "Globalization: Time-Space and Homogeneity-Hetereogeneity." in *Global Modernities*. Eds. M. Featherstone, S. Lash and R. Robertson. London: Sage.

Robinson, Ronald and John Gallagher (with Alice Denny). 1981. *Africa and Victorians: The Official Mind of Imperialism*. London: MacMillan.

Roff, William. 1964. "The Malay-Muslim World of Singapore at the Close of the Nineteenth Century." *Journal of Asian Studies* XXIV, no. 1: 75–90.

———. 1994. *The Origins of Malay Nationalism*. Kuala Lumpur: Oxford University Press.

Roosa, John. 1998. "The Quandary of the Qaum: Indian Nationalism in a Muslim State, Hyderabad, 1850–1948." PhD diss. University of Wisconsin.

Roosens, Eugene. 1989. *Creating Ethnicity: The Process of Ethnogenesis*. Newbury Park: Sage.

———. 1994. "The Primordial Nature of Origins in Migrants Identities." in *The Anthropology of Ethnicity: Beyond "Ethnic Groups and Boundaries."* Eds. H. Vermeulen and C. Govers Amsterdam: Het Spinhuis.

Roseberry, William. 1989. *Anthropologies and Histories: Essays in Culture, History and Political Economy*. New Brunswick: Rutgers University Press.

Russell, Steven. 1996. *Jewish Identity and Civilizing Process*. London: MacMillan Press.

Safran, William. 1991. "Diasporas in Modern Societies: Myths of Homeland and Return." *Diaspora* vol. a, no. 1.

Sahlins, Marshall. 1976. *Culture and Practical Reason*. Chicago: University of Chicago Press.

———. 1981. *Historical Metaphors and Mythical Realities: Structure in the Early History of the Sandwich Island Kingdom*. Ann Arbor: University of Michigan Press.

———. 1985. *Islands of History*. Chicago: University of Chicago Press.

———. 1994. "Goodbye to Tristes Tropes: Ethnography in the Context of Modern World History." in *Assessing Cultural Anthropology*. Ed. R. Borofsky. New York: Macmillan.

———. 2000. *Culture in Practice: Selected Essays*. New York: Zone Books.

———. 2000. "The Return of the Event, Again." in *Culture in Practice: Selected Essays*. M. Sahlins, New York: Zone Books.

———. 2004. *Apologies to Thucydides: Understanding History as Culture and Vice Versa*. Chicago: University of Chicago Press.

Savage, Victor R., Lily Kong, and Warwick Neville, eds. 1998. *The Naga Awakens. Growth and Change in Southeast Asia*. Singapore: Times Academic Press.

Scott, Alan, ed. 1997. *The Limits of Globalization. Cases and Arguments*. London: Routledge.

Sedgwick, Mark J.R. 1998. "The Heirs of Ahmad Ibn Idris: The Spread and Normalisation of a Sufi Order, 1799–1966." PhD diss. University of Bergen.

Sennett, Richard. 1998. *The Corrosion of Character: The Personal Consequences of Work in the New Capitalism*. New York: W.W. Norton.

Serjeant, Robert B. 1951. *Prose and Poetry from Hadramaut*. London: Taylor's Foreign Press.

———. 1957. *The Sayyids of Hadramaut*. London: SOAS.

———. 1963. *The Portuguese off Arabia's Coast. With Yemeni and European Accounts of Dutch Pirates off Mocha in the Seventeenth Century*. Oxford:Clarendon Press.

———. 1993. "Yemenis in Mediaeval Quanzhou (Canton)." in *New Arabian Studies* 1. Eds. R.B. Serjeant, R.L. Bidwell and G.R. Smith. Exeter: Exeter University Press.

———. 1996a. "Yemeni Merchants and Trade in Yemen, 13th–16th Centuries." in *Society and Trade in South Arabia*. Ed. G.R. Smith. Aldershot: Variorum.

———. 1996b. "The Hadrami Network." in *Society and Trade in South Arabia*. Ed. G.R. Smith Aldershot: Variorum.

Sewell, William H. Jr. 1999. "Three temporalities: Towards an Eventful Sociology." in *The Historic Turn in the Human Sciences*. Ed. T.J. McDonald. Ann Arbor: University of Michigan Press.

Shannon, Thomas R. 1996. *An Introduction to the World-System Perspective*. Boulder, CO: Westview.

Sheim, Kassim. 1988. "Israel-Ethiopian Relations: Change and Continuity." *Northeast African Studies*, 10, vol. 1.

Sherwani, Mustafa K. 1993. "Cultural Synthesis in Hyderabad." in *Hyderabad 400 Years (1591–1991)*. Ed. R. Alikha. Hyderabad: Zenith Services.

Siddiqui, Sharon and Nirmala Puru Shotam. 1990. *Singapore's Little India: Past, Present and Future*. Singapore:ISEAS

Siddiqui, Sharon. 1995. "Being Muslim in Singapore: Change, Community and Consciousness." Unpublished paper presented at a conference on Islam and Society in Southeast Asia, in Jakarta, Indonesia.

Silverstein, Michael and Greg Urban, eds. 1996. *Natural Histories of Discourse*. Chicago: University of Chicago Press.

Simmel, Georg. 1990. *The Philosophy of Money*. London: Routledge.

Simon, Robert. 1989. *Meccan Trade and Islam: Problems of Origin and Structure*. Budapest: Akedemiai Kiado.

Simpson, Edward and Kai Kresse, eds. 2007. *Struggling With History. Islam and Cosmopolitanism in the Western Indian Ocean*. London: C. Hurst

Singer, Milton. 1972. *When a Great Tradition Modernizes: An Anthropological Approach to Indian Civilization*. London: Pall Mall Press.

———. 1984. *Man's Glassy Essence: Explorations in Semiotic Anthropology*. Bloomington: Indiana University Press.

Somers, Margaret R. 1999. "Where is Sociology After the Historic Turn? Knowledge Cultures, Narrativity, and Historical Epistemologies." in *The Historic Turn in the Human Sciences*. Ed. T.J. McDonald. Ann Arbor: University of Michigan Press.

Stagl, Justin. 1995. *A History of Curiosity: The Theory of Travel 1550–1800*. Chur, Switzerland: Harwood.

Stewart, Charles, ed. 2007. *Creolization. History, Ethnography, Theory*. Walnut Creek, Cal.: Left Coast Press

Stoller, Paul. 1997. "Globalising Method: The Problems of Doing Ethnography in Transnational Spaces." *Anthropology and Humanism* 22, no. 1: 81–94.

Stookey, Robert W. 1978. *Yemen: The Politics of the Yemen Arab Republic*. Boulder, CO: Westview Press.

Strait Times. 1992. "The Arab Dilemma: are Arabs here Malay?",

Sunday Strait Times. 1994. "Upfront," *The Sunday Straits Times*, 4 September.

Taha, S.A. 1992. "The Jagirdari System in Hyderabad State Under Nizam's Rule." MPhil diss. Centre for Regional Studies, University of Hyderabad.

Talhami, Ghada H. 1979. *Suakin and Massawa under Egyptian Rule, 1865–1885*. Washington: University Press of America

Tambs-Lyche, Harald. 1989. "On the Construction and Form of Ethnic Stereotypes." Paper presented at University of Bergen.

Taylor, Chales. 2002. "Modern Social Imaginaries." in *New Imaginaries* (*Public Culture* 14, no. 1). Eds. D.P. Gaonkar and B. Lee. Durham, NC: Duke University Press.

Taylor, Jean Gelman. 1983. *The Social World of Batavia: European and Eurasian in Dutch Asia*. Madison: University of Wisconsin Press.

Temple, Richard. 1887. *Journals Kept in Hyderabad, Kashmir, Sikkim, and Nepal*. London: W.H. Allen

Therborn, Gøran. 1995. "Routes to/through Modernity." in *Global Modernities*. Eds. M. Featherstone, S. Lash and R. Robertson. London: Sage.

———. 2000. "Globalizations: Dimensions, Historical Waves, Regional Effects, Normative Governance." *International Sociology* 15, no. 2: 151–79.

This Week in Singapore. 1998. "Concierge recommend," 7–13 November.

Thomas, Nicholas. 1991. *Entangled Objects: Exchange, Material Culture, and Colonialism in the Pacific*. Cambridge, MA: Harvard University Press.

Thompson, Edward P. 1991. *The Making of the English Working Class*. London: Penguin Books.

Tibbetts, Gerald Randall. 1956. "Early Traders in South-East Asia." *Journal of the Malaysian Branch of the Royal Asiatic Society*.

———. 1981. *Arab Navigation in the Indian Ocean Before the Coming of the Portuguese*. London: Royal Asiatic Society.

Tiles, Mary. 1984. *Bachelard: Science and Objectivity*. Cambridge: Cambridge University Press.

Tomlinson, John. 1999. *Globalization and Culture*. Chicago: University of Chicago Press.

Troll, Christian W., ed. 1989. *Muslim Shrines in India: Their Character, History and Significance*. Delhi: Oxford University Press.

Turnbull, Constance Mary. 1977. *A History of Singapore, 1819–1988*. Singapore: Oxford University Press.

Turner, Victor. 1967. *The Forest of Symbols*. Ithaca: Cornell University Press.

Udovitch, Abraham L. 1970. *Partnership and Profit in Medieval Islam*. Princeton: Princeton University Press.

Valeri, Valeri. 1990. "Constitutive History: Genealogy and Narrative in the Legitimation of Hawaiian Kingship." in *Culture Through Time: Anthropological Approaches*. Ed. E. Ohnuki-Tierney. Stanford: Stanford University Press.

Van den Berg, Lodewijk. 1886. *Le Hadramout et les Colonies Arabes dans L'Archipel Indien*. Batavia: Imprimirie du Government.

Van der Meulen, Daniel and Herrman Von Wissman. 1932. *Hadramaut: Some of its Mysteries Unveiled*. Leiden: Brill.

Van der Meulen, Daniel. 1947. *Aden to the Hadhramaut*. London: John Murray.

van der Veer, Peter. 1994. *Religious Nationalism: Hindus and Muslims in India*. Berkeley: University of California Press.

———, ed. 1995. *Nation and Migration: The Politics of Space in the South Asian Diaspora*. Philadelphia: University of Pennsylvania Press.

——— and Hartmut Lehmann, eds. 1999. *Nation and Religion: Perspectives on Europe and Asia*. Princeton: Princeton University Press.

Van Hear, Nicholas. 1998. *New Diasporas: The Mass Exodus, Dispersal and Regrouping of Migrant Communities*. Seattle: University of Washington Press.

Vatuk, Sylvia. 1989. "Household Form and Formation: Variability and Social Change

Among South Indian Muslims." in *Society from Inside Out: Anthropological Perspectives on the South Indian Household*. Eds. J. Gray and D. Mearns. Dehli: Sage.

―――. 1990. "The Cultural Construction of Shared Identity: A South Indian Family History." *Social Analysis* 28.

―――. 1996. "Identity and Difference or Equality and Inequality in South Asian Muslim Society." in *Caste Today*. Ed. C. Fuller. Delhi: Oxford University Press.

Vayda, Andrew. 1994. "Actions, Variations, and Change: The Emerging Anti-Essentialist View in Anthropology." in *Assessing Cultural Anthropology*. Ed. R. Borofsky. New York: McGraw-Hill.

Vederey, Catherine. 1994. "Ethnicity, Nationalism and State-Making." in *The Anthropology of Ethnicity: Beyond "Ethnic Groups and Boundaries."* Eds. H. Vermeulen and C. Govers Amsterdam: Het Spinhuis.

Vermeulen, Hans and Cora Govers, eds. 1994. *The Anthropology of Ethnicity: Beyond "Ethnic Groups and Boundaries."* Amsterdam: Het Spinhuis.

―――, eds. 1997. *The Politics of Ethnic Consciousness*. Basingstoke: MacMillen.

Vertovec, Stephen. 2000. *The Hindu Diaspora: Comparative Patterns*. London: Routledge.

Vikør, Knut. 1999. "Jihad in West Africa: A Global Theme in a Regional Setting." in *Muslim Diversity: Local Islam in Global Contexts*. Ed. L. Manger. London: Curzon Press.

Voll, John. 1994. *Islam: Continuity and Change in the Modern World*. Syracuse: Syracuse University Press.

Vom Bruck, Gabriele. 1998. "Kinship and the Embodiment of History." *History and Anthropology* 10, no. 4.

―――. 2005. *Islam, Memory, and Morality in Yemen*. New York: Palgrave MacMillan.

Wallerstein, Immanuel. 1974. *Modern World System (Vol. I): Capitalist Agriculture and the Origin of the European World Economy in the 16th Century*. San Diego: Academic Press.

―――. 1999. *The End of the World As We Know It: Social Science for the 21st Century*. Minneapolis: University of Minnesota Press.

Walters, Dolores. 1987. "Perceptions of Social Inequality in the Yemen Arab Republic." PhD diss. University of New York.

―――. 1996. "Invisible Survivors: Women, Diversity and Transition in Yemen." Unpublished paper delivered at the Annual Conference of the Middle East Studies Association (MESA), November 1996.

Watson, Andrew M. 1983. *Agricultural Innovation in the Early Islamic World: The Diffusion of Crops and Farming Techniques, 700–1100*. Cambridge: Cambridge University Press.

Watt, W. Montgomery. 1953. *Mohammad at Mecca*. Oxford: Oxford University Press.

―――. 1998. *The Formative Period of Islamic Thought*. Oxford: Oneworld.

Weber, Max. 1949. *The Methodology of the Social Sciences*. New York: The Free Press.

Weiner, Anette. 1976. *Inalienable Possessions: The Paradox of Keeping While Giving*. Berkeley: University of California Press.

White, Richard. 1999. *The Middle Ground: Indians, Empires and Republics in the Great Lakes Region, 1650–1815*. Cambridge: Cambridge University Press.

Williams, Raymond. 1977. *Marxism and Literature*. Oxford: Oxford University Press.

Winichakul, Thongchai. 1994. *Siam Mapped. A History of the Geo-Body of a Nation*. Honolulu: University of Hawai'i Press.

Wolf, Eric. 1982. *Europe and the People Without History*. Berkeley: University of California Press.

———. 1999. *Envisioning Power: Ideologies of Dominance and Crisis*. Berkeley: University of California Press.

——— (with Sydel Silverman). 2001. *Pathways of Power: Building an Anthropology of the Modern World*. Berkeley: University of California Press.

Woods, Ellen M. 2003. *Empire of Capital*. London: Verso.

Wuthnow, Robert. 1983. "Cultural Crises." in *Crises in the World System*. Ed. Albert Bergesen Beverly Hills: Sage.

❀ Index